GEORGIA GARDENERS

Also by Laura C. Martin

Gardens of the Heartland
Southern Gardens
Handmade Gifts from a Country Garden
Wildflower Folklore
Garden Flower Folklore
Wildlife Folklore
Bird Folklore

GEORGIA GARDENERS

WISDOM SHARED
OVER THE FENCE

❧

LAURA C. MARTIN

Taylor Publishing Company
Dallas, Texas

Published by Taylor Publishing Company
1550 West Mockingbird Lane
Dallas, Texas 75235

Designed by Hespenheide Design

Library of Congress Cataloging-in-Publication Data

Martin, Laura C.
     Georgia gardeners : wisdom shared over the
fence / Laura C. Martin.
          p.   cm.
     Includes bibliographical references and index.
     ISBN 0878339051
     1. Gardening—Georgia. 2. Gardeners—
Georgia—Interviews. 3. Gardeners—Georgia—
Biography. I. Title.
  SB453.2.G4M37   1996
     638'.09758—dc20   96-12847
                                              CIP

Printed in the United States of America

10   9   8   7   6   5   4   3   2   1

Although the people interviewed for this book
are wonderfully knowledgeable and enthusiastic about gardening,
they are only a select few among hundreds of fine gardeners
found throughout the state. This book is respectfully dedicated
to all Georgia Gardeners, those people who dig and plant and weed
and help make Georgia a place of beauty.

CONTENTS

FOREWORD

Trees, shrubs, flowers, and plants of all varieties delight the senses and bring contentment within the spirit. In the hours spent enjoying my garden, my heart swells with joy and my eyes seldom tire. The cares and concerns of the world are easily erased from the mind as one observes the wonders found in every plant. As you read this book, *Georgia Gardeners*, you will be similarly inspired to love gardening.

Georgia has been acclaimed a garden state since Colonial times. The founding trustees suggested that Georgia lay at the same latitude as the Garden of Eden and the Promised Land. It is true that plants thrive during our long growing season and that we have sometimes taken for granted our plant diversity. We are truly blessed to be able to grow many kinds of plants.

In *Georgia Gardeners*, you will become acquainted with numerous plants and learn to appreciate them more, following the example of Virginia Callaway. Georgia's beloved lady of the gardens encouraged every gardener to know plants by observing them closely.

Georgians have always loved to garden. In fact, the garden club movement began in Georgia. In 1891, the Ladies Garden Club of Athens was founded, and it is still in existence today. This chapter in Athens fostered the garden club movement across America. Now, National Council of State Garden Clubs, Inc. is the largest gardening organization in the world, and The Garden Club of America, Inc. is one of the most prestigious.

Laura Martin is one of Georgia's gardening treasures. Her contributions to horticultural education are extensive. For eleven years, she wrote a weekly gardening column for the *Atlanta Journal/ Constitution*. She has shared her vast knowledge of horticulture in numerous magazines, including *American Horticulturist*, *National Wildlife*, *American Nurseryman*, *Better Homes and Gardens*, *Atlanta Homes and Lifestyles*, *Verandah*, *Garden Design*, and *Southern Accents*. Her lectures on garden subjects have been enjoyed nationwide.

She received the Garden Writers of America Writing Award in 1994, Garden

Club of America Horticulture Award in 1987, National Council of State Garden Clubs, Inc. Publications Awards in 1987 and 1990, and the Alabama Conservancy Award of Excellence in 1987.

In Georgia, we are fortunate to claim Laura Martin as our own. And in this book she has collected the wisdom of thirty-seven other Georgia gardening experts. We are grateful that these select few were willing to share their gardening skills and love of gardening with us.

Mrs. Deen Day Smith
President of The Garden Club of Georgia, Inc.
1987–1989
Second Vice President of National Council of State Garden Clubs, Inc.
1995–1997

INTRODUCTION

"Gardening, reading about gardening, and writing about gardening are all one; no one can garden alone," wrote Elizabeth Lawrence.

Who would want to garden alone? The joy of gardening is in sharing—plants and seeds, tips and advice, stories and experiences. I've never met a gardener who didn't have an experience to relate, from horror stories about root rot to fairy tales about carefree roses. And I've met few gardeners who were not abundantly generous with the plants and produce from their own gardens.

But while we are all "Number One in our own backyards," as Virgil Adams put it, we are not all equal in terms of experience and expertise. Georgia is fortunate to have many gardeners who have spent a lifetime learning about the best ways to grow plants in this state.

It is to these experts that I went for advice—not just on "gardening," not even just on "gardening in the southeast," but specifically on "gardening in Georgia." I wanted to know exactly how Oline Reynolds grows such beautiful roses in Bainbridge, and how Virgil Adams coaxes tender lettuce leaves out of the ground in Jefferson. I wanted to know

how Michael Dirr grows bottlebrush buckeyes in Athens, and how Ashby Angell grows such magnificent ornamental salvias in Savannah—and more to the point—I wanted to know how I could use this information in my own Georgia garden.

The experts I interviewed for this book were impressively knowledgeable and eager to share their hard-earned wisdom, for they understand that a little knowledge goes a long way in the gardening world, and the end result of knowledgeable gardeners is a more lovely world for all of us.

Gardening in Georgia is not without its challenges. Mention hot, humid summers, or clay soils, and otherwise mild-mannered folks begin gnashing their teeth.

It is to solving the problems and reaping the rewards of gardening in Georgia that this book is dedicated. The experts interviewed all had dirt under their fingernails and an eye on the sky watching for rain—both sure signs of a real gardener. The advice they offer is practical, specific, and useful for anyone—both beginner and expert—who wants to participate in that ageless ritual of planting a seed and watching it grow into the miracle of a plant.

The information you find in *Georgia Gardeners* will help in any area of gardening, from designing a garden to growing fruits and vegetables, planting a lawn, putting in flower beds, growing herbs and roses, and planting trees and shrubs. Several experts address the beginner gardener, making suggestions for how to prepare the ground for a new garden, what tools you will need, and which plants are considered easy to grow and "fail proof." Other experts spoke of plants that are, perhaps, more difficult to grow, but which may add depth and a new level of sophistication to an already existing garden.

It is my hope that together, we, the gardeners of Georgia, can transform our small corner of the planet into one continuous garden where everywhere beauty is only a glance away.

1

GETTING STARTED

The nice thing about gardening is that absolutely anyone can do it. You don't have to have acres of regimented vegetable beds and elaborate perennial borders to be considered a gardener. If you've planted a few pansy plants, watered them when they were dry, and admired them when they bloomed, who's to say you're not a gardener?

The problem is, most of us are not content with just a few pansy plants. Most of us dream, at least secretly, of having acres of regimented vegetable beds or elaborate perennial borders. But for many beginner gardeners, the very thought of preparing the soil and planting a bed of flowers or vegetables is overwhelming.

The following tips are compiled from interviews with Georgia gardeners. For the most part, these are observations I heard over and over again from experts in every region of the state. Most are the simple rules of good gardening and are as applicable to the expert as the novice.

GEORGIA GARDENER GOLDEN RULES

Although you are bound to face many challenges throughout your gardening experiences, if you follow these Georgia Gardener Golden Rules, your success rate will be higher and your gardening pleasure increased.

- ✧ Have fun and enjoy your garden.
- ✧ Have a plan in mind before you start.
- ✧ Know what you want from your garden and how much time and space you are willing to devote to it.
- ✧ Start small and be patient.
- ✧ Gardening rarely offers instant gratification. It takes time for plants to grow and mature.
- ✧ Take a soil test and work with the soil you have.

This last was the most often cited piece of advice. Most of Georgia has heavy clay soil that almost always has to be improved for successful gardening. The only way to know the needs of your particular soil is to have a soil test done. Most Cooperative Extension offices will do this for a small fee. (Each county's extension office telephone number is listed in the resource section.)

When the test results are returned to you, they will be accompanied by a list of recommended amendments which, when added to your soil, will improve the health and productivity of your plants.

The term used most often is "working" with the soil and it is a descriptive term. Almost all soil recommendations include adding lime to combat the acidity of our clay soils. The lime (and most other amendments) have to be worked down into the soil to be available to the roots of the plants.

✧ Make and use compost.

Use leaves, garden and kitchen scraps, or whatever you have available to help enrich your soils.

✧ Grow plants suited to the Georgia climate.

Only select plant species and varieties proven to grow in your particular region. You'll have healthier, more productive plants if you choose those suitable for your own region. Trying to grow a plant in the wrong geographic area is inviting trouble. You might have success for a few years, but in the long run the plant will fail.

The plant catalog at the back of this book is a wonderful place to start. This catalog contains all the plants mentioned in the interviews, so all of them grow well somewhere in Georgia. To determine if a particular plant will grow in your region, refer back to the interview. Remember that some of these plants are only now being tested for their usefulness in the garden, and no one knows their exact range just yet. If you have a question, call your county Cooperative Extension Service or a botanical garden close to where you live.

✧ Choose the planting site carefully.

Plant your selections in suitable areas of the garden. Pay attention to the light and moisture requirements of the plants you choose and plant accordingly. For example, if a plant is listed as needing full sun, don't plant it in a shady area. You will be disappointed.

✧ Use more native plants.

Plants already adapted to the growing conditions of a particular region and will generally perform better than plants imported from elsewhere.

✧ If you don't like where a plant is growing, dig it up and move it somewhere else.

Remember that this is your garden and you need please no one but yourself.

✧ Plant for a long season of bloom.

We're lucky that in Georgia we can have something in bloom for most of the year. Choose plant selections that will give color and interest to every season.

PLANT NAMES

Plant nomenclature is sometimes confusing to a new gardener. These definitions ought to help ease the confusion.

Annuals are plants that complete their life cycle within one year. You will see the designation "treated as an annual" for plants that have a longer life cycle but which will not survive the winters (or sometimes summers) in our area. These plants are used for one or two seasons of color only.

Biennials are plants that complete their growing cycle within two years. Generally, these plants, like Queen Anne's lace and Sweet William, will spend the first year putting down roots. They will bloom the second year and die after blooming, although sometimes biennials planted from seed in early spring will produce blossoms by late summer.

Perennials are plants that live more than two years. Some perennials, such as black-eyed Susan (*Rudbeckia hirta*), are considered "short-lived perennials," meaning that they are capable of living more than two years, but generally do not last much longer than that.

Herbaceous plants have soft, fleshy stems and foliage. Most annuals, biennials, and perennials are considered herbaceous plants.

Most, but not all, garden plants have a **common,** or English name, by which they are known. A plant may have several common names. Pansies, for example, have collected dozens of common names through the centuries, including "Kiss Me in the Pantry." Although sometimes confusing, these are the fun names, descriptive and easily pronounced.

To eliminate this confusion, all plants have a Latin **botanical name** composed of a genus and a species. These are written in italics, with the genus capitalized and the species in lowercase letters. (Often the genus name and the common name will be the same. For example, *Coreopsis verticillata* is commonly known as coreopsis.) Although the botanical names of plants are sometimes changed, these names are recognized throughout the world. No two different kinds of plants can have exactly the same botanical name.

Varieties are plants within the same species that show dependable variation generation after generation. Plant varieties often occur within specific geographic ranges. Variety names are preceded by the designation "var." and are italicized. A specific kind of mountain bluestar, for example, is identified as *Amsonia tabernaemontana* var. *montana.*

Cultivars are plants that have been hybridized or selected for certain characteristics. Cultivars, when planted from seed, may or may not stay true to the characteristics of their parents, and are thus propagated by division, stem or root cuttings, or tissue culture. Many garden plants are cultivars. The designation is a name in single quotes, not italicized, as in the watermelon *Citrullus vulgaris* 'Crimson Sweet'. The terms "variety" and "cultivar" sometimes are used interchangeably by gardeners.

Hybrids are plants that occur when two species or genera of plants cross-pollinate, either naturally or as a result of the work of a plant breeder. The designation is the botanical name, and an (×). For example, *Anemone* × *hybrida* is a cross between two species of *Anemone.*

GEORGIA GARDENERS' FAVORITES

Gardeners are generally hard pressed to choose a "favorite" plant, although they are more than willing to list a dozen— or a couple of dozen—favorites. In the course of my interviews, some plant names came up over and over again, indicating that these varieties are real workhorses of the garden. They are reliable, attractive through much of the year, and relatively trouble free.

FAVORITE FLOWERS

Perennials for Full or Partial Sun
Dianthus   *Dianthus gratianopolitanus* 'Bath's Pink'
Purple coneflower *Echinacea purpurea*

Black-eyed Susan *Rudbeckia fulgida* 'Goldsturm'

Swamp sunflower *Helianthus angustifolius*

Goldenrod *Solidago rugosa* 'Fireworks'

Veronica *Veronica* 'Goodness Grows'

Verbena *Verbena* 'Homestead Purple'

Lantana *Lantana* 'Miss Huff'

Salvia *Salvia* 'Indigo Spires'

Yarrow *Achillea millefolium* 'Oertle's Rose' (also known as '1869')

Asteromoea *Asteromoea mongolica*

Russian sage *Perovzkia atriplicifolia*

Daisy *Chrysanthemum* 'Becky'

Bluestar *Amsonia tabernaemontana* var. *montana*

Perennials for Shade

Hosta *Hosta* sp.

Native columbine *Aquilegia canadensis*

Woodland phlox *Phlox divaricata*

Lenten rose *Helleborus orientalis*

Anemone *Anemone ventifolia* 'Robustissima'

Iris *Iris* sp.

Autumn fern *Dryopteris erythrosora*

Southern shield fern *Thelypteris normalis*

Pulmonaria *Pulmonaria longifolia*

Wild ginger *Asarum speciosum*

Astilbe *Astilbe chinensis pumila*

Foam flower *Tiarella cordifolia*

New and Exciting Favorites

Loropetalum *Loropetalum* sp. (Shrub)

Hydrangea *Hydrangea* sp. (Shrub)

Baptisia *Baptisia* sp. (Perennial)

Asters *Aster cordifolius, A. grandiflorus, A. carolinianus* (Perennials)

Salvia *Salvia* sp. (Perennial)

Plectranthes *Plectranthes* (Annual)

Persian Shield *Strobilanthes dyeranum* (Annual)

Stokesia *Stokesia* 'Omega Skyrocket' (Perennial)

Green-and-Gold *Chrysogonum virginicum* 'Eco Laquered Spider' (Perennial)

Sweet flag *Acorus minimus aureus* (Perennial)

GEORGIA GOLD MEDAL WINNERS

The Georgia Plant Selections Committee, Inc., formed in 1992, is a nonprofit organization comprised of individuals from the garden center and nursery industry, botanical gardens, Cooperative Extension Services, and the University of Georgia Department of Horticulture. The purpose of the committee is to identify "superior, yet under-utilized ornamental plants" and to promote their production, sale, and use.

Information about Gold Medal Winners can be obtained by calling the University of Georgia Extension Office at 706-542-2375.

1994 WINNERS

Dianthus gratianopolitanus 'Bath's Pink'

Verbena canadensis 'Homestead Purple'

Fothergilla major 'Mt. Airy'

Japanese Plum Yew *Cephalotaxus harringtonia*

1995 WINNERS

Salvia guaranitica

Lantana 'New Gold'

Lacebark elm *Ulmus parvifolia* 'Athena'

Hydrangea arborescens 'Annabelle'

1996 WINNERS

Petunia 'Purple Wave'

Baptisia sp.

Clethra alnifolia 'Hummingbird'

Crape myrtles *Lagerstroemia* 'Lipan', 'Sioux', 'Tonto', 'Yuma'

1997 WINNERS
Scaevola 'Blue Wonder'
Rudbeckia triloba
Loropetalum chinense rubrum
Cryptomeria japonica 'Yoshino'

2

REGIONS OF GEORGIA

Georgia is composed of a series of beautiful and diverse ecosystems. From the heat and humidity of south Georgia to the early fall frosts of the northern mountains, each region of our state is faced with unique problems and blessed with distinctive opportunities.

It is not difficult to garden anywhere in the state—you simply must be aware of the idiosyncrasies of your individual region and garden accordingly. Although it's difficult to garden according to a rule book, there are general guidelines that make gardening anywhere more rewarding.

Georgians are fortunate to have many experts in the county Cooperative Extension Service offices. These knowledgeable men and women can answer gardening questions, and most have useful, free, printed materials. Phone numbers for agents in each county are listed below.

County lines don't always coincide with horticultural boundaries. Some counties may be in both the Piedmont and the southern zones. Talk with your county extension personnel for specific growing conditions in your area.

For discussion purposes, I have divided the state into four different regions: **Mountains,** north of Rome, Dahlonega,

and Toccoa; **Piedmont,** south of the mountains but above the Fall Line (a line stretching from Macon to Augusta); **South,** below the Fall Line to the Florida state line; and **Coast,** including all of Georgia's coastal areas from Savannah south to Saint Mary's.

MOUNTAIN GEORGIA

The Georgia mountains, at the southern end of the Appalachians, form a region overflowing with natural beauty and rich in native flora. Gardening in this region is rewarding, for the cool temperatures and rich soils result in magnificent plantings. According to Dennis Thompson, superintendent of the Georgia Mountain Branch Experiment Station in Blairesville, soils in the area are varied. Some are quite acidic, most are low in phosphate, and most have a high clay content. The richest soils, according to Dennis, are those in the bottomlands, along rivers and streams.

Georgia mountain weather differs from that of other areas. "We have to be careful to choose cultivars which display winter hardiness," Dennis says. "Our temperatures are significantly lower than in the Atlanta and Athens area."

While most of north Georgia is found in the USDA horticultural zone 7a, with minimum temperatures of 0 to 5 degrees Fahrenheit, a tiny sliver of northeast Georgia is zoned 6b with minimum temperatures between −5 and 0 degrees F.

The idea of planting in a "microclimate" is perhaps more important in the mountain regions than other areas of the state. Microclimates are small pockets of land that present slightly different conditions from the remainder of the garden. For example, a planting bed at the corner of the house may receive full sun and remain protected from drying winds, which could possibly classify it in an entirely different hardiness zone than the rest of the garden. Observe your garden closely, and use these microclimates to your advantage.

Rainfall in the area is generally good, for it is located on the border of the second highest rainfall belt in the United States. At the Experiment Station in Blairsville, the mean annual precipitation is 54.21 inches.

The average last frost date is May 1, although Dennis Thompson urges gardeners to wait at least a few days later for better success in planting summer annuals and vegetables.

MOUNTAIN REGION EXTENSION SERVICE NUMBERS

Northeast District

Louise J. Hyers, director	706-542-2080
Dawson	706-265-2442
Fannin	706-632-3061
Habersham	706-754-2318
Lumpkin	706-864-2275
Rabun	706-782-3113
Stephens	706-886-4046
Towns	706-896-2024

Union	706-745-2524
White	706-865-2832

Northwest District

Susan J. Harrell, director	706-542-2942
Catoosa	706-935-4211
Chattooga	706-857-1410
Dade	706-657-4116
Floyd	706-295-6210
Gilmer	706-635-4426
Gordon	706-629-8685
Murray	706-695-3031
Walker	706-638-2548
Whitfield	706-278-8207

PIEDMONT

Perhaps more is known about gardening in the Piedmont than in any other region of the state. Although there are many rural areas included, major population and academic centers are found here, and much botanical research is conducted. Many horticulture meetings and symposiums are held in this region, and much of the discussion of plants is based on their growth in the Piedmont.

The Piedmont is blessed with moderation—it is neither as cold as the mountains nor as hot as the south. According to the United States Department of Agriculture plant hardiness zone map, this area is 7b, with minimum temperatures between 5 and 10 degrees F.

The greatest challenge to Piedmont gardeners lies in working with the red clay soils, and a soil test is highly recommended. Most soils are acidic and should be limed. (Lime needs to be dug into the soil to be made available at root level, and it takes about six months for it to take effect.)

Randy Drinkard, with the Fulton County Cooperative Extension Service says that urban areas offer their own set of problems. Pavement and decreased green areas increase the ground temperatures, making it difficult to grow plants that like to stay cool. It also might be necessary to water more frequently in urban areas. "Air pollution from cars and trucks might lead to disease or reduced vigor of plants," Randy says. "The white pines are considered a sensor plant for air pollution. You see many of them die along the I-75, I-85 wedge."

The last average frost in the Georgia Piedmont is April 10.

PIEDMONT REGION EXTENSION SERVICE NUMBERS

North Central District

Rose A. Simmons, director	912-825-6414
Butts	770-775-8209
Carroll	770-836-8605
Coweta	770-254-2620
Douglas	770-920-7225
Fayette	770-461-6041
Haralson	770-646-2026
Heard	706-675-3513
Henry	770-954-2060
Jasper	706-468-6479
Jones	912-986-3958
Lamar	770-358-5163
Meriwether	706-672-4235
Monroe	912-994-7014
Newton	770-784-2010
Paulding	770-443-7616
Pike	770-567-2010
Polk	770-749-2142
Spalding	770-228-9900
Troup	706-883-1675
Upson	706-647-8989

Northeast District

Louise J. Hyers, director	706-542-2082
Banks	706-677-2320
Barrow	770-307-3029
Clarke	706-613-3640

Elbert	706-283-2037
Forsyth	770-887-2418
Franklin	706-384-2843
Hall	770-531-6988
Hart	706-376-3134
Jackson	706-367-1199
Madison	706-795-2281
Oconee	706-769-3947
Oglethorpe	706-743-8341
Walton	770-267-1324

Northwest District

Susan J. Harrell, director	706-542-2942
Bartow	770-387-5142
Cherokee	770-479-0421
Clayton	770-473-3945
Cobb	770-528-2464
Dekalb	770-371-2821
Fulton	404-730-7000
Gwinett	770-822-7700
Pickens	706-692-2531
Rockdale	770-785-5952

SOUTH GEORGIA

Gardening in south Georgia is full of both rewards and difficulties. There is no doubt that south Georgia produces some of the most spectacular roses ever grown, and those who have visited south Georgia during camellia season are invariably moved by the experience. Vidalia onions from this region are world famous, and the watermelons ought to be.

But there are also a few drawbacks to gardening in this part of the state. Most of south Georgia below the Fall Line, which stretches from Augusta through Macon and down to Columbus, is ranked USDA plant hardiness zone 8a, with minimum temperatures between 10 and 15 degrees F. The extreme southern border of the state, including Bainbridge, Thomasville and Valdosta, is considered zone 8b, with minimum temperatures between 15 and 20 degrees F.

According to Robert Tucker, landscape designer from Moultrie, Georgia, it is the hot and humid summers that challenge the south Georgia gardener. "We can go four to six weeks with no rain, with both the temperature and humidity near 100. It's pretty awful for us, and really awful for the plants."

Soils in the region are often rich and poorly drained, creating lethal muck pockets. Be sure to have a soil test done before you begin to plant, and amend your soil as needed.

Because of the high summer temperatures and lack of rain, irrigation is generally a necessity, particularly for new plantings. Average last frost is April 1.

SOUTH GEORGIA EXTENSION SERVICE NUMBERS

Southwest Georgia District

John P. Parks, director	912-386-3412
Baker	912-734-3015
Brooks	912-263-4104
Calhoun	912-849-2685
Clay	912-768-2247
Colquitt	912-985-1321
Decatur	912-248-3033
Dougherty	912-436-7216
Early	912-723-3072
Grady	912-377-1312
Lee	912-759-6025
Miller	912-336-2066
Mitchell	912-336-2066
Quitman	912-334-4303
Randolph	912-732-2311
Seminole	912-524-2326
Stewart	912-838-4908
Terrell	912-995-2165
Thomas	912-225-4130
Webster	912-828-2325
Worth	912-776-8216

Southeast Georgia District

James Fountain, director	912-681-0177
Appling	912-367-8130
Brantley	912-462-5724
Bulloch	912-764-6101
Candler	912-685-2408
Effingham	912-754-6071
Emanuel	912-237-9933
Evans	912-739-1292
Jenkins	912-982-4408
Long	912-545-9549
Montgomery	912-583-2240
Screven	912-564-2064
Tattnall	912-557-6724
Toombs	912-526-3101
Treutlen	912-529-3766
Wayne	912-427-5965

South Central District

Darrell Dunn, director	912-386-3413
Atkinson	912-422-3277
Bacon	912-632-5601
Ben Hill	912-423-2360
Berrien	912-686-5431
Charlton	912-496-2040
Clinch	912-487-2169
Coffee	912-384-1402
Cook	912-896-7456
Echols	912-559-5562
Irwin	912-468-7409
Jeff Davis	912-375-6648
Lanier	912-482-3895
Lowndes	912-333-5185
Pierce	912-449-2034
Telfair	912-868-6489
Tift	912-386-7870
Turner	912-567-3448
Ware	912-285-6161
Wheeler	912-568-7138

East Central District

S. Ilene Dailey, director	912-681-0178
Baldwin	912-453-4394
Burke	912-554-2119
Columbia	912-541-0557

Glascock	912-598-2811
Greene	912-453-2083
Hancock	912-444-6596
Jefferson	912-625-3046
Johnson	912-864-3373
Laurens	912-272-2277
Washington	912-552-2011
Wilkinson	912-946-2367

West Central District

G. Melvin Davis, director	912-825-6412
Bibb	912-751-6338
Bleckley	912-934-3220
Chattahoochee	706-989-3055
Crawford	912-836-3121
Crisp	912-276-2612
Dodge	912-374-4702
Dooly	912-268-4171
Houston	912-987-2028
Macon	912-472-7588
Marion	912-649-2625
Muscogee	706-571-4791
Peach	912-825-6466
Pulaski	912-783-1171
Schley	912-937-2601
Sumter	912-924-4476
Taylor	912-862-5496
Twiggs	912-945-3391
Wilcox	912-365-2323

COASTAL GEORGIA

The Georgia coast presents some of the state's most beautiful natural landscapes. Creating a man-made landscape in this area, however, can sometimes be difficult. The combination of wind, salt spray, sandy soils, fog, a shallow water table, and shade from live oaks make growing conditions a little less than ideal.

Rog Ditmer, with the landscaping department of Sea Island Properties, suggests that gardeners in Georgia coastal areas use more native plants, be conscientious about watering, add compost to their soils, and plant more in containers.

Coastal soils generally have very high phosphorous levels and are low in manganese and magnesium. Guidelines for specific amendments to improve garden soils are offered with results from a soil test.

Coastal gardeners are not without good resources, however. The Coastal Gardens, officially known as the Historic Bamboo and Horticultural Collections, has display gardens and offers classes. The Cloister Hotel, on Sea Island, hosts an annual gardening symposium. Carol Krawczyk, Savannah gardener extraordinaire, publishes a wonderful newsletter called the *Coastal Gardener*. For information, or to order a subscription, call 912-920-2531. The Trustees Garden Club of Savannah has published a wonderful book, *Garden Guide to the Lower South*. For a copy, send $12.95 plus $1.75 postage to: Trustees' Garden Club, P.O. Box 24215, Savannah, Georgia 31403-4215.

COASTAL REGION EXTENSION SERVICE NUMBERS

Southeast District

James D. Fountain, director	912-681-0177
Bryan	912-653-2231
Camden	912-576-3219
Chatham	912-652-7981
Glynn	912-267-5655
Liberty	912-876-2133
McIntosh	912-437-6651

3

⚘

DESIGN

DARREL MORRISON, ATHENS: UNIVERSITY OF GEORGIA

In 1983, the state of Georgia gained an invaluable resource when Darrel Morrison left the University of Wisconsin at Madison and came to the University of Georgia in Athens to serve as the dean of the School of Environmental Design, a post which he held until 1992. Darrel's passion for native plant communities and his knowledge and skill in bringing these communities into controlled landscapes

has been a major influence on the field of landscape architecture throughout the country.

Darrel grew up on a farm in southwest Iowa, then attended the University of Wisconsin, where he earned a Master of Science in Landscape Architecture. Throughout his career, Darrel has believed that a convergence of several disciplines best prepares students for landscaping work. The study of horticulture, art, ecology, botany, and field biology, he believes, all contribute to the education of a landscape designer.

Although Darrel modestly describes himself as a "grasslands restoration consultant," his work with native grasses and his pioneering efforts in educating both professionals and laymen about design with native vegetation has led to numerous national awards, including the 1994 "Outstanding Educator" award from the Council of Education in Landscape Architecture.

His many publications and frequent lectures at universities and botanical gardens throughout the country have earned Darrel a well-deserved reputation for excellence.

LCM: I've always been a little confused about terminology—are you a landscape designer or a landscape architect?

DARREL: I prefer the term, "ecological design consultant." The word "architect" reminds me too much of work I did in the Washington, D.C. area early in my career, when we fell into the rut of using the same dozen plants over and over again. I soon became disenchanted. To limit ourselves to such a small number of plants did not seem right.

So, I left Washington and went to the University of Wisconsin, in part, because of the Plant Ecology program on that campus, which interested me even though my degree program was the Master of Science in Landscape Architecture.

A strong influence at this time was a book called *American Plants for American Gardens*, published in 1929. Let me quickly point out, though, that I didn't run into the book until many years after 1929! It was written by Edith Roberts, a plant ecologist, and Elsa Rehmann, a landscape architect, and is now being republished by the University of Georgia Press. The book talks about plant community groupings as a basis for landscape design, a concept which I still hold to be very important.

While teaching plant design at the University of Wisconsin, I often visited the University Arboretum, which included what was probably the earliest and best prairie restoration in this country. I also co-taught a summer field course with a plant ecologist and got out into the field as often as I could to familiarize myself and my students with the botanic and aesthetic characteristics of the region's native plant communities. The more I was out in these settings, the more convinced I became that we should be working with whole plant communities, and not just individual species.

When I came to the University of Georgia, I taught a similar course here with Dr. Sam Jones of the Botany Department. More recently, I've co-taught a course with an artist, Hank Methvin, from Atlanta. In that course, I taught botanical composition and structure of plant communities, and he taught watercolor techniques.

I've begun painting too, and have become very conscious of how much you learn about a plant community when you have to look closely enough to capture it in a painting. It is a whole new way of seeing. It opens your eyes.

LCM: Do you use other kinds of paints, or just watercolors?

DARREL: Just the watercolors. Using watercolors requires you to look for the essential elements. You can't possibly capture every detail with this medium, so you look for the essential lines and patterns. Watercolors are also good because you need to work fairly quickly and because you can't work over it, or you lose something. I like the immediacy of it. You have to decide what's important, and then capture it.

Last fall, I taught at the University of Michigan, and there I didn't have the luxury of working with a watercolor instructor, so I had the students do chalk and pastel drawings of natural settings and they were similarly useful. Whatever the medium, it requires you to process the landscape through your mind and distill it, and this helps you understand the important elements.

LCM: How did the landscaping "giants" influence you, people like Frederick Law Olmsted, Jens Jensen, and O.C. Simonds?

DARREL: They all had a huge influence, but particularly Jensen. When I moved to Wisconsin in the late Sixties, I began going to The Clearing, where he spent the last sixteen years of his life. I have been teaching a course there every other summer since the early Seventies.

Jensen's work has some parallel with Olmsted's in large scale spatial manipulation, such as the meadows and partially secluded views. Jensen was much more adamant about using locally native vegetation, which results in distinctly different landscape characteristics in different regions. I've seen some of his work in Kentucky and some in Wisconsin and they are very different. The spatial configuration may be similar, but colors and textures and forms, which reflect the local vegetation, are different. To me, that is one of the most important things we should be doing, capitalizing on and heightening regional differences rather than standardizing landscapes.

LCM: Do you find that we are evolving into this?

DARREL: Slowly, very slowly. I'm frustrated sometimes because so many landscape architectural programs don't emphasize that idea.

LCM: Why is that true?

DARREL: It's easier and safer the old way. It's a carry-over of an English tradition, which Olmsted supported with his wide, sweeping lawns—an idea which has been abused in this country. As we get into smaller and smaller lots, people still think they have to have a lawn, and often it doesn't function. Lawn is wonderful in an English climate, but in the Midwest and Southwest, and to some extent in the Southeast, a lawn requires a major effort. It tends to eradicate species diversity and certainly regional character,

---

LAWN ALTERNATIVES

Shade
Green-and-gold *Chrysogonum virginianum*
Iris, dwarf crested *Iris cristata*
Hepatica *Hepatica nobilis*
Ginger, wild *Asarum arifolia*

Sun
Broomsedge *Andropogon virginicum*
Bluestem, split *Andropogon ternarius*
Purple top *Tridens flavus*
Indian grass *Sorghastrum nutans*
Coreopsis *Coreopsis lanceolata*
Black-eyed Susan *Rudbeckia hirta*
Beebalm *Monarda fistulosa*
Blue-eyed grass *Sisyrinchium angustifolium*
Bluet *Houstonia caerulea*

---

because a lawn is essentially the same everywhere. That does not even take into consideration the idea of resource use—water, chemicals, and mowers. So, this has become a secondary theme for me, to look for alternatives to massive, unused lawns. I acknowledge the need for lawn for some activities, and sometimes even for design purposes, but I think we've gone about it all wrong, because we put in grasses that have to be watered and fed.

LCM: What are better ways to go about growing a lawn, and what are some of the alternatives?

DARREL: Certainly, if you're going to use it as a play area, then you should use a grass that is more drought tolerant. In the Great Plains, and in Texas, buffalograss is, for example, a good choice of lawn grass.

LCM: What would you suggest for the Southeast?

DARREL: We need to do more investigation in this area. I'm convinced that there are some grasses here with real potential. One is *Stipa avenaceum*, a needlegrass, which is tuft forming and grows about six inches tall. In semishade areas, Pennsylvania sedge, *Carex pennsylvanica*, has great potential: it is clump forming, but almost grows to form a sod. Side oats gramagrass, *Boutelona curtipendula*, is a native prairie grass that extends into extreme northwest Georgia. It is a sod-forming, drought-tolerant grass that I think would be a useful species to test throughout the state.

🌿

The more [I study natural settings], the more convinced I became that we should be working with whole plant communities, and not just individual species.

🌿

I want to encourage turf people to work on the idea. Certainly, among the 3,000 native plant species that we have in Georgia, there must be a grass that would be good for lawns.

LCM: To keep mowed, as a cut grass?

DARREL: Either to be kept mowed, or if it is an area without heavy use, to leave it unmowed, as they use buffalograss in Texas and the Plains states. That's the simplest solution where you want to have a monospecies cover.

Beyond that, there's an array of possibilities. In the shade, you can have mixes of native groundcovers. In semishade you can have green and gold, *Chrysogonum virginianum*; crested iris, *Iris cristata*;

hepatica, *Hepatica nobilis*; and wild ginger, *Asarum arifolia*. These all form a diverse cover in the woods and spread well. Given the opportunity, I would certainly want the diverse mixture of plants as opposed to using a single species.

In sunny areas, too, there's a wide variety of species to create a perennial meadow in the Southeast. A good backdrop for such plantings could come from native grasses such as broomsedge, *Andropogon virginicus*; split bluestem, *Andropogon ternarius;* purple top, *Tridens flavus;* and Indiangrass, *Sorghastrum nutans.* For diversity and color, you can add coreopsis, black-eyed Susans, showy evening primrose, butterfly weed, and monardas, to name a few.

Something else I am interested in working on is a short flower mix for sunny areas. I've used some of these—such as blue-eyed grass, bluets, and green and gold, in front of the Atlanta History Center.

LCM: The wildflower meadow idea seemed to have boomed and then lost steam. What happened? Did the consumer try it, fail, and give up on it?

DARREL: That's a big part of it, often because the wildflowers were not perennial natives. There's still much work to be done on the idea. Some of the seed companies are putting together mixes which don't include native grasses, and you really need the grasses to hold the whole thing together, from the standpoint of erosion control and for visual purposes.

The North Carolina roadside plantings have solid masses of a single kind of flower. It dazzles people for two weeks, and then it's gone. Greater diversity, including these native grasses, will bring more sustainable plantings.

Having observed the prairies in the Midwest and some grasslands in the

Southeast, I'm convinced that grasses need to make up about 80 to 90 percent of the vegetation. Flowers are there for sprinkles of color. What you really need to be doing is establishing a long-lasting plant community.

I've gone back to prairie restoration projects that I did in the Midwest over twenty years ago, and they're thriving because they have native perennials, and an appropriate mix of grasses and forbs [herbs].

A big problem comes in when you introduce aggressive weedy species like dame's rocket, *Hesperis matronalis*, and Queen Anne's lace, *Daucus carota*. I don't know where you stand on Queen Anne's lace, but I worry about it because it spreads so aggressively.

LCM: In the Midwest, people are adamantly opposed to the introduction of non-native species in a prairie restoration area because they will destroy the delicately balanced community. Is that something we have to worry about in the Southeast?

DARREL: I think there are any number of potentially invasive species. In the Southeast, I've seen it more with the woody and semiwoody species, like kudzu, of course, and privet, which is one of the worst in the world, and Japanese honeysuckle. I really believe that even though we have many invasive non-native species around us, we are obligated not to bring more in, certainly if we know that they are potentially invasive. I think we should be much more stringent about introducing new plants into the environment without observation and testing. I don't think that there are any regulations in Georgia now on bringing in new garden plants.

LCM: Why do people insist on non-natives?

DARREL: Ninety percent of it is education. I'm convinced, for example, that most people, if they knew the reason for not planting purple loosestrife, or Queen Anne's lace, would be very willing to listen to alternatives.

But people don't question it, and growers and landscape architects haven't made them question it. There is the feeling, I think, that by adding these exotic plants, you are increasing diversity. But if these plants get out of hand, as many of them have, it's going to lead to a net loss of diversity. I think the key will be breaking old habits and educating people why various plants might be a problem.

If you already have some native plants growing, then it's beneficial to encourage them and add other compatible natives.

In the Atlanta area, and probably all over the Southeast, many broad-leafed evergreen shrub species have been introduced, and in my opinion, overused. People have come to believe that they are a requirement for the landscape. They may be from China or Japan—or the coastal plain—but they are still not native to the Piedmont. It leads to a year-round, luxuriant-looking landscape, but it is no longer a distinctive Piedmont landscape.

The phenomenon of the Japanese azalea is so prevalent in the urban areas here, and it's unfortunate, because we have such beautiful native azaleas. But they are not evergreen, nor quite as showy. People are open to being educated if we make the effort. Many clients don't even know that there are native azaleas, and if they knew it, and could be shown, they would be very willing to use them.

LCM: Do you find that we're a better educated public than we were, say ten years ago?

DARREL: Oh, I think so. The environmental movement has done a lot for the use of native plants. But I also think that people respond to the beauty of using plants which belong to a certain environment, and knowing that in planting them, they are making more ecologically sound landscapes, with a more subtle beauty. And again, it comes with education and exposure. I was excited that I was able to do this when designing around the Atlanta History Center building.

LCM: Tell me about the design around this building.

DARREL: Initially, when I was approached to work on it, the area

❧

We should be . . . capitalizing on and heightening regional differences, rather than standardizing landscapes.

❧

around the museum had been designated the "Twenty-first Century Garden."

When I was asked to do the design, I asked just what was a "Twenty-first Century Garden," and was told that it was to be a sustainable landscape that would require little in the way of chemicals and water—no lawn—and one which used regionally native plants throughout. So, the framework was set for me to do a project the way I like to.

I walked over the site many times, and eventually divided it into different zones of community types, some natural, some more cultural. For example, the entrance next to Slaton Drive is a roadside community like one might find in Georgia. That implied native grasses and a number of wildflowers, which are then backed up by

sumac, sassafras, Chickasaw plum, and redbuds, so in a fairly compressed manner, we have a roadside community.

On the east side, I put in an early successional pine forest with fairly closely spaced loblolly pines with grasses and sumac beneath them. In an area with high canopy with oaks and mature loblolly pines, I went into more of a climax forest look with red and white oaks, black gum, and American beeches, with dogwood, fringe tree and redbuds as understory.

In the circle in front of the building, where we have full sun, I drew on the granite outcrops, which are a native phenomenom. This site was once a granite quarry, and the entrance was paved with granite blocks from an old Atlanta street. It just made sense to do that circle as a stylized granite outcrop, and perhaps that's the most exciting part of the whole project because it is truly new and it hasn't been done before, to my knowledge.

LCM: What kind of plants did you put in?

DARREL: Plants that grow naturally in granite outcrops. A little broomsedge, and ragwort, *Senecio tomentosus*, which blooms in late March; pineweed, *Hypericum gentianoides*; and some sedums. We dug all the plants where we got the stones, and I think of it as a rescue mission because the plants would have been destroyed with the next wave of quarrying.

LCM: Are all the plants in this garden native to the Piedmont?

DARREL: Yes, with the exception of the verbena, which I included for midsummer color in the roadside zone. It is a naturalized species, able to withstand the rigors of the roadside environment.

LCM: For the real purist, then, it's not enough to be native to Georgia? A plant should really be native to the region, and the plant community to which it belongs naturally?

DARREL: Yes. Not only for the health of the plant, but because plants ought to reflect our own specific region and its plant communities. But the roadside community is a cultural phenomenon, and for that reason, a naturalized species may be acceptable.

LCM: What advice would you give to homeowners who want to establish a plant community in their home landscape?

DARREL: There are an increasing number of native plant nurseries, so it is becoming easier to find native plants. Go out and look at natural models. Observe from the ground up and notice where they grow. You might even want to make a map of a particular natural area showing the distribution of trees and shrubs.

LCM: Can you suggest specific places to go and look at different ecosystems in our area?

DARREL: For granite outcrops, see Panola Mountain, east of Atlanta. For forested areas, see Thompson Mill Forest near the floodplain, along the Chattahoochee River; for the slope forest of the mountains, look at Blood Mountain. For the luxuriant cove forest, look at Sosebee Cove. The latter two are within National Forest land. Closer to Atlanta, the Atlanta History Center now serves as a demonstration garden for native plantings.

LCM: What are your goals, what do you hope to do from here?

DARREL: If there's one thing we are obligated to do, it is to not continue to diminish the biotic diversity that we inherited. Unfortunately, we have historically taken a piece of land which may have fifty species per acre, and landscaped it and diminished it to ten to twenty species. It seems overwhelming to think that we can stem the tide of homogenization, but if everyone, on their own bit of land—and the land that they influence—would try to maintain the biotic diversity, we would do a lot better.

There was a study quoted in *The New York Times* last fall (1994) about the vegetation on Staten Island. In 1780 a study was done identifying 1,100 native species. Two hundred years later, in the 1980s, another study was done and 430 species are gone, replaced by 100 species of exotics. That's a 4-to-1 ratio.

People, and particularly professionals, need to be conscious of these issues. We talk about loss of species in tropical rain forests, but it happens right here, too. If there's anything I hope to do, it's to help reverse that trend.

JIM GIBBS, CHEROKEE COUNTY: GIBBS LANDSCAPE COMPANY

Drive around Atlanta and it's impossible to miss the white vans and trucks bearing the Gibbs Landscape logo. They seem to be everywhere, from the Atlanta Botanical Gardens to Jim Gibbs's own home and garden in Cherokee County, north of Atlanta.

Undoubtedly, Jim Gibbs has had tremendous influence on landscape design in Georgia. Jim was chosen Georgia Nurseryman of the Year in 1983, and in 1991, he won a National Landscape Association Award for his own home and garden. In 1994, he was awarded Person of the Year by the Metro Atlanta Landscape and Turf Association. And Gibbs Landscape Company has won over 150 awards on the regional and national level.

Having worked closely with Atlanta Botanical Gardens from its inception, and currently serving on the Board of Trustees, Jim recently gave one hundred acres adjacent to his Cherokee County home to the Gardens to be used as a north Georgia extension.

Jim grew up in a gardening family. He says that his mother and her four sisters were all very good with color and all loved to garden. "It's in the genes. If you grow up gardening and listening to people talk about gardening all the time, you grow up loving it. All of a sudden I realized that if I wanted to participate in a family conversation, I had better learn a little about gardening."

LCM: You have an obvious love of plants. Is this what led you into designing gardens?

JIM: No, not really. I had a great aunt, Mrs. Edgar B. Dunlap, who had a beautiful garden in Gainesville, Georgia. She loved plant material and was fascinated with it. And my parents and both my grandmothers were great gardeners.

When I went off to college, I knew I wanted to do something creative, so my great aunt suggested that I talk with Hubert Owen, who was the dean of the School of Landscape Architecture at the University of Georgia. So I did, and I liked what he said, and ended up going into landscape design.

But my aunt kept insisting that I learn plant material as well. After my junior year in college, I spent the summer in California visiting gardens. The gardens I liked best were ones created by people who did both design and installation. This was very different from what I had experienced in Atlanta. At that time, there were few design/building companies here which did both design and installation. But I thought this was really important, so I shifted gears and studied horticulture as well.

The older I get, the more I see if you don't know the horticulture, you can never really put the plants together. You have to know how the plants will grow, and what colors and shades work well together. You need to know how to move the eye from one bed of color to another. I call this trailing color, color echo, or plant marriages.

LCM: Do you find that the need to know plant material is a prevalent attitude among landscape designers?

JIM: Not as much as it should. You can learn basic design techniques, but once you have that on paper, you have to have knowledge of horticulture to know which plants to use to fill the spaces.

People who don't know plant material tend to do great big masses of plants because they don't know what else works. That's what takes so much study.

Every day, I pick up a book and learn something. I used to think that if I read enough and studied enough, I'd learn it all, but now I know that I'll never learn it all. I'm going to die before then. You just can't learn everything because every day people are discovering new things.

Look at Gertrude Jekyll and what she wrote, and compare it to some of the writers today. They have read everything she wrote, and added to that everything that has been learned since then—and we've learned a lot. She was a great gardener, but we've come a long way.

LCM: Are there other writers whose work you really admire a great deal?

JIM: There are so many of them—John Brookes, Vita Sackville-West, Rosemary Verey, Elizabeth Lawrence.

LCM: Tell me about the property here.

JIM: I named it Arbor Crest because this is the highest crest in northeast Cherokee County, and an arbor is a place covered with trees, vines, and shrubs, thus the origin of the name. We built an arbor at the top of the hill and from there down to the ponds at the bottom is an elevation change of 145 feet. We have eleven different levels, with walkways on each level, so you can walk and enjoy each part of the garden.

The ponds are on the bottom level. There's a lot of water on the property. Every time we would dig for a pond, we would hit five or six springs.

I have so much to learn about aquatic plants. But getting out there and actually digging in the dirt and gardening with the plants is really the only way to learn. That way it's easy and fun, rather than academic.

LCM: Will you use native plants in any of the ponds?

JIM: Oh yes. I have a large area that is naturally landscaped with ferns and native plants, and it is just beautiful. All I'm doing is putting in curved walkways and making sure the native plants are featured. People come and look at this area

and ask me how long it took to put in all these ferns and plants, and I tell them thousands of years, since they were here naturally.

We have native azaleas, and mountain laurel that has grown 25 feet tall; some rare native orchids; and hundreds of native hydrangeas. In the fern glade, as the sun moves throughout the day, the light on the ferns changes, and it is just beautiful.

LCM: You've spent many summers in Europe studying landscapes. What influence did that have on your philosophy of landscape design?

❧

Color groupings and color echo are so important—without these groupings, the garden just looks busy. It's hard to do in a small garden.

❧

JIM: When I was in college I had a textbook called *Design on the Land*, by Norman Newton, which showed the original landscape plans of the big European gardens. I wanted to take that book and revisit each of these gardens to see how they had changed over hundreds of years.

After a while, my wife Sally and I were able to do that. Each year for seventeen years, we visited the gardens in Europe. It was amazing to see how the large gardens had evolved. I was fascinated by these gardens, but then I would see a small garden, for example, in the English countryside, and I'd think, "This is somebody's garden, and this is the scale

I want to work with," so I began learning about these gardens and the plants in them. The best education I had was traveling and visiting other gardens. I think that is invaluable. You can get a lot out of a book, but to really see a garden, you have to stand there and experience it all.

LCM: What design mistakes do you see people making in their home gardens?

JIM: Color groupings and color echo are so important; without these groupings, the garden just looks busy. It's hard to do in a small garden, and people often get little spaces too busy.

I think people should start with the bones of the garden—the plants that provide winter interest. I try to first think about winter, the bleakest time of the garden, and take care of that, then move to spring, summer, and fall.

❧

I think people should start with the bones of the garden—the plants that provide winter interest. I try to first think about winter, the bleakest time of the garden, and take care of that.

❧

Russian sage is beautiful in winter, with the silver stems coming up. The stems stay silver until March when you cut it back, and immediately it comes back out. And now, in summer, it has a beautiful lavender color.

I think sedum 'Autumn Joy' is another good winter plant because it has enough of an ornamental bloom to be interesting. 'Fairy' roses and dianthus 'Bath's Pink' have great winter interest. The stems of

the roses stay green, and the blue-grey foliage of the dianthus is exciting. Rosemary is wonderful, as are ornamental grasses, and nandinas for the red berries.

Under these plants we do an underplanting of bulbs that begin to bloom in January—snowdrops, aconites, and crocus. Bloom from bulbs continues through May. As the perennials fill out, they cover up the unattractive foliage of the spring bulbs. The garden here was designed for twelve months of color.

At this location, even this close to Atlanta, things are different. I think it's the altitude, and the change in temperatures. We're about seven degrees cooler here. People forget about the effect of reflective heat in Atlanta. When you think of all the houses in the neighborhood, and the paving from the streets and drives, some temperatures really get up high.

We don't have to deal with that out here. I think the cooler temperatures actually result in more beautiful color shades in the plants. For example, the purple coneflower always looks more beautiful, and the lythrum is also a more intense color.

The more I work with plants, the more I am amazed that what works well in one area, will not necessarily do the same thing in another. You just can't put a plant in another place and expect it to do the same thing. You have to experiment with gardens and be willing to dig things up and move them around.

LCM: What are some other gardens that you've designed?

JIM: One of my favorites is Deen Day Smith's. I was involved with that from the time she built the house. We did a lot of berming and mounding to get undulation through the garden. We wanted different focal points and had enough space to do nice color echo. It makes you want

❧

to keep going farther and farther into the garden.

Other favorites are the gardens that I designed for Mr. and Mrs. Tom Cousins, one at their Atlanta residence and one at their plantation in Albany.

LCM: What advice do you have for people who are trying to design their own gardens?

JIM: Have fun and enjoy it. I have one client who loves plant material so much that she wants to put everything in a small space, and it tends to look busy. I told her that if it pleased her, not to worry about it. She is the one who sees it every day.

But, in general, if you have a small space, why not make it a view garden, so that you have a magnificent view of the garden from different angles and different locations? Just don't try to do too much in a small space.

LCM: Have you met some interesting people through your work?

JIM: We do a lot of commercial landscaping, but I love working with residential people. They love gardening, and they become so involved. Sometimes they'll see something in a magazine and think that they want just that, and it may be completely wrong for their space or their topography, so they need a little guidance.

They don't always take my advice, but I try to make suggestions and guide people in the right direction. I don't tell people what to do; I always try to make them feel that they've made the correct decisions.

LCM: Any last philosophy or advice?

JIM: Just have fun with gardening. I don't know which I enjoy more: actually installing a garden or planning a new project. There's so much fun in both for me. While I'm working on a project, I always have another in mind.

A person's garden has to please that person. The easiest way to change a gar-

den is to keep moving things around until you're happy with how things look. No perennials are set in concrete.

RYAN GAINEY, DECATUR

Every time I visit Ryan Gainey's garden in Decatur, I come away thrilled with the experience. My senses are well pleased, and my mind is alive with inspiration.

I am hardly alone in my enthusiasm over Ryan's garden. It has been photographed and written about in numerous magazines, including *Veranda*, *Southern Accents*, and *House Beautiful*, and is also on the annual "Gardens for Connoisseurs" tour sponsored by the Atlanta Botanical Garden.

Ryan, originally from Hartsville, South Carolina, studied Ornamental Horticulture at Clemson University. Well known for his garden designs, which are found throughout the eastern United States and southern France, Ryan says that these gardens "embrace the ideas of classical garden style and design with the exuberance of romance and color."

Atlantans probably best know of Ryan's work through his shops, The Potted Plant, The Cottage Garden, and The Connoisseur's Garden, and his creations at various prestigious fund-raising events, such as the annual Garden of Eden Ball, benefiting the Atlanta Botanical Garden.

❧

A garden has to have good design, thoughtfully laid out beds, and . . . order. A garden brings order to our lives because it involves the issue of controlling nature.

❧

Ryan has shared his creativity and knowledge through many different media, including a PBS documentary, a book entitled *The Well-Placed Weed*, and a highly acclaimed video, *Creating the Romantic Garden*.

LCM: You are known internationally for the gardens you have created. What do you consider the essential elements of a landscape design?

RYAN: A garden must have good design and thoughtfully laid out beds, and should have some order to it. A garden brings order to our lives because it involves the issue of controlling nature.

The whole process of designing a garden allows for constant refinement. For example, in this garden, we removed the old greenhouse that was here and made a large addition to the garden space. We now have beds for growing cut flowers, which gives us a constant supply of zin-

nia, cosmos, sunflowers, and salvias throughout the summer. It's laid out in rectangular spaces, so even in a flower bed there is order, which is essential to a garden.

LCM: Do you think that a basic mistake that gardeners make is in not having a design before they begin to garden?

RYAN: Oh, very much so. People put in plants, and then all of a sudden say, "This is a mess, and I need a plan."

LCM: What are some things to consider when creating a design?

RYAN: Be conscious of the plants you are putting in and the ultimate size they will attain. How do you know this? How can you learn to judge what the garden will look like twenty years from now? By observing nature and seeing what other people have done in the making of gardens throughout history.

The elements of design come from nature and are based on how plants grow. If you are going to put the picture together correctly, you must observe nature, and you must be patient. In nature there is a natural succession, starting with grasses and annuals, and progressing all the way up to the hardwoods; it takes a long time. You can't build a forest and create an instant overstory.

Another element to consider is the architecture of the house. Whether it is a little bungalow in Morningside, which may allow for a charming picket fence and nice steps, or something more formal, you need to be conscious of how you move through the space and how it all fits together. For example, the garden may be Italianate or Mediterranean, which may or may not match the architecture of the house. When the garden doesn't have anything to do with the house, then you have a difficult juxtaposition. A good design integrates the garden setting and the structures. The house and garden should be one design.

LCM: Do you think people ignore good design concepts because they get caught up in gardening fads and simply want what's hot and new?

RYAN: Yes. I think we get bogged down in wanting to have, but not necessarily in wanting to have what is right. Even if you have the best intentions and a good design, gardening is still a difficult task.

LCM: You've obviously had tremendous influence in the gardening world, through your work with the Atlanta Flower Show, your books and lectures, and your shops. What do you feel has been your greatest influence?

RYAN: Making a statement for doing that which is correct for the individual—what you wear, what you eat, what you eat off of—it's all personal expression. Many people have the key to personal expression in hand but don't know how to use it.

LCM: Why?

RYAN: We're too dictated by trends and lack confidence in our own creativity. To be creative doesn't mean you have to do everything yourself. The creative process involves other creative minds. I don't create anything, but I can take the creative ideas and the imagination of other craftsmen, and I can put it all together and make something wonderful to look at. People say that I'm a genius, and I say, not really. I just happen to have eyes and can put these things together. Part of the creative process is in recognizing what other people do. For example, choosing a garden designer is a reflection of yourself.

As a designer, I can only give my client what he or she can control, or what can be controlled for them. The worst thing you can do is to lose control

of something because you can no longer take care of it. A garden will not take care of itself. Well, it will take care of itself in the most astute way, in that it will revert totally back to nature, and that can happen in three weeks. Even in an uncultivated garden, there will be areas where, unless you nurture them, nature will take over. Making a garden is a combination of cultivating that which is not natural, and allowing that which is natural to become cultivated. It works both ways.

For example, you can have an absolutely wonderful stand of *Aralia spinosa*, and when it blooms and makes berries, there is really nothing any pretti-

❧

I think we get bogged down in wanting to have, but not necessarily in wanting to have what is right. Even if you have the best intentions and a good design, gardening is still a difficult task.

❧

er. Someplace else in the world, people may think that a single plant of carefully cultivated *Aralia spinosa* coming to fruit beside a purple aster is a brilliant and wonderful combination. Here, it tends to be an invasive weed, and we don't consider it as special. In either case, it does not detract from the fact that this is a beautiful plant when the berries start to form and contrast with the stems which are chartreuse, turning to purple.

LCM: How do you teach people about designing their own gardens?

RYAN: The demonstration gardens I have done for the Southeastern Flower

Show in the past few years still bring people good ideas. I believe that good design involves the unification of man and nature, and a knowledge of plants and

❧

If you have a nice place to sit and eat outside, with pots of plants for change in color for different seasons, that's all you need.

❧

which ones will look good and grow well in your garden. There is often a difference between what you want in your garden and what you need.

I tell people to look for something simple and pleasing and in balance. If you have a nice place to sit and eat outside, and pots of plants for change in color for different seasons, that's all you need. If you want extras in the garden, buy pretty pots, or add water and a fountain, a pretty sculpture, or an arbor and trees.

Evaluate what a garden can give you other than flowers. Trimmed plants, both woody and evergreen, even without flowers, give you a nice structure. Realize that there is foliage, fruit, berries, and flowers that grow just as wonderfully on woody shrubs as they do on sunflowers and zinnias.

One of the most satisfying ways of gardening is with trees, shrubs, and shade. The more sun you have, I can tell you, the more work it is. If you are trying to grow a rose in the sun, there are also other things that want to grow in the sun—weeds.

LCM: What changes have you seen in gardening during your professional career?

RYAN: We have seen tremendous environmental changes in our lifetime. We have long periods of rain, then long periods of drought. We don't live by horticultural zones anymore. We just know that we can grow things here successfully now that we would never have dreamed of five years ago because of changes in our climate.

I lecture all over the country, and what I try to tell people is to have their enthusiasms, but put them in order. It's a tenuous struggle to balance the passion to have all these plants with the original idea of creating order out of nature.

I tell people to let a fewer number of things give them greater pleasure. It's an ancient, Old World idea which works well for the garden. Gardening is all about pattern making. Every single thing, every flower or tree, is a combination of patterns. And pattern is about design, and design is all about order.

ROBERT TUCKER, MOULTRIE

Like many plant people, Robert Tucker has found himself in the landscape and horticulture business not through a grand design and early aspirations, but through a love of plants and the natural world, which brought him to this point almost in spite of himself.

Robert grew up in the southwestern part of the state, in Moultrie. After graduating from Emory University with a degree in English, he made his way back to Moultrie, where he began to create landscapes of great beauty.

Robert learned his craft well. As a true artist, he felt that he needed to know his medium as well as possible, and launched an intensive self-study program to learn what he could about the plants which grow and thrive in his portion of the state. The result is his extensive knowledge about the plants native to his region of the state, and the ecosystems to which they belong.

"Helping my clients understand the interrelationships of plant material is vital to their understanding of what we are trying to accomplish. A natural ecosystem in south Georgia is created largely by the canopy above, which provides much needed shade. In a home landscape we try to incorporate this, rather than just install shrubs around a residence."

And why does Robert landscape for a living? "Because it allows me to be creative and to work with both plants and people. In a short time, I can see the transformation from disturbed dirt to finished landscaping. This is truly rewarding."

LCM: Gardening in south Georgia is obviously a challenge. The weather yields bountiful harvest for some kinds of plants, but makes growing other plants very difficult. You often speak of gardening below the "gnat line." What is the "gnat line" and what is it like to garden here?

ROBERT: As Yankees travel south, around Cordele they get out to gas up the car, and all of a sudden, gnats cover their faces. Then they know that they are down south. The gnat line runs just below Macon and the Fall Line.

Below the gnat line, and including the region fifty miles south of Tallahassee, is a horticultural zone all to itself, which can be very hot and dry in summer. We can go four to six weeks with no rain, both the temperature and humidity near 100. It's pretty awful for us, and really awful for plants. You have to make sure that the plants you install will be able to survive that heat and drought cycle.

It's almost essential to have irrigation if you're going to garden here. It is so hot that when we don't get rain, the roots close to the surface dry out quickly.

LCM: Do most people put in irrigation systems?

ROBERT: Most of my clients do. In southwest Georgia, we have incredible resources of water underneath us, though we are becoming increasingly aware of the water table and the need for conservation. Many big companies, as well as farmers in the area, use a lot of water. The shallower wells are beginning to have a lot of sulfur in them.

But it is so hot for so long that you really need an irrigation system to help the plants through at least that first summer. In the mountains, we say that the critical point for the plants is that first winter. Here, we say it's the first summer.

When we put together a landscape design, we try to be aware of the moisture requirements of the plants, and plant accordingly. However, we still experiment. For example, we use bald cypress,

SOUTHWEST GEORGIA PALETTE OF PLANTS

Shrubs

Indica azaleas *Rhododendron* sp.

Florida leucothoe *Agarista populofolia*

Florida anise tree *Illicium floridium*

Wax myrtle *Myrica cerifera*

Tea olive *Osmanthus fragrans*

Camellias *Camellia sasanqua* and *Camellia japonica*

Spiraea *Spiraea* × *Vanhouttei*

Oak-leaf hydrangea *Hydrangea quercifolia*

Viburnum *V. watteri, V. obovatum, V. rufidulum*

Sweetspire *Itea virginica*

Native azaleas *R. canescens, R. speciosum, R. austrinum*

Perennials, Bulbs, and Grasses

Iris (Siberian and Japanese) *Iris* sp.

Daylilies *Hemerocallis* sp.

Daffodils *Narcissus* sp.

Black-eyed Susans *Rudbeckia fulgida, R. hirta*

Sunflower, narrow-leaf *Helianthus angustifolia*

River oat grass *Chasmanthium latifolium*

Yellow star jasmine *Trachelospermum asiaticum*

Black mondo grass *Ophiopogon planiscapus* var. *arabicus*

Lantana *Lantana camara* 'New Gold'

Blue-eyed grass *Sisyrinchium angustifolium*

Blazing star *Liatris graminifolia*

Phlox *Phlox divaricata*

Columbine *Aquilegia canadensis*

generally considered a wetland species, in drier areas and it's done fine—it just grows more slowly. But willows will not grow in a site like this at all. Some plants are more adaptable than others.

We also have wet times, and our soils are much richer than, for example, they are north of Macon. When it rains a lot, the soil holds its moisture, gets mucky, and simply does not drain as well. In the mountain, you can plant a dogwood by a stream bank and the soil will be moist and damp, and you'll say this soil is wonderful. Here, if you plant it in a moist spot by a stream, the soil stays mucky, never drains, and the plant will die. Conditions are pretty tough for plants. I try to use as many native plants as possible.

LCM: Why do you like using native plants?

ROBERT: Not only do I think that they are better suited for our environment, I also feel that it is important for people to know what's here and what's beautiful around us. We, in rural southwest Georgia, need to wake up and realize what beautiful natural resources we have here, instead of feeling that we have to drive to Callaway or Atlanta Botanical Garden to see beautiful plants. If I can help people become excited about native plants in the landscape, then hopefully they'll get excited about their own woods as well.

For example, if I introduce a client to the beauty of *Hymenocallis*, which grows naturally in TyTy Creek in south Georgia, then he or she might be better able to appreciate ecological changes that affect this creek.

LCM: By native you mean native to southwest Georgia?

ROBERT: If we can, we try to get the species native to the region, but often we have to pull from a broader area because nurseries don't always have exactly what's native to this particular region.

One of our most beautiful natives is spider lily, *Hymenocallis latifolia*, which is just stunning. It is white, with a lemony fragrance, and foliage like amaryllis. Just the foliage is exquisite, even though it dies down in winter. These lilies like a lot of moisture, but they do very well off-site and are used most effectively in a mass planting. The foliage stays attractive throughout the summer. It's a wonderful, wonderful plant.

The bulbs are fairly large, and you might be able to grow them as far north as Atlanta, though you would have to plant them deeper. Other species, such as *Hymenocallis occidentalis* and *H. crassifolia* are native to North Carolina.

LCM: What other native plants do you use?

ROBERT: There are some wonderful shrubs, like Florida leucothoe, Florida anise tree, native yaupon holly, and native azaleas, *R. canescens, R. speciosum,* and *R. austrinum.*

Of course, there are some great non-native shrubs to use as well. Why limit your palette? We can grow beautiful camellias and tea olive, forsythia.

LCM: Which native trees do you incorporate into your landscapes?

ROBERT: The long-leaf pines, which are native here, are just beautiful. We also use a lot of oaks—live, red, and willow—and Florida maple, red buckeye, southern magnolia, native river birch, and dogwoods.

As for non-natives, dwarf green Japanese maple, Natchez crape myrtle, and Japanese magnolia all add a lot to the landscape.

LCM: When do you begin to get really cold weather here?

ROBERT: We usually have our first hard freeze right around Thanksgiving,

Trees
Flowering dogwood *Cornus florida*
Buckeye, red *Aesculus pavia*
Pine, long-leaf *Pinus*
Oak, live *Quercus virginiana*
Oak, willow *Quercus phellos*
Oak, southern red *Quercus falcata*
Black gum *Nyssa sylvatica*
Florida maple *Acer floridanum*
Chalkbark maple *Acer leucoderme*
Japanese red maple *Acer palmatum*
Crape myrtle *Lagerstroemia indica* 'Natchez'
Cryptomeria *Cryptomeria japonica*
River birch *Betula nigra*
Pine, spruce *Pinus virginiana*
Tulip poplar *Liriodendron tulipifera*
Magnolia, southern *Magnolia grandiflora*
Silverbay *Magnolia virginiana*
Crabapple *Malus angustifolia*
Winged elm *Ulmus alata*

but it can be as late as Christmas. The last frost is generally in early March.

LCM: How do you begin to create a landscape design?

ROBERT: I'll share with you what I do with a client who is building a new home. I visit the site, hopefully before construction begins on the house, and then ride around looking at landscapes with the clients. They tell me what they like and don't like so that I can begin to design a plan with their tastes in mind. I work within their guidelines, but I also try and work with nature as well. I help educate my clients—and myself—about what happens with these plants naturally, and then try to make the landscape respond.

I help my clients learn to look. A college course on the history of art is one of the most valuable I've ever taken. We used a book called *Learning to Look*, and I often refer back to that. It's about perspective and what you see when you look into a painting or a landscape.

❧

It stays hot for so long, you really need an irrigation system to help the plants through the first summer. In the mountains, we say that the critical point for the plants is the first winter. Here, we say it's the first summer.

❧

Sometimes my clients don't really know what it is they want, though some have a very clear idea. Sometimes they want many different kinds of plants and have no idea how to fit them together. To me, design and knowing the plant material have to be absolutely integrated.

There's no substitute for hands-on work. People like to sit at a desk and design a garden, but you've got to get out there and experience what the plants will do in a particular region before you know how they will fit together in a design. The only way to help solve someone else's problem, whether it's a garden design or a community problem, is to get out there and work alongside them.

There are also practical considerations that have to be dealt with. Not the least of these is the amount of time and money a client is willing to spend on garden maintenance.

They also need to understand how they will use the garden space. Will they use it for a children's play area, or to attract wildlife? Will they entertain here, or do they just want something pleasant to look at?

Perhaps the most important concept to be considered is how the landscape can complement the house and become an integral part of the overall site. Too often, landscape designers work in a vacuum, only working with the idea of filling remaining empty space with plant material.

LCM: What are some of the challenges of gardening in this area?

ROBERT: People have to understand how important it is to get water to the new plantings during that first hot, dry summer. This is a time of real stress for these plants, so you must water them.

Another problem is Indian summer, where temperatures stay around 65 degrees during the day and only drop to 45 to 50 degrees at night for about three weeks. Then one night the temperature will go down to 15 or 20 degrees. The plants are like plumbing pipes full of water and when they freeze, they will burst. You may not see the damage until next spring, or until it gets hot again.

Fungus is a big problem here, too. Redbuds in Atlanta grow thirty to forty years. Here, they grow seven to ten years because of the fungus, and cannot be used as a major feature of the landscape.

It's also important to know the needs and life cycles of the different plants and to site them correctly in the garden. Shade-loving plants have to be planted in the shade, and sun-loving plants need to go in the sun. One of the worst mistakes that people make down here is to plant dogwoods in the sun. They just won't make it.

❧

LCM: What are some of the goals you have for your work?

ROBERT: To learn about and enjoy the plant world in southwest Georgia, and to help my clients learn to enjoy gardening.

RESOURCES FOR DESIGN

BOOKS

The American Horticultural Society Encyclopedia of Garden Plants. Macmillan Publishers, 1989.

Brookes, John. *The Garden Book.* New York: Crown Publishers, Inc., 1984.

————. *The Small Garden.* New York: Crown Publishers, Inc.

————. *The Book of Garden Design.* New York: Macmillan, 1991.

————. *The Country Garden.* New York: Crown Publishers, Inc., 1987.

Brown, Jane. *Vita's Other World.* New York: Viking Press, 1985.

Church, Thomas D. *Gardens Are For People*, 2nd Edition. New York: McGraw-Hill, 1983.

Cox, Jeff. *Plant Marriages.* New York: HarperCollins, 1993.

Gainey, Ryan. *The Well-Placed Weed.* Dallas: Taylor Publishing Co., 1993.

Hobhouse, Penelope. *Color in Your Garden.* Boston: Little Brown, 1985.

Jekyll, Gertrude. *Garden Ornament.* (Reprint.) Suffolk, England: Woodbridge, 1982.

Jekyll, Gertrude, and Lawrence Weaver. *Gardens for Small Country Houses.* (Reprint of 1912 edition.) Suffolk, England: Woodbridge, 1981.

Lawrence, Elizabeth. *A Southern Garden: A Handbook for the Middle South, Revised Ed.* Chapel Hill, North Carolina: University of North Carolina Press, 1967.

Verey, Rosemary. *Rosemary Verey's Good Planting Plans.* Boston: Little Brown, 1993.

MAGAZINES

Garden Design
American Society of Landscape Architects
1733 Connecticut Avenue
Washington, D.C. 20009

CLASSES

Atlanta Botanical Garden 404-876-5859

Gwinett Tech 770-962-7580, ext. 148

State Botanical Garden, Athens 706-542-1244

4

FLOWERS: ANNUALS AND PERENNIALS

LUCINDA MAYS, PINE MOUNTAIN: CALLAWAY GARDENS

Though born in Nebraska, Lucinda Mays now calls Georgia home. As a child, she was always encouraged to garden, and this led her to a lifetime of work and play in the garden. She served as assistant director of Kalmia Gardens at Coker College in Hartsville, South Carolina, and in 1988 joined the Callaway Gardens staff. For two years she served as horticulture instructor for the Education Department, and in 1990 was named Horticulture Department Curator.

Soon after she came to Callaway Gardens, she became the behind-the-scenes gardener with the television show, *The Victory Garden*. She now serves as one of the hosts for this popular PBS series. Callaway includes Victory Garden South, a demonstration garden Lucinda tends. Thousands of viewers have grown to know and love Lucinda's enthusiasm for her work, and have come to depend on her advice and inspiration.

In addition to her television work, Lucinda lectures and writes articles on various horticultural topics. Recent publications include a book on vegetable gardening, which she co-authored with her colleague, David Chambers.

She and her husband Roger live in rural Georgia where, Lucinda says, "I cannot imagine *not* gardening."

LCM: What is it like to do *The Victory Garden* show from Callaway Gardens?

LUCINDA: I love doing it, but it's sometimes tough to get everything in. It's as if I take a thirty-minute lecture or demonstration and condense it to six minutes. When I'm working in the garden at Callaway and visitors walk up and ask me questions, I know that these are probably the same kinds of questions our viewers have, so these will make good television segments.

For example, if you walk through the garden today, you'll see lots of hanging containers made from gourds. People see something like this and respond. They want to know what the gourds are and how to grow them, and where you find the seeds. It becomes an instant lesson, not only on growing gourds for a container, but also on growing plants in a container.

LCM: How do you grow plants in a container?

LUCINDA: Begin with the right kind of container. Pots that are wider than they are tall retain water longer and are really better for holding plants, but containers can be made from almost anything—terra cotta, washtubs, whatever.

Once you have a good container, you need the right kind of soil. Soil out of the garden isn't good to use in a pot because it's too heavy, it crusts up, and doesn't drain well. I suggest that people buy a soil-less potting mixture made of vermiculite and peat moss. This is a very light mixture, and will feel light in the bag.

When I plant the containers, I don't put the new plants into a dry potting mix because the dry soil will wick the moisture right out of the roots and away from the plants. I put the mix into the container, moisten it, cover it and let it sit overnight. The next day, I put in the plants, water, and add a slow-release fertilizer. Fertilizer is important because the only nutrients available to the plants are from the soil in the pot. Peat moss and vermiculite contain no nutrients. For container plants, you have to provide all those goodies that garden plants get from the soil.

LCM: What kinds of plants are found in the garden at Victory Garden South?

LUCINDA: A wide variety, including trees, shrubs, herbs, annuals, perennials, bulbs, and vegetables. It's constantly changing. The Home Demonstration Garden [Victory Garden South] receives about 600,000 visitors every year, so we always have something new for them to see. Right now, we have a flower border planted with fragrant daffodils. When the daffodils die back, poppies will come up. We have twelve or thirteen different varieties planted this year. We hope that visitors will see this display, then go home and plant them in their own garden in the fall.

SOW IN AUGUST FOR SPRING BLOOM (MIDDLE AND SOUTH GEORGIA)

Poppy *Papaver orientale, P. rhoeas, P. nudicaule*
Hollyhock *Alcea rosea*
Dianthus *Dianthus chinensis*
Parsley *Petroselinum crispum*
Linaria *Linaria purpurea*
Larkspur *Consolida orientalis*

LCM: How hardy are the poppies you grow in the garden here? Will they grow well in north Georgia?

LUCINDA: Poppies will grow nearly everywhere, they just bloom later in the north. We've found that they can take temperatures in the 20s, but much lower than that and they start losing their root system. We've also found that if the soil around them stays wet, the plants are not as cold tolerant as they are when the soil is dry and well drained. We build our poppy beds up three inches higher than the surrounding beds.

Here at Callaway Gardens, we sow poppy seeds in August, either in flats or directly into the soil and are very conscientious about watering them. In the lower south, if the seeds are sown in late summer, the first-year plants will bloom in spring. In zones 7 and up, you should wait until March to sow the seeds, and expect blooms the following year.

To get good poppies, work up the soil just as you would if you were planting a tomato. Rake it smooth, sow the seeds, cover with one-half inch soil-less potting soil, and be sure to keep it moist.

LCM: What other seeds can you sow in August to overwinter?

LUCINDA: Old-fashioned hollyhocks will bloom the first year from seed sown in late summer. Sometimes in winter they'll respond to unseasonably warm days and throw up a flower spike which is killed when it turns cold again, but it doesn't really hurt the plant.

I like to set out parsley plants in August. It winters over and stays evergreen at least as far north as Helen, Georgia. During mild winters, it even stays green in my dad's Nebraska garden.

Dianthus is another great plant to start from seed. Any variety of *Dianthus chinensis* does well. Try cultivars like 'Ideal

Violet', which is a neon magenta color, 'Pink Flash', or 'Color Magician', which has different colors all on the same plant. 'Scarlet Splendor' is as red as they get.

LCM: Should you pinch back the seedlings if they begin to put on good growth in the fall?

LUCINDA: No, just let them go. If you clip back the plants, this will spur on even more growth, which will be more tender. It's better just to let winter do what it will do to the plants.

LCM: What are some of your favorite plants for a fall display?

LUCINDA: We get beautiful displays from annuals sown directly in the garden in late July and early August. I love to use cosmos, particularly *Cosmos bipinnatus*, the orange and yellow species. Marigold and zinnias are also beautiful fall bloomers.

Some of the best fall flowers are the native perennials. My favorites are *Helianthus angustifolius, H. gigantus* and *H. salicifolius*. These three sunflowers bloom in sequence, beginning with *H. angustifolius* in mid-September.

Another great plant is *Salvia leucantha*, velvet sage or Mexican bush sage, and *Verbena canadensis*, which gets powdery mildew in July, but looks great by fall if you shear it back in mid-summer. The goldenrods are also good, especially something like *Solidago rugosa*, rough-stemmed goldenrod. It never becomes invasive or looks ragged. I like the cultivar 'Fireworks'.

One of my all-time favorite plants is vining aster, *Aster carolina*, which is native to Georgia and blooms in October here at Callaway. After the first frost, when everything else begins to look a little tired, the foliage of this plant turns a beautiful plum color. The name is misleading, though. It doesn't really twine, though I do have to trellis it to give it support.

SOW IN JULY AND AUGUST FOR FALL COLOR

Salvia *Salvia splendens*

Cosmos *Cosmos sulphureus* 'Bright Lights'

Cosmos *Cosmos bipinnatus* 'Early Wonder'

Marigolds *Tagetes* 'Golden Gate'

Zinnias *Zinnia* 'Zenith' hybrids

Sunflower, annual *Helianthus annuus* 'Inca Jewels', 'Giant Grey Stripe'

LCM: Do you have favorite plants, either for practical or philosophical reasons?

LUCINDA: Most of the plants which are my favorites for Victory Garden South end up being so for practical reasons. The plants I just cannot live without are the workhorses, but some of the plants I am attracted to are difficult ones that I have to fuss with. If I had to be limited to a certain palette of plants, everything would be a workhorse because they usually have a long bloom period, are easy to care for, and always look great.

I could not be without *Phlox stolonifera*. It is a great native plant, rampant but not aggressive enough to choke out other plants. It begins to bloom in February and blooms through April every year. It has reddish-lavender flowers that stand about four inches tall.

Another favorite is *Artemisia* 'Powis Castle' which will grow anywhere I put it and softens the color and texture of anything I put it next to. It will make the hottest landscape look cool. When it starts to look rangy, I cut it back, water it, and it comes back out within a few days.

The old-fashioned plants, those that have been around for ever and ever amen, seem to go in and out of favor. The tea plant, *Camellia sinensis*, was popular at the turn of the century and you can still see it around old country houses. It's a wonderful plant if you grow it in full sun. When it blooms it looks as if it's covered with little fried eggs. It's hardier than people think; I've seen it growing in Nashville, Charlotte, and Chapel Hill.

LCM: Do you have a gardening philosophy you'd like to share?

LUCINDA: I'd say, just do it. People seem to spend a lot of time trying to find out the best way to do something, but no amount of research can come close to the actual experience of gardening.

FAVORITE FALL PERENNIALS

Willow leaf sunflower *Helianthus salicifolius*

Giant sunflower *Helianthus giganteus*

Swamp sunflower *Helianthus angustifolius*

Mexican sage *Salvia leucantha*

Goldenrod, rough-stemmed *Solidago rugosa* 'Fireworks'

Aster, vining *Aster carolina*

When I am on television, I try to get across that anyone can garden. I like to encourage people to garden because it's such a healthy thing to do, both physically and psychologically.

For me, personally, I cannot imagine *not* gardening. I think it would be a life devoid of pleasure. To think that I would never garden again would be really awful. Gardening is a wonderful thing.

MILDRED PINNELL, ATLANTA: ATLANTA BOTANICAL GARDEN

Mildred Pinnell, enthusiastic horticulturist at the Atlanta Botanical Garden, has combined a love of plants and a love of people to help educate Atlanta gardeners for the past ten years.

While still in school at the University of Georgia, Mildred worked as a student intern at the Atlanta Botanical Garden. "This internship led to my decision to pursue a degree and a career in horticulture and public horticulture, respectively. The South, and Atlanta in particular, had a bright future in gardening and horticulture in the mid-80s."

Another internship, this one through the Garden Club of America Interchange Fellowship program, allowed Mildred to work and study in England for a year. After graduating from the University of Georgia with a Master's Degree in Horticulture in 1987, Mildred joined the staff of the Atlanta Botanical Garden as horticulturist.

TIPS FOR BEGINNER GARDENERS

1. Start small.
2. Look at other gardens.
3. Start with perennials, then add shrubs, trees, and annuals.
4. Join organizations such as the Georgia Perennial Plant Society or Atlanta Botanical Garden.

Her job at the Garden covers many diverse areas and includes developing the outdoor plant collections, supervising the gardening staff, planning and managing the spring and fall plant sales, and coordinating the landscape exhibit for the Southeastern Flower Show.

In 1993, Mildred was named Young Professional of the Year by the Georgia Green Industry, and in 1996, was elected Chairman of the landscape division for the Association. Although Mildred considers it a privilege to be a part of the Atlanta Botanical Garden, gardeners throughout the state consider it a stroke of fortune to have Mildred in a position of leadership in the Georgia gardening world.

LCM: As horticulturist at the Atlanta Botanical Garden you must meet many beginner gardeners. How do you advise people who have never gardened before?

MILDRED: I suggest that they start small and choose a little area to work on. I tell them to go look at other gardens, either a public garden, a friend's garden, or commercial plantings, and to look at the plants and how they blend together. Most people seem to want to start with perennials, so I recommend that they choose some that are easy to grow. After that, they can begin to add trees, shrubs, and accessories such as annuals. I also encourage people to join an organization like the Georgia Perennial Plant Association because it is a wonderful source of information.

LCM: Do you feel that the Georgia Perennial Plant Association addresses the needs of the beginner as well as those of the experts?

MILDRED: Yes, because members have a wide range of experience and are willing to share their knowledge. Everyone can learn something.

LCM: To learn to identify plants, people can go to places such as the Atlanta Botanical Garden or other public gardens where most of the plants are labeled. But how does one learn more about a plant—

whether it is an annual, or perennial—
and how to grow it? Are there basic
resource books suitable for the beginner?

MILDRED: The Georgia Cooperative
Extension Service has a series of booklets
that are good basic resources. These offer
information on many different subjects:
perennials, landscape materials, and
native plants.

Any library will have basic resources
such as Allan Armitage's book,
Herbaceous Perennial Plants. I also like
the *Southern Living Gardening Guide*.
It's an older book, but a good introduction to gardening here. The Ortho series
of books are all good, although they are
not necessarily written for the South.
They are concise, though, so people don't
become overwhelmed. These are printed
in separate volumes on different topics:
shade gardening, native plants, annuals,
perennials, etc.

I encourage people to take classes. We
offer many basic gardening classes here
on annuals, perennials, or how to amend
your soil. We try to offer a wide array of
programs pitched at different levels of
expertise.

You can also take advantage of the
free information sheets available at places
such as Callaway Gardens, or even at
nurseries or garden centers. I think professionals are responding to this need for
basic information. If people mess up the
first time, then they don't want to continue, so those of us involved with horticulture education want to make sure that
people get as much information as possible, and that the information they get is
as accurate and easy to understand as
possible.

Our most important job is to be
encouraging and say "don't get frustrated,
don't get overwhelmed. It takes time to

learn. We're all still learning—as long as
you garden, you'll be learning." I think
that particularly in Georgia, and really all
over the Southeast, interest in gardening
is exploding. We're just now beginning to
explore what we can do.

LCM: Do you think that part of the
increase in interest in the Southeast is a
new confidence in our own native plants
and in our own gardening techniques? It

❧

*We're trying to make the garden
not only a place for plants, but a
place for people too.*

❧

seems that suddenly the South is *the*
place to garden.

MILDRED: I think so. While we can't
grow many plants which thrive in
England, we can grow things they can't,
and I think we're beginning to accept
that trade-off. We are also learning to deal
with our lousy clay soils, which is our
number one challenge.

LCM: Okay, I'm a home owner with a
sunny, grassy spot and I want to put in a
flower bed. What do I do?

MILDRED: First, you need to lay out a
basic design, either with landscaper's tape
or a garden hose. It can be any shape.
Look at it from the outside, and then go
back inside the house and envision how
it will look from indoors. You'll be spending as much, if not more, time looking
at this from inside as you will be from
outside.

If it's a grassy area, you need to kill
the grass with something such as

Roundup™, which is a basic herbicide commonly sold in local garden centers. It will not stay in the soil, and it's a safe product as long as you follow the manufacturer's directions. Be sure to spray when the wind is not blowing, and when temperatures are at least 70 to 75 degrees—and don't forget to wash your hands and clothing after you spray.

It takes a couple of weeks for the grass to die.

Then have a soil test done by the Cooperative Extension Service. Take a sample from about five different areas and mix it up in the bag so you have a profile of your soil. If you have a huge area, you might want to take several different samples, or if you have a shady area versus a sunny area, you might want to keep them separate. The extension service will give you clear instructions, and then they will send back information about the pH and nutrient levels of your soil.

Then the best thing you can do is to really work on the soil. If you want to grow annuals and perennials you need to amend the soil throughout the bed.

LCM: How do you amend the soil?

MILDRED: Add organic matter such as aged, ground-up, composted pine bark. This is readily available in products like Nature's Helper™. You can also use aged kitchen compost or composted leaves from the yard.

Organic matter is really the key. It adds nutrition and improves the structure of the soil. We don't recommend peat moss because it's a nonrenewable resource and it breaks down too quickly in our climate anyway. Some people recommend adding sand or granite dust, but I'm not a big fan of either of those. You have to be careful in adding straight granite dust or granite sand to clay, because sand and clay make cement, as we always

tell people. If you're going to add sand, you need to add a significant amount of compost too. Maybe one-eighth to one-fourth parts sand and three-fourths parts compost.

LCM: Do you need to do another soil test after you amend the soil?

MILDRED: If you've followed the original recommendations you ought to be okay.

LCM: Is pH the biggest factor in the soil test?

MILDRED: Yes, because it affects the availability of nutrients. If you have a low or a high pH, certain nutrients will not be released to the plant. In our area, 6.0 or 6.5 is a pretty good pH level, unless you're growing plants such as azaleas or rhododendrons, which like more acidic conditions.

You also want to watch the drainage in your garden area. You may have runoff from the house or gutter, which needs to be diverted in another direction. Or, if you're in a low-lying area you might want to build the soil up in a raised bed above the ground level. You can berm or mound it, or use bricks or landscaping timbers to hold the soil up, depending on your preference and your budget.

Particularly near the foundation of a new house, where trucks may have completely compacted the soil, poor drainage can be a real problem.

Once you've worked with the soil, then you want to make your plant selection.

LCM: Do you have a favorite collection of annuals and perennials that you would recommend for beginners? The easiest, the ones that give the best results with the least frustration?

MILDRED: Yes. For spring, *Dianthus* 'Bath's Pink' is a great plant for our area. It is perennial, evergreen, and makes a good groundcover with fragrant pink flowers.

Ox-eye daisy, *Chrysanthemum leucanthemum*, is a great naturalized plant that blooms early in the spring. These look good with blue bachelor buttons, *Centaruea cyanus,* or English daisies, *Bellis perennis*, though the latter probably won't last through our summers. Our native columbine, *Aquilegia canadensis*, is good if you have a shady spot, as well as the blue woodland phlox, *Phlox divaricata.*

Also, some bulbs, such as daffodils, which are perennials, or tulips which are treated as annuals here. Our climate is not cold enough for most tulips to bloom well after the first year.

LCM: Are there tulips which put on a perennial display here?

MILDRED: Yes, and some of them work pretty well. Researchers at North Carolina State University have been evaluating cultivars of tulips to determine which ones repeat from year to year. Some of the species tulips, such as *Tulipa chisiana,* seem to be more dependable in coming back every year. In general, we treat tulips as annuals, and after they bloom, take them out and put in summer annuals.

In the summer, you certainly can't beat the black-eyed Susans, *Rudbeckia hirta.* Purple coneflower, *Echinacea purpurea*, is another great plant, as well as butterfly weed, *Asclepias tuberosa*, or the *Baptisias*, either the blue, yellow, or white species.

In shady areas, try *Astilbe, Digitalis*, or *Hosta.* There are many hosta cultivars to choose from now, from little tiny ones to the broad-leafed ones.

In fall we use *Calendula*, or pot marigold. If the winter is mild, they'll stay around.

For winter color, you can't beat pansies. Plant them in October, and they'll bloom even into May or June. As it gets hot, they stretch and look ragged.

For additional color, we use wallflower, *Cheiranthus cheiri*, but it doesn't bloom until January. Snapdragons have good bloom in fall, although they seem to stop in December. After winter, they bounce back and look good until June. We use them as annuals because they tend to peter out during summer.

LCM: Are all these readily available through the nursery trade?

MILDRED: More than they used to be. Certainly in the Atlanta area you can get these. The Atlanta Botanical Garden plant sale, and many specialty nurseries in the area, always offer a nice array of unusual plants, both new varieties and old favorites.

It seems that many of the old-fashioned plants are coming back, and people are beginning to realize why they were grown for so long. They're reliable plants and good performers.

LCM: Where do you hope to see the Atlanta Botanical Garden go in the future?

HOW TO GET STARTED:

1. Lay out the design with garden hose or landscaper's tape.
2. View the proposed design from indoors and out.
3. Remove any existing grass, if necessary.
4. Take a soil test.
5. Amend the soil with organic matter. Add lime and nutrients as necessary.

MILDRED: I would like to see us focus on developing specific collections. We don't have much room for woody plant collections here, but since we've been given another hundred acres in Cherokee County, north of Atlanta, that possibility is there for the future.

LCM: What will that location be called?

MILDRED: We call it the Yellow Creek Arboretum of the Atlanta Botanical Garden. It was given to us by Jim Gibbs and will be a combination of home demonstration gardens, plant collections, and the site of conservation projects.

The home demonstration gardens are still in the planning phase, but hopefully will include seasonal selections for the homeowner, displaying different plants at their peak blooming time.

There will also be a big emphasis on education, and we plan to offer several classes there. Atlanta seems to be moving in that direction, and the new site will be convenient for many people. We feel that there's a big audience for us north of Atlanta. This site will also give us room to do some conservation work and grow more plants for our native plant conservation program. Right now we're involved in projects such as one in which we grow pitcher plants for the Department of Natural Resources to plant back in the wild. With more room, we can expand such programs.

At the same time, we're taking a hard look at the downtown property and trying to make the best use of the thirty acres we have here. Future plans include a new education building, a new wing on the conservatory, a children's garden, and developing the woods to a ten-acre shade and water garden. So, significant changes will occur here too.

LCM: Is all this building on the work of the first director, Ann Crammond?

MILDRED: I think it is. Ann and the initiators of the Atlanta Botanical Garden helped build a strong base of volunteers, as well as community and corporate support. Our goal is to build on this support and make the gardens more accessible to everyone. Some people think we're elitist because we're a botanical garden, but we're not. We're for everyone. We're trying to make the Atlanta Botanical Garden not only a place for plants, but also a place for people.

STEVE WHEATON, ADAIRSVILLE: BARNSLEY GARDENS

Steve Wheaton's enthusiasm for plants and horticulture is perhaps rivaled only by that of the originator of Barnsley Gardens. Godfrey Barnsley, wealthy cotton merchant from antebellum days had, as Steve puts it, a "fire deep in his belly" for the plants that he collected from around the world and displayed in the gardens in Georgia. This fire has remained lit at Barnsley Gardens through the passion and knowledge of Steve Wheaton.

Steve originally hails from New York. After graduating from the University of Vermont, he interned at Harvard's Arnold Arboretum and the New York Botanical Garden. For ten years he served as director of grounds and assistant director of Scott Arboretum at Swarthmore College.

While at Swarthmore, Steve began plant collection trips to the southeastern United States. His goal of creating a collection of native azaleas for the Scott Arboretum frequently brought him to Georgia, and he soon fell in love with the natural beauty of the state.

Steve's interest in heirloom plants and his knowledge of and enthusiasm for naturalistic landscape design—particularly the work of Andrew Jackson Downing—brought him to Barnsley Gardens soon after Prince Fugger, the current owner, bought the property in 1989. And although he began pruning the plants on the property with a chainsaw, he and his staff have quickly tamed the wilderness, as evidenced by the stunning gardens at the estate today.

I interviewed Steve at Barnsley Gardens in early September when the mixed border was still overflowing with the colors and textures of plants I recognized from my grandmother's garden. To visit Barnsley was to borrow a day from another era and to indulge in the slow and lazy pace of antebellum Georgia.

LCM: Tell me a little bit about Barnsley Gardens—how it began and how it developed.

STEVE: In 1823, Godfrey Barnsley came from England with only a couple of

❦

Many of the properties around here are virtual horticultural museums. Because the homesites have stayed in the same families, the gardeners are still growing the pass-along plants, or grandma plants. They have annuals, perennials, and especially bulbs that essentially dropped off the horticultural wagon generations ago—plants which you can't find commercially anymore.

❦

shillings in his pocket, but he was full of energy and ambition, and soon began to buy and sell cotton. He never grew it himself, but he developed an entire fleet of ships to transport it, and eventually had offices in Liverpool, New Orleans and Mobile. He married into the Scarborough family of Savannah, and became one of the wealthiest men in Georgia, but he always maintained his English citizenship.

Godfrey Barnsley had an avid passion, maybe even an obsession, for horticulture. Once he began buying land in this part of Georgia, he accumulated 10,000 acres. This was formerly Cherokee Indian territory, which was sold through a lottery. Barnsley did not obtain the land himself through the lottery, but bought it from people who did. He was apparently a very cultured and well-traveled man who was on the cutting edge of technology, landscape design, and architecture.

LCM: The British influence at Barnsley Gardens is unmistakable. Were the original gardens planted in an English style?

STEVE: Most people would probably call it an English style, but the landscape really followed the principles of Andrew Jackson Downing, who was a popular landscape designer from the Hudson River area.

The landscape at Barnsley Gardens almost slavishly adheres to his principles. This is illustrated in the way the rockeries are done, the way in which the Gothic-style manor house sits on top of the hill, and the way the boxwood parterre is oval and uses a rambunctious combination of perennials, annuals, bulbs, and shrubs, which is not a bedding-out scheme. Other Andrew Jackson Downing features are found in the water cascades, the brooks, fern glades, and woodland gardens, which we would call the natural English style woodland garden.

PLANTS FOR WINTER INTEREST

Hellebores *Helleborus* sp.
Winter honeysuckle *Lonicera fragrantissima*
Daphne *Daphne odora*
Apricot, flowering *Prunus mume*
Witch hazel *Hamamelis* × *intermedia*
Winter sweet *Chinonanthus praecox*

At the time Barnsley installed this kind of landscape, it was quite revolutionary, particularly in the South because Andrew Jackson Downing was not yet popular here. But Barnsley liked to be on the cutting edge. In the manor house he had water closets and flush toilets, as well as fountains in the front boxwood gardens. Unfortunately, like other grand Southern homes, Barnsley Gardens suffered greatly from the Civil War. Godfrey Barnsley died a pauper in New Orleans in 1873.

LCM: How much of the original landscape has been restored?

STEVE: Quite a bit. In a way, it was fortunate that there was such an economic depression here. In the northeast, families had enough money so that each successive generation could repair, replant, and follow the latest gardening fads, so most of the original gardens are now gone. Here at Barnsley Gardens, the family went through severe economic depression after the war and had no money for the gardens.

The years following the Civil War were difficult ones for Barnsley Gardens. In 1906, a tornado took the roof off the manor house. Soon after this, the rest of the house fell in, and nature took its toll. Since they had no money for repairs, the Barnsley family, who still lived here, moved into the kitchen wing and servant's quarters. They were land rich and cash poor. The estate slowly mouldered away and fell into disrepair, but it remained in the same family until 1942.

Along with the house, the gardens were neglected. During the next fifty years, they became almost completely overgrown. Trees grew up through the boxwood gardens. The sunken gardens and bog gardens filled in with silt and were like swamplands.

As we began work to recover the gardens, we peeled aside layer after layer of trees and underbrush. We were surprised at the size and grandeur of the gardens which we were uncovering. It took about two years for us to realize what we had here.

For the first eighteen months we used backhoes, front end loaders, and chainsaws to reclaim the garden areas from the wilderness. There are 1,100 acres here now, and we had about 25 to 30 acres covered with brambles, poison ivy, and honeysuckle. The house ruins were shrouded in wisteria, and the east side of the garden was covered with kudzu.

LCM: Did written records exist of what had been here?

STEVE: We think so, through his letters. Barnsley was an obsessive person, and he had a burning passion deep in his belly. He put everything he had into these gardens. He was often away on business, but sent a lot of plant material back with detailed letters saying exactly what he wanted done here and there. These letters are now scattered in Barnsley collections at the University of North Carolina, the University of Georgia, and other places. We're still finding all these letters and documents. We also have a lot of photos, which are really wonderful.

LCM: When did the gardens here begin to decline?

STEVE: We consider the Barnsley period to have ended in 1873, though generations of the Barnsley family gardened here to a much lesser extent for years. Addie Saylor, Godfrey Barnsley's granddaughter, died in 1942, and the property was finally sold.

Although we try to be as accurate as possible, we have areas of the estate which we have converted to gardens which were not originally gardens, and vice versa. For example, the third wing of the house, which was torn down in the 1950s and '60s occupied the site where we have planted a lawn and heirloom herbaceous and rose border. This area provides a perfect place for parties and receptions. Even though Barnsley did not originally plant this part of the garden, we tried to create a garden setting in a "Godfrey Barnsley" style.

Barnsley Gardens is not a strict historical reproduction like Monticello, where if they can't absolutely document the fact that Jefferson used a particular plant, they won't put it in. I think what we're doing is probably re-creating a sense of period, of place, and time.

LCM: What is the restoration philosophy? Do you use only period plants, and where do you find these?

STEVE: We try to use as many period plants as possible. We've had a lot of help with documentation. The Southern History Society has worked with us, as well as Jane Simms, Don Shadow from Tennessee, and Don Franklin from Atlanta.

We've gone to several of the old homesites in the area, many of which are virtual horticultural museums. Because the homesites have stayed in the same families, these people still growing the pass-along plants, or grandma plants. They have annuals, perennials, and especially bulbs that essentially dropped off the horticultural wagon generations ago and which you can't find commercially anymore.

Barnsley disseminated a lot of plants around here. For example, the green rose, which he introduced to the area, can be found at several homesites. We've also obtained plants and seeds from Peggy Newcombe at Monticello.

We are trying to maintain a period heirloom garden in the sense of style according to Andrew Jackson Downing. When possible, we use the kinds of plants that Barnsley used. But to do the kind of massive gardening we do, we've had to bend and compromise just to keep something in bloom.

We plant a 120-foot-long mixed border. When we just can't get big enough numbers in the plant material we want, we might have to substitute some things. A surprising number of plants fall into an heirloom category though. For example, *Zinnia linearis* is actually an old-fashioned flower that has come around again.

LCM: What are some of the plants you include in the mixed border?

STEVE: One of my favorites is the old-fashioned reseeding petunia. Why would anyone grow another petunia, except maybe *Petunia integrifolia*, which is another old-fashioned petunia? The reseeding petunia just keeps blooming. It has a wonderful fragrance and a beautiful moth comes to pollinate it at night. We also put in *Celosia* 'Princess Feather' along with some old-fashioned bulbs in spring.

We've also included an old-fashioned butterfly bush, *Buddleia lindleyana*, which looks a little ratty by late summer, but the flowers are very pendulous and fine—a much more finely textured plant than the more common butterfly bush.

LCM: Do you find that there is a lot of interest in period and heirloom plants?

STEVE: Yes. We work hard to help educate visitors who come here. For example, we have rock gardens that appear bizarre and unusual to some people. They're definitely period pieces, and not what most people think of as a rock garden today. We have to interpret this for people. We have to explain who Andrew Jackson Downing was, and why

these rock gardens are significant, and why that was such a turning point in the history of landscape architecture—what it meant and how Barnsley did it here.

LCM: What are some of the most important components of the Downing landscape?

STEVE: Basically, his ideas became a whole philosophy and turning point in American landscape design. The Hudson River school of landscape art was all about man's relationship to nature. In other words, it was no longer thought that nature was a wilderness to be feared and closed off with formal, geometric, and orderly gardens. Instead, it was believed that the best types of gardens reflected the hand of Mother Nature; that you worked with nature and tried to re-create a naturalistic feel in the garden.

Barnsley also lived during a time when the western world was being flooded with new plants from all over the world, from China, Korea, Japan. Wonderful treasures were coming in, and the repertoire of plants he could use in a garden setting expanded geometrically.

Barnsley used these new plants, mixing them with native plants and Old World plants brought by the colonists. Barnsley did not believe in putting in a traditional rose garden, but roses were combined with annuals, perennials, and bulbs in the landscape setting.

In the mid-nineteenth century, this was really quite revolutionary. It reflected what Capability Brown and others were doing in England. Andrew Jackson Downing popularized and Americanized it. Instead of taking English ideas and trying to adapt them to American soils, he began creating American gardens.

LCM: Did Barnsley introduce a lot of plants not previously grown in Georgia?

STEVE: Yes, there's no doubt about it. For example, the Chinese fir at the top of the hill was probably the first ever grown in the area. Remember that Barnsley had his own fleet of ships and had the ability to do a lot of plant collecting on his own. It was obvious that there was a lot of trial and error going on, especially if you read his letters and look at the photographs. Barnsley was bringing in seed or small plants and really had no idea how things would do in this area. And probably no one knew what the mature plant would look like. It had to be a tremendously exciting period of time.

One of the most beautiful gardens here was the boxwood parterre, which was apparently a riot of colors and fragrances reflecting a combination of hardy reseeding annuals, such as the hardy reseeding petunias; herbaceous plant material, and woody plants, such as spireas, smoke trees, roses, mock orange, and hibiscus. This is a strict departure from what you normally think of in a parterre garden. Andrew Jackson Downing really deplored the monotonous bedding-out that had to be changed periodically.

Other Andrew Jackson Downing features at Barnsley include glades of ferns and woodland plants, babbling brooks, and thickets of climbing and rambling roses. Closer to the manor house things would have been more orderly, with more formal garden areas, but still done in a naturalistic way.

LCM: How does this compare or contrast with Olmsted and his influence?

STEVE: Olmsted was really a disciple of Andrew Jackson Downing. Olmsted took his [Downing's] principles and brought them to a higher degree in that he was able to take it to a commercial level. Andrew Jackson Downing died while still in his early thirties, in a boating accident on the Hudson River. Olmsted, on the other hand, lived to a ripe old age and was able to exert a strong influence. But Olmsted strongly reflected the ideals of Andrew Jackson Downing with landscapes such as Central Park, and the park systems in New Orleans and Boston. Andrew Jackson Downing was the inspi-

---

HEIRLOOM PLANTS AT BARNSLEY GARDENS

Narrow-leaf zinnia *Zinnia linearis*

Petunia *Petunia*

Celosia *Celosia spicata*

Butterfly bush *Buddleia lindleyana*

Rose, green, double cabbage, sweetheart ('Cecile Bruner') *Rosa* sp.

Spiraea *Spiraea* sp.

Smoke tree *Cotinus coggygria*

Mock orange *Philadelphus coronarius*

Hibiscus *Hibiscus coccineus*

---

ration that plowed that ground. Olmsted reaped the benefits.

LCM: Do you think Barnsley was influential in the horticultural world?

STEVE: No, he was too isolated here. The only letters we have are to his overseer and his daughter. We don't have any record of his corresponding to any other gardeners.

LCM: What is your mission for the gardens here?

STEVE: I hope that we will become a real drawing card for people interested in heirloom plants.

LCM: Can you tell me about some unusual plants that you grow here?

STEVE: We know that Barnsley grew over sixty varieties of garden roses. These included old-fashioned favorites such as the chestnut rose, which is a big double cabbage rose that blooms heavily in June and then again in fall; the green rose; the sweetheart rose 'Cecile Bruner'; and the old moss roses.

He also grew crinum bulbs, which are wonderful plants. Many people didn't realize they could be grown this far north.

Then there's the old-fashioned reseeding petunia, which we sell here in the garden shop. The new petunias have been so hybridized they don't much resemble their ancestors.

There are several plants we consider Barnsley signature plants. Our garden shop tries to focus on the heirloom plants that do well and which are just as appropriate for today's gardening situation. These are especially good for people who don't have the time to mess with fussy plants, or for those who want to get away from heavy pest and disease control.

Barnsley also had fruit orchards and a big vegetable garden. It was a gentleman's estate, designed after the English style.

LCM: I understand your own gardening background was primarily in the northeast. Do you find gardening here drastically different than, say, Pennsylvania?

STEVE: It's a whole different ball of wax. The basic principles are the same, but much of it is drastically different. Here, rains come in downpours during the winter. In Philadelphia, we had about the same amount of rain, it was just more evenly distributed. And of course, the soils are quite different. The clay soils here erode quickly, so you can't leave the soil naked at all, you have to keep it planted.

Although the temperatures may be the same, the intensity is different because the heat really builds up. I love the pleasant Georgia winters. We get a lot of warm, sunny days that are good for winter-blooming plants such as winter honeysuckle, daphne, flowering apricot (*Prunus mume*), witch hazels, and winter sweet, *Chimonanthus praecox*, which is wonderful and may even be a rare old homesite plant.

Lonicera fragrantissima, goldflame honeysuckle, has translucent yellow, waxy flowers that just pump the air from about Christmas until February—it's a great plant. It's deciduous and tends to be a little sprawly, but you just tuck it away somewhere.

I'm also trying to introduce some plants down here which we grew in Pennsylvania, such as the lilacs. Generally, lilacs don't do so well here. The heat and humidity wreaks havoc with them, but when I came down here from Swarthmore I brought a few lilacs with me. One of them was 'Swarthmore' and another was 'President Lincoln'. I forgot about them and they sat around in containers for about two years just blooming away. I thought that was strange because I didn't think they would live. I planted them out and they did fine.

Then Ruth Dix mentioned that researchers at the U. S. National Arboretum were doing lilac breeding for the South, for heat and powdery mildew tolerance. I decided to see what we could do with lilacs here at Barnsley. I now have planted here over thirty varieties of lilac, *Syringa* × *hyacinthiflora*, which we will be evaluating.

BARRIE CRAWFORD, COLUMBUS

Soft spoken and lovely, Barrie Crawford is the epitome of the Southern gardener. The gardens at her gracious home in Columbus reflect Barrie's love of plants. The formal front garden is an English design with a large grassy center area, bordered on four sides with beds of mixed perennials, annuals, bulbs, and shrubs. In the back of the house, towering oak trees provide shade for a variety of wildflowers. Barrie wrote of these gardens and flowers in her book, *For the Love of Wildflowers.*

For many years, Barrie and her sister, Kay Reeves Van Allen, who lives in New Jersey, have spoken on the phone almost daily, and inevitably their conversations turned to the garden. In comparing notes, they noticed when different things bloomed and which plants did best in which garden. They finally pulled their conversations together into a book entitled *The Gardens of Two Sisters.* It is a

delightful and useful collection of conversations and information from two sisters who garden in two very different climates.

Barrie Crawford continues to share her knowledge of gardening with the Columbus community and beyond through her weekly radio show, classes at the local college, and lectures to garden clubs and other groups.

LCM: How did you become interested in gardening?

BARRIE: Like most people hooked on gardening, I think it must be in my genes. Both my mother and grandmother gardened here in Columbus. My grandmother had a really wonderful garden, which my mother eventually took over. It was featured in one of the first issues of *Southern Accents* magazine.

I grew up digging in the flower beds and weeding, particularly out in the country where we had a summer home about twenty-five miles from Columbus, in Harris County. As soon as school was out for the summer, we left Columbus and went to the country, where we would stay out until Labor Day. In an effort to entertain all of us, Mama took us walking along those old back country roads. She knew all the wildflowers by name so, we got to know them too and became interested in them.

I grew up in this house where I live now. It was my parents' house, then my grandmother's, and then mine, and I raised my children here. Although I moved away for a while, now I'm back living in this same house.

In the back is an oak tree seventeen feet in circumference. I started my wildflower garden there. The whole back yard is a shade garden. I brought things like blue phlox and wild geranium from the country and they have spread beautifully.

Although I've been interested in growing wildflowers all my life, recently I've also become interested in annuals and perennials. My son, Philip, designed the formal front garden for me. You should have seen the neighbors' faces when we started digging up foundation shrubbery and pulling up zoysia! They thought we'd lost our minds.

Now neighbors love to walk by and see what's coming up in the garden. It's as if I'm gardening for the whole neighborhood. Once a year, in mid-June, I have an "English Open Garden" and invite all the neighbors and anyone else interested in gardening. I serve tea and orange juice on the front porch from eight to ten in the morning.

LCM: What a lovely tradition! Are there plants that grow in the Atlanta area but you cannot grow here?

❦

Actually, if you learn to work with it, clay is a wonderful soil to garden because it holds the nutrients so well.

❦

BARRIE: We really can't grow peonies or astilbes here because of the heat and higher humidity. The climate in Atlanta is far enough north to make a difference. On the other hand, several plants, such as lantana and Mexican sage, which are not reliably hardy in Atlanta, will usually survive our winters. Plants such as tea olive

and banana shrub, which are borderline hardy in Atlanta, we seldom lose.

LCM: When you were talking to your sister about gardening in New Jersey, and then later when you were writing the book together, did you discover that gardening in the North is quite different from gardening here?

BARRIE: Yes, it's a whole different ball game. One thing predictable about gardening in the South is that it's totally unpredictable. There's no such thing as a normal spring or winter. We have huge swings of temperatures. This year we had almost no spring. It turned hot so early and so quickly, the daffodils only lasted a week.

I think that the biggest difference is in the soil. In areas south of Columbus, you might run into some sandy soils, but most of us here deal with clay soils. Actually, if you really learn to work with it, clay is a wonderful soil to garden because it holds the nutrients so well. In sandy soils, everything leaches out quickly.

LCM: How did you improve the soils in your garden?

BARRIE: When I put in the front garden, I used six cubic yards of mushroom compost and tilled it in eight inches. The plants practically jumped out of the ground.

In the fall, I used it again as a mulch and again worked it into the soil. You have to be careful about using straight mushroom compost on established plants, though, because it might burn them.

I fertilize with Osmacote™ during the first week in April and it lasts throughout the entire growing season.

The secret to having successful annual and perennial beds is good soil preparation and choosing the right plant for the right spot. You might not get the right spot the first time, so keep trying things in new places. I grow beautiful cardinal flower, atamasco lily, and Jack-in-the-pulpit in an area that is fairly dry, even though you wouldn't expect them to do well there.

Don't take what the books say as gospel. Go ahead and experiment on your own. And if you don't like something someplace, dig it up and move it. I've moved everything in this garden at least ten times, including full-sized bushes and small trees. I do try to get everything moved by June, but as long as you continue to water, you can transplant anytime.

I also recommend that people use a lot of native plants because they are generally so adaptable.

I love to try something different every year. Whatever the new plants are, I have to have some of them. Sometimes they work, and sometimes they don't, but I don't want the "same old, same old" every year. My front garden is totally different every year.

LCM: Do you have a basic dozen favorite plants?

BARRIE: There are so many . . . I love *Veronica* 'Icicle', *Artemisia* 'Powis Castle', and *Verbena canadensis* 'Rosea', which is evergreen here and will throw a few blooms in January and February and then really kicks in the first of March. I like *Verbena* 'Silver Anne', which has the most wonderful fragrance and blooms for about two to three weeks. Then I cut it way back and it blooms sporadically all summer.

I like salvias and lantana and hardy geraniums, shasta daisies, the pink fall-blooming michaelmas daisies, lilies, dianthus, spiraea, goldenrod, and an alpine aster called 'Happy End'. Catmint, *Nepta cataria*, is good, as well as the pur-

ple coneflowers, *Echinacea purpurea*, 'White Swan' and 'Bright Star'. The little toad flax, *Linaria*, has beautiful deep lavender flowers and evergreen foliage.

I love dianthus 'Bath's Pink' for its delightful fragrance; soapwort, *Saponaria ocymoides*; and 'The Fairy' rose, which is totally carefree.

ADVICE FOR BEGINNERS

Grow a combination of annuals and easy perennials like daisies and daylilies.

Work on soil preparation.

Put the right plant in the right place.

Use a lot of native plants.

Keep trying new things in new places.

Don't take what the books say as gospel. Experiment on your own.

If you don't like how a plant looks, dig it up and move it.

Read all you can and stay in touch with other gardeners.

I try to keep the beds looking good all the time. I've become fascinated with grasses such as *Miscanthus sinensis* and *M. variegatus* and use them as background foliage for winter interest. I'm also interested in unusual shrubs like loropetalum, Indian hawthorn, viburnum, hydrangea (particularly the cultivar 'Tardiva'), and fothergilla. I try different things. Sometimes they work and sometimes they don't.

LCM: Any other advice that you have for gardeners?

BARRIE: Stay in touch with other gardeners, go to symposia and classes, read all you can, and stay up to date with the gardening world.

ALLEN SISTRUNK, LOGANVILLE: VINES BOTANICAL GARDEN

A self-proclaimed non-purist, Allen Sistrunk is a man who loves flowers and plants. "South America, Africa, Asia—it doesn't matter where they come from, I love them all," he says, rubbing his hands together as if he can't wait to put his hands on yet another plant.

The results of Allen's creativity are obvious at the Atlanta History Center, where he was Director of Gardens for over fourteen years, and at Vines Botanical Garden, where he became Executive Director in 1994.

Allen, a native of Columbus, Georgia, credits his grandmother Helen Sistrunk, and his best friend in high school, Phil Caudle, for getting him hooked on plants. His grandmother had an old-fashioned garden full of flowers that she had collected and traded through the years, but it was Phil's home-grown terrarium that really fascinated Allen.

For years, he said, he wanted to grow indoor plants, so his parents finally built him a greenhouse. "Now," he laughs, "the only reason I would use a greenhouse would be to start plants to grow outdoors. I love to garden outside."

Although he began his school career as a pre-vet and biology major, it only took a few botany courses before Allen had second thoughts. When he discovered the magical world of plant communities during a field botany course, the world lost a budding veterinarian and gained a gifted horticulturist.

LCM: You served as Director of Gardens at the Atlanta History Center for many years. What changes did you see in the grounds during your tenure?

ALLEN: I began the job in 1980, at a time when little emphasis was placed on the grounds or gardens. I fell in love not only with the place, but with the potential it presented. By the grace of God, we ended up with seven gardens that create a ramble through the landscape history of Atlanta. While the museum tells the story of Atlanta's history inside a building, we tell of the landscape history outdoors.

Some of the gardens, such as the Swan Woods Trail, had been created years before I arrived. But my staff and I designed others, such as the Cherry Sims Asian-American Garden. Together, this collection of gardens tells the story of how the land has changed from primeval time to the present, and even looks toward the future.

The most challenging task I faced was to transform a thirty-two acre site into a mission-focused public garden. Some public gardens lack a direction or focus and remain a collection of plants. At the History Center, we wanted to narrow the focus to include only plants relating to Atlanta and the region, and I feel that we have done that.

In the Quarry Garden, we try to include indigenous plants, those that were here before the pioneers. In the Tullie Smith House Garden, we have re-created an early European settlement, which is primarily English.

The Swan Woods Trail shows vestiges of once terraced agricultural land, and tells the story of how natural succession changes the landscape. The plantings around the Swan House, built in the early twentieth century, were influenced by the Italian or French landscape school. The "great house" era was characterized by great expanses of lawns, flowers, and evergreen shrubs.

In the Cherry Sims Asian-American Garden we used plants that explorers found in China, Korea, and Japan in the late nineteenth and early twentieth cen-turies. Because the climate of the south-eastern United States is similar to that of parts of the Orient, many of these plants thrive here. The significance of this gar-den is to show Asian counterparts to our native plants, and the impact of these plants on our landscapes today.

The newest area, designed by Darrel Morrison, is in front of the museum building. It displays [both] a design and plant material which will hopefully with-stand the challenges Atlanta gardeners will be faced with in the coming decades, including decreased chemical applica-tions, increased maintenance costs, and limited natural resources such as water.

LCM: Are these the landscaping prin-ciples which you include in your own personal garden?

ALLEN: Yes. I have a half-acre in Brookhaven, and it is a plant collector's

paradise. I killed all the grass and began to install my favorite plants. I tried to blend and wed trees, flowers, and shrubs so that I would have color and interest from January through December.

Atlanta is the most wonderful place in the world to garden because the possibili-ties here are limitless. Almost anything can be grown here, but for whom is any-one's guess. I've seen beautiful stands of heath and heather in a front yard, and I stop and think, "How do they do that? That's not supposed to grow here." Even if someone tries to tell you how they did it, it still might not work. I think garden-ers are like cooks with a secret recipe: they don't always tell you *exactly* how they do it.

☙

There's no question about it, hydrangeas are going to be Atlanta's plant of the future. They come in white, pink, red, and blue—and you can plant successively to have color for a long time.

☙

Even though I had a landscape plan in mind when I pulled up all the grass in the front yard, I'm sure my neighbors thought I was crazy. They would stop and ask what had happened to the yard. Now they stop and want to know what the dif-ferent plants are and how to grow them. What I'm doing is creating a tapestry beneath the trees. I have hosta, fern, and lots of *Pulmonaria.*

LCM: What can you tell me about *Pulmonaria?*

ALLEN: What a great plant! When it's in bloom my yard looks like the inside of a jewelry box filled with blue and white. It's a highly adaptable plant. It can take wet or drought. When it's stressed, it just shuts down shop and waits to grow again the next year. Last summer [1994], when it was so wet, it sort of melted away. I thought I had lost it, but after a couple of weeks, I looked and saw just a little activity and in another couple of weeks, it looked great.

There are some great cultivars like 'Roy Davidson', which has early blue flowers, or 'Bertram Anderson' which has a blue, blue flower that comes in April. 'Sissinghurst White' looks great all season long. The flowers last about four weeks, but the foliage stays attractive for months.

LCM: What kind of plants do you use with *Pulmonaria?*

ALLEN: Hostas, ferns, and spike moss, *Sellaginalla*—and what a great plant that is. It's a low-growing, prostrate plant that spreads by runners. The leaves are best in heavy shade where they look iridescent blue-green. In the sunlight, it's still attractive because the foliage is lacy, but it loses that iridescence.

And ferns. I never met a fern I didn't like. I personally prefer the spreading ferns like New York or southern shield, although some of the clumping ones look good too. Even the common Christmas fern, with a little maturity, is special.

LCM: Do you find it difficult to garden in the shade?

ALLEN: It's not hard if you know the kinds of plants to put in and the conditions they need. And you can't expect too much. You can get great flowering from shade plants, just not all the time. If you plant wisely, though, you can have an entire season of color in the shade, but you have to depend on the perennials. Annuals in the shade just don't bloom that well. If you start with *Scilla* and *Pulmonaria* in early spring, then follow it with *Hydrangeas, Phlox,* and *Rudbeckia goldsturm* or *R. triloba*, you can have a long season of color.

LCM: How about more traditional shade plants, such as impatiens?

ALLEN: Most people think that impatiens are the best choice for shade, but even these need at least two hours of sunlight before they flower well.

LCM: What are some of the best shrubs for shade?

ALLEN: Hydrangeas. There's no question about it, hydrangeas are going to be Atlanta's plant of the future. In the Cherry Sims Garden, we have one of the most complete hydrangea collections anywhere, and it's exciting. They come in white, pink, red, and blue—and you can plant successively to have bloom for a long time.

Too many people think that the gardening season in Atlanta is over when

---

ALLEN'S FAVORITE SHADE PLANTS

Hostas *Hosta* sp.

New York fern *Thelypteris noveboracensis*

Southern shield Fern *Thelypteris normalis*

Spike moss *Sellaginalla uncinata*

Scilla *Scilla sibirica*

Pulmonaria *Pulmonaria longifolia*

Phlox *Phlox divaricata*

Hydrangea *Hydrangea macrophylla*

Rudbeckia *Rudbeckia goldsturm, R. triloba*

the azaleas and dogwoods are through blooming, but hydrangeas will fill that gap so you can have another explosion of color during the summer months. We haven't even touched on the hydrangea thing yet. We plan to have a wonderful collection at Vines Botanical Garden as well.

LCM: Tell me a little about Vines Botanical Garden.

ALLEN: Our mission statement says that our goal is to "promote gardens and gardening as a universal language, to collect, evaluate, and exhibit plant material suitable for the home, commercial, and public landscape, to offer opportunities to people of all ages and backgrounds to learn more about the science, technique, and joy of successful gardening."

It is going to be garden oriented. The collections are going to be for the garden, rather than the other way around. By that I mean, if we have fifty viburnums, we won't have them grouped all at the same site. We'll have them distributed throughout the garden so we can show visitors how to use different varieties of plants in their own gardens.

This is a ninety-acre site, with twenty-five developed acres. We have a three-acre spring-fed lake, which will be a perfect place to showcase our native wetland plants. Behind the developed area are meadows, hardwoods, granite outcroppings, and wetlands. In front of the house we will plant an American year-round mixed border with small flowering trees, shrubs, perennials, and annuals for all-season interest.

We also have an Asian-influenced garden, a rose garden, a white garden, vegetable garden, a flower garden, an herb walk, and a woodland terrace. It's already an exciting place to visit, but the potential is tremendous.

❦

I think gardeners are like cooks with a secret recipe. They don't always tell you exactly how they do it.

❦

LCM: Do you have any advice for beginner gardeners?

ALLEN: Remember that anything is possible. I used to tell people to fit their landscape design to the architecture of the house, but now I'm inclined to think that when you begin to garden, it's more important to match the style of the garden to your own personality. Some people like to weed for hours and mow the grass twice a week, others don't. If you don't have a garden that suits you, you're going to be frustrated.

RICK BERRY AND MARC RICHARDSON, LEXINGTON: GOODNESS GROWS NURSERY

Perhaps no one in the state has brought as much joy and satisfaction to Georgia gardeners as the owners of Goodness Grows Nursery, Marc Richardson and Rick Berry. These two men, who met and became friends while at the University of Georgia, have spent the last two decades finding, propagating, growing, and selling incomparably beautiful plant material. They began at a time when people were saying, "Perennials? It's too hot to grow perennials in the South." and since then have helped raise the awareness and educational level of gardeners throughout the state.

Although neither has a formal background in horticulture—Rick was a math education major and Marc was in biology—they found a common interest in growing plants, and it was this interest which led them to create a nursery whose name says it all. Goodness does grow—and flourish—and reproduce abundantly in their nursery near Lexington, Georgia.

Today, hundreds of gardeners throughout the southeastern United States eagerly await the arrival of the new Goodness Grows catalog, for it signals the time for garden dreams to begin as we read breathlessly about the newest, hardiest, and most beautiful plants which Marc and Rick have made available for our gardens.

I first spoke with Rick about the history of Goodness Grows and the floral industry in Georgia. And then listened as Marc shared information about some of his favorite plants to grow in the state.

LCM: Goodness Grows has been a wonderful source of plants and inspiration to gardeners throughout the region. How did you and Marc first decide to go into the nursery business?

RICK: We met in college and lived in a house in Athens with several people. We both liked gardening, so we began planting flowers for the people in the neighborhood and growing things from seed to sell, just to make a little money on the side.

After a couple of years of growing the same old material that everyone else was growing, we decided to do something more interesting. This was in the late Seventies when people were really not growing perennials in their garden, except maybe the old-fashioned ones like lilies, daylilies, or bulbs. Perennials weren't even considered a part of the horticulture curriculum in the schools.

People told us we couldn't grow perennials in the South because it was too hot. Marc knew that wasn't true because his grandmother grew perennials in her garden, so we began looking for gardeners who would share not only cuttings from their perennial plants, but also information about the plants.

People were wonderful. They gave us plants and tips and knowledge gained from their own experience. Many gardeners in the Athens area loved to garden, but were forced to get perennial plants by trading with other gardeners, or by buying bare root plants from a mail order source. These people were eager for us to start a nursery.

So we started growing more and more perennials, and tried to figure out which ones would grow here and which wouldn't, and what their cultural requirements were in the state of Georgia. Back then, there were few reference materials. The only books were from England, or those written by Southern gardeners such as Elizabeth Lawrence and William Lanier Hunt.

There were no local nurseries from which to buy plant material, although we did get some from mail order sources. Many catalogs listed plants as perennials which were not always winter hardy in our area, or offered plants which were not very attractive. We began growing many different plants just to see what they would do here.

We learned a lot as we went along. We knew we could root woody shrubs and plants such as *Coleus,* but we didn't know you could root *Achillea*, for instance, or *Coreopsis verticillata* from stem cuttings, so we learned ways to propagate things vegetatively, and we learned different ways to start plants from seed. For example, some seeds need to be covered, others need to be surface-sown, some need cold treatment. It was all trial and error because no one really knew how these plants would perform in our climate.

We also began to look around at the roadsides and the native landscape and found many herbaceous perennials growing wild, which were quite lovely. How could people say herbaceous plants wouldn't grow here in the South? We began collecting native plants to find out what was garden worthy, and we discovered that many plants growing wild in the southeastern United States are very garden worthy.

Another thing we did was to develop trial gardens to determine what would happen with different soil preparation and cultural conditions. The trial beds gave us the opportunity to study the plant material and watch as it developed over a period of a couple of years. They also gave us the chance to show different plants to our customers and to educate them about the life cycle of the plant. Not only did we learn from these beds, our customers did, too.

In the early Eighties, some of the University of Georgia professors became interested in what we were doing. People were talking about us and the unique plants we were selling. We were growing plant material that no one expected. We even had big beds of lupines, which you're not supposed to be able to grow in the South. We found that you can grow many unusual plants—you just have to know what to expect. For example, lupines won't have a long life in the South, but if you plant them correctly, they will put out one or two years of bloom before they peter out from the heat.

❧

We were growing plants no one expected. For example, lupines won't have a long life in the South, but you can grow them and enjoy one or two years of bloom before they peter out from the heat.

❧

Fortunately for us, we are located in a part of Georgia where it gets cold enough in winter to kill plants back. Some perennials, such as columbine and foxglove, need a dormancy period to set a bud. If you keep these in a warm greenhouse all the time, they will never flower. But on the other hand, it's warm enough here to grow some of the more tropical perennials like *Salvia leucantha* or *Hibiscus mutabilis*. If you live in Tennessee, for instance, you can't grow *Hibiscus muta-bilis* because it will freeze before it comes into flower, whereas in south Georgia, this plant starts flowering in August and will bloom for a couple of months before freezing weather comes.

The state of Georgia is a wonderful place to garden because it has so many different types of microclimates and ecosystems. Gardening on the coast is different from gardening in the mountains, and gardening where we live is different than gardening farther south. You can still grow pretty much the same thing throughout the state, you just have to know what to expect from the plants.

LCM: Why do you think people finally embraced the idea of gardening with perennials?

RICK: People became excited because it was unique. Some gardeners had never seen these plants before. Others said they remembered them from their grandmothers' gardens but they had never been able to find them. Back in late Seventies, the plants available to gardeners were boring. Our landscapes consisted of little green balls at the base of the house, and if you wanted color in the yard, you bedded out annuals like impatiens, marigolds, begonias, or pansies and that was about it, except for the avid iris or daylily grower.

All of a sudden, people wanted something different in their yards. Organizations such as Callaway Gardens began sponsoring symposiums on perennials, and things began to snowball and they're still going strong.

We're fortunate to be in the Southeast where we have a long growing season and conditions which can accommodate an extremely wide range of plant material. We certainly have our frustrations with heat, drought, and bugs, but the overall climate is wonderful, and right now the availability of plant material to gardeners is greater than it's ever been in the history of horticulture.

LCM: Where do you hope to go from here?

RICK: We hope to do more, moving in the same direction. We feel that we've accomplished a lot in less than twenty years. We feel that we've been influential in the gardening world by making plant material available to people and helping to inspire other professionals to do what we're doing.

LCM: Aren't you just amazed at what you've done and how it's all come together?

RICK: We really are. Even within the horticulture industry, we feel that we've been influential. We were the first to offer perennials in containers. People who sold perennials did so as bare root, but not in a pot. We began growing plants in pots so we could sell throughout the year and people could plant any time during the year. That inspired other growers to grow things in pots.

LCM: Any bit of advice you give to people when they begin to garden?

RICK: Take your time, be patient, and start slowly.

LCM: Whenever I ask that question, I always get the same answer!

RICK: That's because it's true. Another thing is that people need to understand their limitations. It's easy to get excited and try to do more than you can handle. That's true with any part of life. People need to understand their environment and their location and where they really want to put their plants. They need to understand their ecosystem— when it receives the best sunlight and how long it lasts, how the soil drains, and their capability of watering. I don't think you can really garden successfully in this state without being able to supplement with water.

Then gardeners need to decide what they want out of the plant material. Do they want it to be evergreen? To bloom all year long? To be fragrant? They need a clear understanding of where and how they can best use each plant they purchase. And they need to be realistic about their own lifestyle. If someone likes to go out and weed, dead-head, mulch and groom, they can use a little pickier plant. But if they just want to stick it in the ground, get it established, then sit back and watch it grow, that's fine too. They'll just need a different kind of plant. It's important to choose plants that suit your own personality.

✧   ✧   ✧

LCM: Do you come from a gardening family?

MARC: I'm from Donaldsonville, Georgia, and my mother's family is from Bainbridge, and every one of them had gardens. When my grandfather retired he built a huge nursery on Springcreek near Dothan, Alabama. A lot of people were into camellias at the time, and that's basically what he planted, too. Even though it hasn't been kept up, if you visit there in winter, it's still a stunning sight.

LCM: So, you're not surprised that you ended up doing what you're doing?

MARC: No, not at all, though I loved embryology, which was my major in college. My college background is certainly helpful, though. For example, I can pick a unique seedling out of a million of them, and sometimes those seedlings develop into something special. That's where

Veronica 'Goodness Grows' and *Digitalis* 'Emerson' came from, both of which are our introductions.

LCM: Tell me about some other Goodness Grows introductions.

MARC: We've introduced twelve labels that are now being grown all over the United States and in Europe. Some of these were uniquely ours, some were things gardening friends stumbled on and shared with us like *Achillea* 'Oertel's Rose', which is a dwarf yarrow. If you cultivate it in the sun, it stays compact. Generally, if you cultivate *Achilleas* in rich soils, they will get huge and flop around, but this little plant makes a wonderful groundcover and it's something someone shared with us.

MARC'S ADVICE TO BEGINNER GARDENERS

1. Take your time and be patient. Start slowly.
2. Understand your limitations. Don't get excited and try to do more than you can do.
3. Understand your environment. Know the amount and duration of sunlight, how the soil drains.
4. Have a water source.
5. Know what you want from the plant material and put it in the right place.
6. Choose plants to suit your own personality: picky plants for those who like to work with them, hardier plants for those who don't.

Veronica 'Goodness Grows' was a volunteer in our garden. We were growing several species of *Veronica* to determine which would perform well in the hot weather. We watched some of the seedlings for a couple of years, and when they began to bloom, the blossoms were blue and the plant was very floriforous. It begins blooming in spring and, with dead-heading, goes through the season. We named it *Veronica* 'Goodness Grows' and believe that it is a hybrid of *Veronica alpina* 'Alba' and *Veronica spicata* 'Rosea'. It is now number six on the top selling list in America.

COMMON MISTAKES

❖ Putting plants together that have different watering or light requirements.

❖ Poor spacing: crowding plants because of not understanding how large some plants become.

❖ Not preparing the soil correctly.

❖ Not understanding the life cycles of different plants. Some early plants go dormant and seem to disappear during summer, leaving empty spaces.

❖ Planting only for spring. Too many gardens are all bloomed out by mid-summer. Gardeners should balance their gardens with late performing selections. Spring is easy: consider fall first.

We found another exciting plant with Ryan Gainey while cultivating *Digitalis mertonensis*, a hybrid foxglove. He had planted *Digitalis purpurea* a good distance away, and we did not think they would cross pollinate. But when the seed germinated, three seedlings in 1,000 looked unique, so I plucked them out. They turned out to be a huge, white-flowering, weather-tolerant foxglove. We

named it after the street Ryan lives on, 'Emerson'.

Dianthus 'Bath's Pink' is a superb plant that another gardener shared with us. Jane Bath brought it to us. We planted and watched it, and determined that it was sterile and would not seed. It is an amazing plant. It will go through 105-degree summers. Even kudzu was browning out, and this plant still looked great. We named it after Jane Bath.

LCM: Do you have a top ten list of perennials?

MARC: Just ten?

LCM: Okay, I'll give you twelve.

MARC: Good. I lean toward species plants.

LCM: Why?

MARC: They're natural for the area, and if they have ornamental value, we like to use them because they seem to do better. I also like high performance plants, such as verbena, which begins flowering early and continues throughout the season, and we have a very long season here. It starts in March and lasts until frost in late October. I also like things that flower freely. *Coreopsis verticillata* 'Zagreb' is one of my favorites. It is dwarf, with small bright yellow flowers, and will outlive you if you don't crowd it out.

Dianthus 'Bath's Pink' is a good ever-green plant for the front. *Oenothera perennis* is a day-flowering yellow primrose. When the flowers go out, it produces little evergreen rosettes. *Veronica* 'Goodness Grows', of course, and *Veronica* 'Sunny Border Blue' are both good, long-flowering plants for the border. For fall color, I like *Hibiscus mutabilis*, which has large flowers that open white and then fade to pink, or *Hibiscus coccineus*, which is another plant indigenous to the South. These plants wake up in spring and grow to full size in one season, so you have to remember to leave enough space for it.

Salvia leucantha, Mexican bush sage, is a good plant which is hardy and dependably perennial south of Macon. Even though it's not reliably hardy north of that, I had one that lived eight years.

I like all the *Verbena* hybrids, and we've introduced a couple of varieties. Our introductions include a red one called 'Evelyn Scott' and another called 'Abbeville', which is lavender with a little white and a bit of fragrance. It's a mainstay for us because it flowers freely and lives through drought. And of course there's 'Homestead Purple', which Michael Dirr and Allan Armitage introduced.

There are several *asters* that are wonderful that are not yet available for the market. We are currently building stock on *Aster laevis*, a wonderful plant with purple foliage and blue flowers with yellow centers.

Lantana 'Miss Huff' is a top-of-the-line shrub. This came from the home of Mrs. Ruby Huff, a woman who lives just down the road from us. It is the only hardy shrub lantana in our area. It even survived zero-degree temperatures. It loses all its leaves and is late to wake up in spring, but then it begins to put out foliage at ground level. At this time, the gardener can cut out all dead wood. By mid-spring it's flowering and continues until frost. It's great for attracting butterflies and hummingbirds all season. It is not thorny and generally does not fruit.

LCM: That's a wonderful list of perennials. What do you think of using annuals?

MARC: I think annuals are very necessary for the garden. They are just as important as perennials.

I love the white *Zinnia linearis*, Mexican zinnia. For years only the orange form was available, and it was frustrating trying to blend it into the color scheme of the garden. But these little plants are easy to work with and are free flowering, even in our heat.

I also like the Swan River daisy, *Brachycome iberidifolia*, which takes full sun and flowers fully. Although it's actually a perennial and may be hardy in coastal areas, we treat it as an annual here. Gomphrena is another good annual which goes all season.

LCM: Do you have pest and disease problems with many of these plants?

MARC: Well, everything is subject to something. For years and years we grew *Anemone japonica* without a bug on it, but two years ago a leaf-eating beetle showed up, so now we have to spray these plants. There is no such thing as a disease- or insect-free plant.

It helps to keep the plants healthy, though. Don't garden without irrigation. You're wasting your time.

LCM: What kind of plants do you recommend for shade?

MARC: I like to use species plants, like woodland phlox, *Phlox amoena*, which outlives and outperforms even *Phlox divaricata*. It begins flowering in February and continues through spring and into summer.

Virginia bluebells, *Mertensia virginica*, is a wonderful performer. It flowers and produces seed, and then it gets ugly, which is natural. The plant only lives to reproduce. The plant's protection against a hot, dry season is to shrivel and go dormant. At this point, the gardener needs to groom it.

LCM: What do you think of *Pulmonaria*?

MARC: In strong, filtered light and the right soil, *Pulmonaria* does fine and ought to be a mainstay for a shade garden, though it is prone to slug damage. Generally, if a gardener loses *Pulmonaria*, it's due to slugs and not heat. In a bad season, it goes dormant, but because it has a woody root, it can regenerate.

LCM: What do you see as "up and coming" in the horticultural world?

MARC: Baptisias. We've made selections from a pink form of *Baptisia australis* that are going to be wonderful.

SELF-SOWING PLANTS FOR A NATURAL-LOOKING GARDEN

Peony poppies *Papaver somniferum*
Larkspur *Consolida orientalis*
Violas *Viola* sp.
Biennial foxglove *Digitalis purpurea*
Ox-eye daisy *Chrysanthemum leucanthemum*
Forget-me-nots *Myosotis scorpiodes*

"When flowers become weeds, you know you really have a garden."

Baptisia pendula is better for smaller gardens, but for larger areas, *Baptisia australis* is wonderful. There is also a dwarf yellow *Baptisia vertis*, not to be confused with the yellow baptisia in south Georgia which has small, insignificant flowers. *B. vertis* has canary yellow inflorescences that measure twelve inches long.

Another good new plant is *Amsonia tabernaemontana* var. 'Montana', which has blue flowers in spring. This selection is nice for the garden because it is low growing, compact, and doesn't fall over in the rain.

LCM: What general mistakes do you see gardeners making?

MARC: One of the biggest mistakes is in water compatibility, that is, putting plants together which have different watering requirements. For example, planting astilbes with German iris. The amount of water astilbes require causes German iris to rot.

Another mistake is putting plants together that have different light requirements—putting shade-loving plants in the full sun. And people make design mistakes because they don't know, or they don't pay attention to, the size these plants attain at maturity. For example, before you plant a young eight-inch tall lythrum, you need to remember that at maturity, these plants reach a height of two and a half to three feet.

We also need to know about the life cycles of the plants we use. For example, oriental poppies can be cultivated here. They become green in late fall and remain so through the winter and into spring when they elongate and flower. After that they turn brown and go dormant in summer. A lot of people think that they're dead and pull them up, but if left alone, they'll revive again in fall. So, knowing the plant's life cycle and using the plants correctly in the garden is crucial. These are mistakes professionals make as well.

Soil preparation is also important, and that's a custom thing. Two things you need to remember. Soil needs amending, and plants use up soil. Here at the nursery, we build the soil for three years before anything goes into the ground. The soil drains well here, but the nutrients are depleted because this was once a cotton farm.

LCM: What other mistakes do you see?

MARC: People like to use self-sowing plants, but they can be dangerous. One year we had a huge *Baptisia australis* in full bloom surrounded by about a thousand peony poppies and it looked stunning. What people don't realize is that those thousand peony poppy plants were what remained after I filled three thirty-gallon trash cans with poppy seedlings that I pulled up. Self-sowing plants can be wonderful, but gardeners need to know what they're in for. I've seen cleome, which is a great annual, totally take over a garden.

Johnny-jump-ups, *Viola tricolor,* will reseed too, and can be a lot of work. Another reseeding plant is *Lychnis coronaria*, or mullein pink. It is a magenta-colored (or white) biennial, with a silver-grey rosette in winter. It flowers in late spring through early summer and reseeds everywhere.

Celosia is another that readily reseeds, and forget-me-nots, *Myosotis scorpiodes*, and the ox-eye daisy, *Chrysanthemum leucanthemum*, which we grow with the understanding that it's not a long-lived plant and that it will migrate through reseeding.

If you want an easy plant—a daisy that stays put and doesn't reseed—try *Chrysanthemum maxima* 'Ryan', or 'Becky'. It's a wonderful plant that flowers July Fourth, has succulent foliage, and is long lived. We've seen it a lot in old homesites.

Another good one is *Chrysanthemum nipponicum*, a shrub chrysanthemum that flowers in fall with white flowers and a yellow center.

LCM: How about larkspur?

MARC: Most gardeners don't have a problem with larkspur overseeding. We really push the larkspur that Thomas Jefferson cultivated, *Consolida orientalis*, because it is a species plant and over-winters beautifully.

If you don't allow them to get out of hand, using reseeding plants is a wonderful way to establish a natural-looking garden. When flowers become weeds, you know you really have a garden.

ALLAN ARMITAGE, ATHENS: UNIVERSITY OF GEORGIA

From his native Canada to his current home in Athens, Georgia, Allan Armitage has spent a lifetime digging in the dirt and working in greenhouses, influencing and teaching students, gardeners, and professional growers. All have benefited greatly from his inspiration and expertise.

COLOR FOR THE SHADE GARDEN

Hellebores *Helleborus* sp.

Silenes *Silene* sp.

Pulmonarias *Pulmonaria longifolia*

Columbine *Aquilegia canadensis*

Anemone *Anemone vitifolia*
    'Robustissima'

Iris *Iris virginica*

Celandine poppy *Chelidonium majus*

Asarums *Asarum* sp.

Trillium *Trillium* sp.

Jack-in-the-pulpit *Arisaema triphyllum*

Although interested in, and knowledgeable about, many fields of horticulture, perhaps Allan's greatest contribution has been in the area of herbaceous plants. Not only has he written several books and numerous articles about bedding plants, cut flowers, and perennials, he was also instrumental in founding a professional growers organization. He is in charge of the University of Georgia Horticulture Garden, one of thirty All-American Selection trial gardens in the United States. This garden provides information and guidelines for growing perennials and annuals in climates with high heat and humidity.

Lecturer, teacher, researcher, and writer, Allan's first love is the garden where it all began. His own garden in Athens is an eclectic collection of new potentials and old favorites.

When asked if he grew up in a family of gardeners, Allan laughs. "Gardening? We cut the grass and that was it."

Since that time, Allan has broadened his horticultural horizons to include the world, for he has lectured in the rest of the United States, Canada, New Zealand, and Europe.

We Georgians are the fortunate recipients of Allan's untiring search to find better, more beautiful, hardier, more fragrant flowers for our gardens.

LCM: I understand that you grew up in Montreal, Canada. You've said that your family had little interest in gardening. How did you happen to get into horticulture?

ALLAN: During college, I had a summer job as a grave digger: literally digging graves with a spade—we had no backhoe. It was a perpetual-care cemetery, and in Montreal this meant planting the grave site—not around it, but on it—and planting with an array of flowers. They were works of art.

I would see people grieving in the cemetery, but when they saw the flowers it seemed to make them happy. Witnessing the joy that flowers brought to people showed me what flowers could do.

Although I was in school and worked at other jobs, I kept finding myself in greenhouses. I was really into ecology at the time, and almost went to northern Canada with a professor to study northern black bears. The day I was to interview for the job, my wife and I started wandering around the campus and I found myself in the greenhouses. I thought, why am I going to northern Canada when I would really rather be in a greenhouse? So, that was the turning point, and I went back to school in horticulture.

LCM: So that was it? From cemeteries to bears to being a world famous horticulturist?

ALLAN: Well, more or less.

LCM: Tell me about the trial gardens at the University of Georgia. When were they installed?

ALLAN: The gardens have been in about ten years, but we redid everything last year and made it more user friendly. We added new beds and walks and a wonderful gazebo, donated by the Georgia Commercial Flower Growers Association.

Each year we evaluate the plants every two weeks, checking for size, bloom, color, hardiness, [and the like].

LCM: What are some of the plants you've tested here?

ALLAN: For a start, we look at all the major classes of annuals, such as petunias, geraniums, marigolds, and vincas, because growers are constantly working to improve these and develop new cultivars.

The goal of this garden is to display plant varieties adjacent to one another, so when breeders—or gardeners—come to look, they can tell immediately what works—and what does not work in this region.

For example, the petunia 'Fantasy' series includes varieties with small flowers on dwarf plants. We have found that this type of plant, which has smaller flowers, work well for us here because they take the heat so much better. In general, what works best for us are the multifloras rather than the grandifloras—varieties with smaller, more numerous flowers rather than fewer, bigger blossoms.

This is true of the pansies as well, although people still love the giant-flowered hybrid, and that remains the best-selling pansy. It is a matter of education. We need to educate both the breeders and the gardeners about what does best in our own region.

The small-flowered petunia 'Purple Wave' is a great plant and grows well here. You can see it all over the University of Georgia campus. We're working to develop a similar variety with white flowers.

We are looking at plants that tolerate the heat well and are evaluating many relatively unknown groups of plants, such as *Pentas*. We've had good success with one called 'Nova', which is easy to grow from cuttings and seems to take heat and sun. After a summer like 1995, you can easily tell which plants can take the heat and which can't.

Another little known plant is *Duranta*, or pepper berry, which is from south Georgia where it produces dozens of blue flowers and blooms for most of the growing season. In north Georgia it seems to grow well, but we treat it as an annual and replant it each year.

LCM: What are some of the more well-known plants that are good for our region?

VINES FOR THE SHADE

Allegheny vine *Adlumia fungosa*
Yellow dicentra vine *Dicentra*
Clematis *Clematis texansis*
Climbing aster *Aster carolinianus*

ALLAN: Dianthus is a great plant for us because it tolerates our winters and then flowers profusely when it begins to warm in spring. Most selections can also take the heat. The best for fall planting and spring flowering are selections such as 'Ideal' and the 'Telstar' series, which are hybrids between the annual *Dianthus chinensis* and the winter hardy *Dianthus barbatus.* The result is the best traits of both parents and a terrific plant.

We've also done a lot of work with coleus, and all of a sudden coleus is a hot item. We introduced another group of coleus, the 'Sun Lover' series, which includes popular varieties such as 'Freckles', 'Red Ruffles', 'Olympic Torch', 'Rustic Orange', and 'Gay's Delight'. Another favorite is 'Thumbelina', which has tiny leaves.

HEAT-TOLERANT ANNUALS

Purslane *Portulaca oleracea*

Gomphrena *Gomphrena globosa*

Celosia *Celosia spicata*

Sweet potato vine *Ipomoea batatas* 'Blackie'

Petunia *Petunia hybrida* 'Fantasy', 'Purple Wave'

A grower from Florida also sent me a series from Indonesia, which are beautiful and will tolerate sun, so we have called these the 'Solar' series.

Plectranthus is closely related to coleus, and is going to be a great plant for Georgia gardens planted as an annual. The *Plectranthus* growing in my own garden produced a sport, an offshoot with brighter yellow leaves. We developed it and named it 'Athen's Gem'.

I also love the ornamental salvias. *Salvia guaranitica*, blue anise sage, has violet-blue flowers and has performed well all season. It was chosen as a Georgia Gold Medal winner in 1995. *Salvia* 'Cherry Queen' has been flowering since June, and *Salvia leucantha*, which has beautiful blue and white blossoms in the fall.

Purslane is something else we've been working with because it is similar to *Portulaca*, which is not a good plant for our region. Purslane, however, tolerates our heat and performs well for us.

Chinese foxglove, *Rehmannia elata,* is a plant that not many people know, but they ought to. It is an attractive plant that grows in the shade and produces large, tubular flowers. It has the potential to be invasive, however, as it puts out seedlings everywhere.

We are looking at some new *Celosias* and some of them are going to be terrific. One called wheat celosia produces long, slender, cream-colored plumes that look like wheat. The new pink variety, called 'Pink Candle', is probably even better known.

Tithonia, Mexican sunflower, has impressed a lot of people because it's so big, but many gardeners find it difficult to use. We tried the dwarf forms in the Trial Garden, but they were shaded out by the tall form, so we don't know how they will perform.

LCM: Do you find that there is a lot of interest in the ornamental grasses?

ALLAN: Yes, but not as much as there was. The real "got to have" phase seems to be over. Ferns are becoming much more important commercially, especially in the South, where everyone wants to know which ferns to plant.

The movers and shakers of the horticulture world are interested in the Southeast because they know it's a big gardening region. There's a strong network of gardeners in the South, and growers know that if they can find plants that do well here, they will sell well throughout. Particularly in north Georgia and the Carolinas, word of mouth is quick to pass on information about new plants.

LCM: What does your home garden look like?

ALLAN: It's an area with a lot of oak trees that produce shade for an abundance of wildflowers underneath. In spring I have *Helleborus* and ferns, *Silenes*, *Pulmonarias*, and *Aquilegia*, the native red-and-yellow columbine. There is also *Polygonatum*, Solomon's seal, and *Tovara* called 'Painter's Palette', and a foam flower with great foliage, *Tiarella* 'Dunvagen'.

I also like vines, though I don't have a lot of places for them. I just train them over and around and through the trees. I have a great biennial vine called *Adlumia fungosa* or Allegheny vine; and a yellow *Dicentra* vine; and *Clematis texansis*, which produces seed heads as pretty as the flowers. The climbing aster, *Aster carolinianus*, flowers in September and October. It's a vigorous climber and grows as if it wants to take over the world.

Anemones flower in late summer. One of my favorites is *Anemone vitifolia* 'Robustissima', which is a fine plant and easier to grow than the hybrids.

I have a zillion different kinds of iris. *Iris virginica* forms a huge plant. I prune it way back every year and it still keeps coming back.

In the only sunny area in my garden, I have planted *Aster tartaricus* and *Aster laterifolius, Amsonias,* and *Baptisias,* which are all wonderful plants.

LCM: Which ferns do you grow?

ALLAN: One unusual one is East India holly fern. This is evergreen through most of the winter. If it gets really cold, it goes down, but I think that in general it's a great looking plant with brown on the back of the yellow-green fronds.

I also grow a netted chain fern (*Woodwardia* sp.). The reproductive part is thin and wiry in the center and it has broader fronds on the outside. Other good ferns for the South include the good old Christmas fern, autumn fern, lady fern, and southern shield fern.

I don't do well with the bigger ferns like cinnamon and royal. I think they might do better farther north. I have only moderate success with maidenhair and spleenworts because my soil is not rich enough.

Next to the ferns, in a really shady spot, I also have *Trilliums, Asarums,* and *Arisaema* (Jack-in-the-pulpit), celandine poppy, and lots and lots of hosta.

LCM: Why do you love to garden so much?

ALLAN: I just love to learn. There's just no getting old when you're a gardener. You can get mature, but not old. A garden always gives you something to look forward to. The hue and cry of the gardener is "Just wait until next year!"

BOBBY SAUL, ATLANTA: SAUL NURSERIES

Artist? Horticulturist? Grower? Designer? It's hard to classify Bobby Saul. This multi-talented, many-faceted man, along with his wife, Kathy, and his brother Richard, started Saul Nurseries in 1986. The result of this endeavor is a wonderfully rich source of plant material for the Southeast. The nursery supplies garden centers with the new and unusual, as well as the tried and true plants for every season.

A native of Atlanta, Bobby received a degree in agronomy and horticulture from the University of Georgia, then returned to Atlanta to work in the landscaping industry. He soon realized that his greatest enjoyment came from growing plants, so he and his partners bought a piece of land in the north Georgia mountains to start the nursery and "it became a fever."

Bobby Saul loves change—thrives on it, as he puts it, and he has taken great delight in watching the world of horticulture and gardening change here in the South.

PERENNIALS TO START FROM SEED

Helianthus *Helianthus angustifolia*
Purple coneflower *Echinacea purpurea*
Black-eyed Susan *Rudbeckia hirta*
Ox-eye daisy *Chrysanthemum leucanthemum*
Verbena, upright *Verbena bonariensis*

"My old landscaping boss told me how people used to garden around here," he says. "In the Sixties it was a solid green landscape; the flowers were on azaleas, dogwoods, and magnolias—and they called it gardening! And then they began to add bulbs, then annuals, then perennials, then flowering shrubs. Gardening in Georgia really received a boost when Post Properties began doing the tulips. People began to see the need for color, and wanted something more than hollies and junipers.

"Now we grow all kinds of things at the nursery—ornamental grasses and ferns, and about five or six hundred varieties of perennials. We also started growing annuals and that was a big jump. We grow all the basic things, but we started growing some weird plants too. That's what makes it fun."

LCM: Saul Nurseries is well known for the unusual plant material you supply to the landscape industry and garden centers throughout the region. What types of plants are people particularly interested in now?

BOBBY: There seems to be great interest in unusual annuals. In fact, the newest trend is the tropical look. In Atlanta, the summers are more tropical than temperate, and we can grow a lot of tropical material, if we treat it as an annual. Plants such as mandevilla, plumbago, and bananas, combined with annuals and perennials give you a great look.

LCM: Do you think it's a look that will really catch on?

BOBBY: Yes. It's a very Victorian look—antebellum—like the palms on the front porches or beside the white columns.

LCM: So, there's really nothing new in the gardening world?

BOBBY: Right. We've gone back to an old look. But there are some new twists on old plants. For example, you saw many new cultivars of *Coleus* everywhere this year. One of our growers has eighty different varieties. One of the best is a miniature, 'Thumbelina', which gets only about twelve inches tall.

LCM: What are some of the hot new annuals—or hot old ones?

BOBBY: One of the wildest annuals this year was *Strobilanthes,* or 'Persian Shield', which has metallic purple foliage and a real tropical look. There's nothing like it. We've seen a move toward using unusual foliage plants in big commercial beds in office parks, which get a great deal of public exposure. There are really no rules anymore. You can follow styles, but to me it's like modern art. You don't want to go backwards. We're trying to create something very new.

LCM: Do you find that people are willing to try new things?

BOBBY: Now they are. You can see it in the landscape industry, in particular. Of course Post Properties is a big player in this game. They're not afraid to use anything. They have incredible designers.

Another great designer is Dottie Myers. She contends that since you have to work with the soils so much in preparing these beds, the shape of the beds really never changes. The only creativity, then, is what you put into the beds. We love change. We thrive on it.

LCM: Winter annuals seem to be a relatively new passion for gardeners. What do you recommend?

BOBBY: Pansies, of course. But we now have what we call pansy accessories. Dianthus, snapdragons, giant red mustard, and parsley are all good to plant with pansies. Black-seeded Simpson lettuce looks good in fall, but it generally won't make it through the winters here.

LCM: How about native plants?

BOBBY: That's a big part of our business—we have about one hundred varieties of natives, depending on how you define native.

LCM: How do *you* define native?

BOBBY: To me, there are three ways. You can include only local, indigenous plants, or you can include the ones which have become naturalized over a period of time, or you can also include selected varieties which come from natives. There is a big debate throughout the country as to what a native plant really is. We've introduced several selected varieties from native plants, such as new colors of native phloxes.

LCM: So now we have "manipulated native" as well?

BOBBY: Right.

❦

There are really no rules anymore. You can follow styles, but to me it's like modern art. You don't want to go backwards. We're trying to create something very new.

❦

LCM: Which plants are easiest to start from seed?

BOBBY: Plants such as larkspur and poppies can be sown in fall. Plants such as melampodium, upright verbena (*Verbena bonariensis*), cleome, cosmos, reseeding or wild petunias should be sown in spring. Lychnis and bachelor buttons can be sown either spring or fall.

The highway department has found out that they could get a better naturalized look if they used some cultivated varieties. The highways looked beautiful this spring.

LCM: Why do you think the cultivars look better than species?

BOBBY: Because they are bred for color. Species plants are only trying to attract whatever it is that pollinates them. Many of the plants I just mentioned are not natives, but they will reseed here.

LCM: Should gardeners use caution when planting reseeding plants?

BOBBY: I think you can run into trouble with plants such as Queen Anne's lace, honeysuckle, English ivy, and kudzu, which take over no matter what else you have. Kudzu is actually not a terrible plant. It is, at least, a nitrogen-fixing plant that puts down roots every three feet, so it's breaking up subsoil. But it's amazing how quickly it spreads.

It's been said that 8,200 acres a day in this country are being overtaken by introduced plants.

LCM: A day?

BOBBY: Yes. It's outrageous.

LCM: Do any of the perennials reseed as well?

BOBBY: Yes, there are quite a few, such as helianthus, purple coneflower, rudbeckias, ox-eye daisy, native columbine, calamint, sun drops, stokes aster, coreopsis, verbena, dicentra, and several ornamental grasses.

LCM: Can you propagate by taking stem cuttings as well?

BOBBY: It depends on the family of the plant. Sedums are easy to root, as well as members of the mint family. Rooting from stem cuttings tends to get technical, though, because certain times of the year are better for doing this than others, and you need to use growth hormones. You also need to mist several times a day to keep the ambient humidity high. Usually, when a plant goes into heavy bloom, it's not a good time to root it.

Probably the easiest way for a gardener to propagate a plant is by division. Daylilies, hostas, astilbes, and monardas are all very easy to divide. You can divide plants anytime of the year, as long as you keep the newly planted divisions watered.

LCM: Do you have problems with mildew on monarda?

BOBBY: Aha! No, because the only one we sell was given to us by Gene Cline and it has no problem with mildew. It is named for his son, Jacob Cline, and you can rub mildew on this plant and it won't get it. This plant has now made its way to the northeast, and they're going crazy over it. You can even plant it in close quarters, with little air circulation and it will do fine. It's a red variety which gets about six feet tall. It is a great plant.

We try new materials all the time, and there are several people we communicate with about these, such as Jimmy and Becky Stewart, Ozzie Johnson, Carol Hooks at Post Properties, and Mildred Pinnell at the Botanical Garden.

There are some great new plants coming out such as the 'Becky' daisy. It is a short-lived Shasta daisy with uniform foliage, a strong stalk, a long blooming time, and big flowers. We don't even grow the variety 'Alaska' anymore because the blooms are not uniform and do not last long enough.

A new lamb's ear, 'Helene von Stein', is also called 'Big Ears'. It has a bigger leaf than *Stachys lanata*, but it doesn't melt out as much in the humidity. The leaf is huge, and the plant grows eight to twelve inches tall.

There are new phloxes, like a wild purple, *Phlox paniculata*, that bloomed three times this year and never got mildew.

LCM: Do you have a group of, say, the top ten favorite plants that a home gardener could grow successfully?

BOBBY: By "successfully" do you mean material that's long blooming, no trouble, and spreads readily?

LCM: Naturally. And inexpensive too!

BOBBY: Of course, the old standbys like purple coneflower and rudbeckias would still fall into that category. We also have an *Achillea* or yarrow that we call '1869', which may be the same plant that Goodness Grows calls 'Ortel's Rose'. It was found locally, but in a different spot. It's fuschia pink, blooms a long time, divides quickly, doesn't need to be fertilized or bed prepared, and is adaptable to varying conditions.

An old plant mentioned by Elizabeth Lawrence is *Asteromoea*, which I think is one of the best. It is incredibly adaptable; it will grow in full sun down to about one hour of sun, and it blooms its head off from mid-May to October. You have to have well-drained soil or it will rot in the winter.

A lot of people like cannas, a lot of people don't. The new ones are really wild. We have one called 'Bengal Tiger' which Dottie Myers used last year on a Taylor-Mathis property, and the world went crazy over it. This year we sold about 2,500 of them. It was something new and fun. You'll see them all over the place next year.

Another great plant, which is more a groundcover than a flowering plant, is *Dianthus* 'Bath's Pink', introduced by Rick Berry and Marc Richardson at Goodness Grows Nursery. It's one of the best groundcovers now. It needs little soil preparation and just looks great. The bloom, to me, is just an extra.

We've also introduced a selection of *Dianthus* which we call 'ItSaul White'. It has double white blooms and silvery foliage.

As for the *Echinaceas*, it depends on how you're using them. If you're planting an English cottage garden, either the purple or white are good.

In more moist ground, *Lythrum* is a great one. We don't see a problem with it spreading here like it does in the Midwest and Northeast. We only grow one variety, 'Morden's Pink', and it's supposed to be sterile, so it doesn't reseed.

Russian sage, *Perovskia*, is one of the best plants ever. It needs full sun because if you have it in shade, it will lean. It also needs to be in well-drained soil, because winter wetness will hurt it.

Another great plant we introduced is the 'Moon Traveler' daylily, which my brother Richard crossed probably fourteen or fifteen years ago. One of the parents is 'Stella D'Oro'. It blooms as well as 'Stella', but has a much better color. It's a beautiful citron yellow.

ANNUALS TO START FROM SEED

Larkspur *Consolida orientalis*
Poppies *Papaver somniferum, P. rhoeas*
Melampodium *Melampodium* sp.
Bachelor buttons *Centaurea cyanus*
Cleome *Cleome Hasslerama*
Cosmos *Cosmos bipinnatus,*
    C. sulphureus
Coleus *Coleus* sp.
Petunia, reseeding *Petunia*

Another long blooming plant is *Salvia guaranitica*, blue sage, which we consider more of an annual than a perennial, but it blooms well. Also 'Indigo Spires', which is hardier.

LCM: How about the penstemons?

BOBBY: I think it's too hot here. The one that made the national perennials list is 'Husker's Red'. In England, they're great, and in the Midwest, but it's just

BEST OF THE NEW

Daisy *Chrysanthemum maxima* 'Becky'
Monarda *Monarda didyma* 'Jacob Cline'
Lamb's ear *Stachys lanata* 'Helene von Stein'
Purple phlox *Phlox paniculata*
Persian shield *Strobilanthes dyeranus*
Coleus, miniature *Coleus* 'Thumbelina'

too hot and humid here. You can't put them in the shade because they'll all fall over, and they can't take the hot sun. They will survive, however.

LCM: But there's a difference between "survive" and "thrive"?

BOBBY: Yes. Yes. Yes. Many people say, "it lives . . ." and you want to say, "Great. Does it bloom?"

LCM: What else is new and exciting?

BOBBY: There are a couple of new plants coming out that look like they're going to be great. Ron Deiterman, at the Atlanta Botanical Garden, and Ozzie Johnson found a stokesia native to Georgia that has blooms 36–40 inches tall. The foliage stays close to the ground. This may revolutionize the cut flower industry in regards to stokesia. It has big blooms that won't fall over, which is exciting.

I think we have a new and improved *Chrysogonum* to offer this year. 'Eco Laquered Spider' is a selection that has silvery green foliage and will make a beautiful groundcover.

The plant world is going crazy over new plants, and finally homeowners are realizing that they can be totally different from the next person. And that's what keeps the artistic value of the garden, not to limit yourself to any one kind of gardening plant, but to try new and exciting things.

LCM: Don't you think that as we gain confidence as Southern gardeners we will become more comfortable using a wider variety of plants and not try to emulate a Northeastern garden or an English garden? It's as you said about modern art— an artist has to have a certain level of self confidence before he, or she, is willing and able to do something different.

BOBBY: Here at the nursery, we talk about supplying the paint—and the gardener is the artist. The artist has to know what the paint is made of and what it will do.

LCM: Are there basic mistakes that you see people doing over and over?

BOBBY: One of the biggest mistakes is site selection. As we have more and more plants available to us from all over the world, we have to remember that many of them are limited to specific microclimates. We know, for instance, that native maidenhair fern grows best out of the wind.

Mediterranean plants such as rosemary and santolina need a hot area and they don't mind the wind. And when you plant these, you need to prepare the soil with a lot of gravel and chirt to get better drainage. If you do these things, they'll work.

Or take tropical plants. The side of my yard looks like I live in a jungle with bamboo, palms, and bananas—you almost need a machete to get through it. I enjoy that part of the yard immensely. For that you need heavy watering capacity.

Gardening is a lot more exciting than it used to be. Container gardening is probably one way you can be the most creative in the garden and be acceptable, if you want to be acceptable. You can get some great combinations. An idea about design that I stress is to find three or four plants that you love and that look good together, and use them. If you are doing a long perennial border, place your favorite combinations at intervals throughout the border, then fill in with other things that come in and out of bloom. I think that's the best way to do it. Plants enhance other plants, and I don't think people use that concept enough.

SAM AND CARLEEN JONES, WATKINSVILLE: PICCADILLY FARM

Sam and Carleen Jones have combined their considerable talents and energies to create Piccadilly Farm, a nursery specializing in shade plants, near Watkinsville, Georgia.

Sam grew up in Roswell, Georgia, in a family of horticulturists. After receiving his B.S. degree in horticulture from Auburn University, he worked with his parents in the family business, but his desire to teach led him back to college to pursue graduate work in botany.

After receiving his doctorate, Sam taught botany at Auburn University, Southern Mississippi University, and then finally at the University of Georgia where he stayed for twenty-seven years.

"The genesis of Piccadilly Farm resulted from seeing my colleagues reach retirement age and realize they had nothing to do. Since we both enjoyed gardening and trying new plants, Carleen and I decided a nursery would provide us with something to do when we retired.

"We talked to Fred Gallee at Callaway Gardens, and he suggested that we get into hostas and hellebores. We never dreamed that the business would grow so large."

Carleen's introduction to plants occurred when she was assisting Sam in his botanical field research. Although she loved her job teaching high school biology in Athens, Carleen took early retirement in 1987 to devote full time to developing Piccadilly Farm. In 1991, Sam also retired, allowing for more time in the field to locate and propagate plants. The nursery began to grow quickly.

Growth and popularity have brought much pleasure—and a new set of problems. The display gardens are so magnificent that people began trekking to Watkinsville to visit the gardens, thus limiting the time that Sam and Carleen could spend in the nursery. They solved this problem by opening the nursery and gardens to the public only on specified days, generally Thursdays through Saturdays during spring and fall, but visitors are encouraged to call to confirm the hours (Piccadilly Farm: 706-769-6516).

LCM: In a very short time Piccadilly Farm has become quite well known throughout the Southeast as a specialty plant nursery. Although there were many plants you could have chosen to specialize in, you selected hellebores and hostas. What was it about these plants that caught your interest?

CARLEEN'S FAVORITE HOSTAS

'Antioch'

'Aspen Gold'

'August Moon'

'Betsy King'

'Blue Angel'

'Blue Cadet'

'Brim Cup'

'Fort. Aureo-Marginata'

'Frances Williams'

'Gold Standard'

'Great Expectations'

'Hadspen Blue'

'Halycon'

'Love Pat'

'Midas Touch'

'Tardiflora'

'Tokudama Flavorcircinalis'

'Zounds'

CARLEEN: At first, we knew little about them, but a friend told us that they were good plants that were hard to find in the trade. When we started learning more about the hostas, we found that they were excellent plants to work with in the shade, and have wonderful variation in color, size, and texture.

SAM: We began the nursery during the "hosta explosion," when tissue culture came into play and new cultivars were becoming readily available. Prior to this, plants had to be divided, which is slow and labor intensive, and some of the new cultivars cost $300 or $500. With tissue culture, a new one cost about $25 to $30, so an average gardener could afford these plants.

We were probably the first nursery in Georgia to really get into growing hostas and hellebores, and through the years, we've built up a good customer base. Our clients seem to be serious gardeners. People from all over the Southeast come here during hosta season to visit the demonstration gardens and purchase plants.

LCM: Can you tell me a little about the lenten rose, or hellebore, and why so many people are attracted to it?

CARLEEN: Hellebores are wonderful evergreen plants that are long-lived and easy to grow. The flower color ranges from white to pink to plum. People in the South are accustomed to being outside so much of the time, and they're fascinated with a plant that blooms during the winter months. Every year we sponsor a Helleborus Day in late February or early March. People seem to have a good time exploring the gardens and seeing the many different kinds of hellebores which we grow.

SAM: People like to come here because the garden is pleasant to walk around. We're not like a garden center, which is often surrounded by acres of asphalt. It's an educational experience for people to visit here. The plants are labeled, and our customers come to learn as well as buy plants. Unfortunately, we have to limit the hours we are open to the public, but we encourage people to come and visit during the times we are open.

We specialize in shade plants for the Georgia Piedmont region. We have one of the largest selections of shade perennials in the Southeast, and some unusual woody plants as well.

It's important to us that we are actively involved in learning, so in addition to the pleasure of gardening, we are also continuously testing plants and new ways to grow them. We try not to sell anything that does not do well in this region. People buy from us because they know the plants we have are going to work.

CARLEEN: People sometimes aren't sure how to use the plants they have, and which plants to use together, and I think the display gardens help them with this.

LCM: What plants do you recommend for grouping with the hellebores and hostas?

CARLEEN: We've been experimenting with different combinations for years. We have discovered that even with the wide variety of textures and sizes found in hostas, if you just have hostas, it gets boring.

I think ferns are wonderful to use with hostas and hellebores because they have such nice textures. *Pulmonarias* are great too, and *Carex* and *Acorus* provide nice grass-like texture.

Native woodland flowers look beautiful in spring and early summer. Plants like *Cimcifuga* (bugbane), *Smilacina* (false-Solomon's-seal), *Chelidonium majus* (celandine or yellow wood poppy), *Phlox divaricata* (wood phlox), *Heuchera* (alum root), and *Lobelia* (cardinal flower) are all good choices. We also include shrubs such as pieris, anise, and rhododendrons.

LCM: What varieties of hellebores do you sell?

SAM: We sell *Helleborus orientalis*, which, under the same growing condi-

tions, presents great variation in flower color from white to deep plum. You'll hear people talk about named cultivars, but these plants come from seed and do not always stay true to the parent plant, so they're not predictable in the trade.

We also grow *Helleborus argutifolius*, which needs a little more light, and Bear's Foot hellebore, *H. foetidus*, which has nice texture and acts like a biennial. It reseeds so readily, though, that once it is established, it persists to make a nice specimen plant.

LCM: What cultural conditions do hellebores require ?

SAM: They like ample organic matter and need well-drained soil. A hillside is an ideal place to grow these plants because drainage is better. Because the heads nod, it's easier to see the flowers if you're looking up at them.

PLANTING HOSTAS

1. Dig the entire bed and work ground well, taking care not to disturb tree roots.
2. Avoid water-hungry trees such as water oak or maple.
3. Work in five to ten inches of organic matter. Add 10-10-10 fertilizer, sand, or granite dust.
4. Raise beds where possible.
5. Fertilize in April with Osmacote™.

Hellebores don't like to be moved, so it's important to choose your site carefully. When planting, if you want the clumps to overlap, space them eighteen inches apart. If you want each clump to stay separate, plant them twenty-four inches apart.

LCM: Do you clip back the dead leaves at the end of the season?

CARLEEN: It depends on how particular you are. If you're fussy and have a small garden, you can cut off the leaves, just for aesthetic purposes. My garden is large and I have too many hellebores to do this. I describe my garden as a natural woodland garden, and I just let the leaves stay and work around them. It's never going to be in pristine condition, although I do try to stay ahead of the weeds and work hard to get them out before they go to seed.

SAM: I call it an informal Southern shade garden, and I feel that it reflects our personalities. We like plants, but the garden is not fluffy.

LCM: Are the cultural conditions necessary for growing hostas the same as for hellebores?

CARLEEN: I would say yes. Once established, the hellebores will take dry conditions better than hostas, though. Hostas seem to take a little more care than the hellebores.

❦

A garden is a very personal thing. If you like it, then it doesn't matter what other people think. It should fit your own personality.

❦

LCM: How adaptable are hostas to other areas of Georgia?

SAM: As you travel north, the hostas get a little larger. The farther south you go with the hostas, the less success you have. Past the Fall Line, south of Macon, some people have good luck with them,

but it's an exception. Our plants do a bit better in Macon than they do when you drop down into the sandy soils in the south.

People in south Georgia may have special microclimates that allow them to grow hostas. We have customers in Savannah who say they have good luck with them, but it takes a lot of work and effort.

LCM: Are there varieties of hostas bred for higher temperatures?

SAM: No, not really. It's not only the heat of summer that bothers them, it is also the lack of cold. Hostas need a dormant period during the winter months.

CARLEEN: There are several conditions to consider. In south Georgia, both temperatures and humidity are higher, and the soil is different.

LCM: Are you surprised at the popularity of hostas?

CARLEEN: No. I think people react as I did when I first discovered hostas. The old common varieties weren't very exciting, but then some of the new cultivars came out with different colors and textures, and I became very interested.

People like hostas for different reasons, though. We have one customer who lost her daughter this year. She said that she liked the hostas because they were like a rebirth. She would watch them die in fall, and then in spring, watch them come up again.

I get excited anticipating how much bigger they're going to become every year. Hostas are perennials that do not need to be divided. If you want a nice, big clump, just let it go.

LCM: What are your favorite hosta selections?

CARLEEN: There are so many. 'Blue Angel' is the largest blue hosta, but you must have a large space for it. 'Antioch' is a good simple, variegated one. 'Great Expectations' has good coloring, and 'Zounds' has beautiful texture for a gold. 'August Moon' is beautiful for a gold, especially if you can get a little light on it during certain times of the day. It's also reasonably priced.

SAM: No matter what your budget is, you can find some nice hostas for the garden. It takes a lot of plants to make a garden, and that can get expensive. I tell people to put in some of the less expensive ones, and then add a new, hot variety as a focal point.

LCM: How do you advise people about choosing hostas?

CARLEEN: I try to determine what kind of gardener they are first. If they seem as if they are impatient gardeners, I recommend something that will multiply fast, like the plain old *H. undulata,* which is an all-time favorite variegated hosta. It doesn't always hold up as well as some others, but people seem to like it.

When you're planning a bed, look at it as a whole and think about the colors. You need both uniformity and variety. I recommend that people include some of the greens or dark blue greens next to the variegated or gold varieties.

LCM: What are the planting requirements for hostas?

SAM: The entire bed should be dug, taking care not to harm the tree roots. Don't put hostas at the base of a large water oak, or maple, or anything that will pull water away from the hostas, because they just won't do well. They need to be some distance from the tree.

You need to work the ground well. Take a rotary tiller or a mattock and work on the soil, then work in five to ten inches of organic matter such as Mr. Natural

or Nature's Helper. If you have bad red clay, you might want to discard the soil.

One of the most important things you can do is to raise the beds. We've raised beds in the woodland area by terracing them up with rocks.

Preparing the beds is a lot of work, but I tell people that if they don't want to spend the time, effort, and money to do good soil preparation, they might as well go away.

TREES AND SHRUBS FOR A WOODLAND GARDEN

Maple *Acer* sp.

Camellia *Camellia japonica*

Dogwood *Cornus florida*

Winterhazel *Corylopsis glabrescens*

Witch hazel *Hamamelis*

Oak-leaf hydrangea *Hydrangea quercifolia*

Anise *Illicium floridanum*

Sweetspire *Itea virginica*

Viburnum *Viburnum* sp.

Daphne *Daphne odorata*

LCM: How about fertilizing?

SAM: We add 10-10-10, superphosphate, and sand or granite dust when we first work the soil. After that we use Osmacote™, which is a slow-release fertilizer. Everything receives a treatment of Osmacote™ the first of April. We don't want to overfertilize or overwater, because too much nitrogen or moisture will make the plants floppy.

LCM: Do you have a gardening philosophy?

CARLEEN: A garden is a very personal thing. If you like it, then it doesn't matter what other people think. It should fit your own personality.

SAM: One of the nice things about gardening is that you're always learning things. There's no way you can know everything about gardening. I've been working with plants in one form or another for longer than I want to think about, but I'm constantly learning and seeing new things, which is a real personal thrill. I'd be very unhappy if I wasn't doing what I'm doing now, even though I'm working harder than ever before in my life.

RESOURCES FOR FLOWERS

BOOKS

Armitage, Allan. *Herbaceous Perennial Plants: A Treatise on Their Identification, Culture, and Garden Attributes*. Athens, Georgia: Varsity Press, 1989.

Chapman, Lois Trigg. *The Southern Gardener's Book of Lists*. Dallas: Taylor Publishing Co., 1994.

Halfacre, Gordon, and Anne Showcroft. *Landscape Plants of the Southeast*. Raleigh, North Carolina: Sparks Press, 1989.

Harper, Pamela, and Frederick McGourty. *Perennials: How to Select, Grow and Enjoy*. Los Angeles: Price Stern Sloan Publishers, 1985.

Lawrence, Elizabeth. *A Southern Garden: A Handbook for the Middle South. Revised Edition*. Chapel Hill, North Carolina: University of North Carolina Press, 1984.

Reader's Digest Illustrated Guide to Gardening. Pleasantville, New York: Reader's Guide Association, 1981.

Southern Living Garden Guide. Birmingham, Alabama: Oxmoor House, 1981.

Welch, William C. *Perennial Garden Color*. Dallas: Taylor Publishing Co., 1989.

PERIODICALS

Fine Gardening
Taunton Press
P.O. Box 355, 63 S. Main Street
Newtown, CT 06470

Flower and Garden
Modern Handcraft, Inc.
4251 Pennsylvania
Kansas City, MO 64111

Horticulture
P.O. Box 2595
Boulder, CO 80323

Southern Living
P.O. Box 523
Birmingham, AL 35201

SOCIETIES

Georgia Botanical Society
Mikell Jones
2490 Windsor Wood Drive
Norcross, GA 30071

Georgia Horticulture Society
Joyce Latimer
Horticulture Department
Georgia Experiment Station
Griffin, GA 30223
770-228-7243

Georgia Perennial Plant Association
P.O. Box 13425
Atlanta, GA 30324

Middle Georgia Botanical Society
Dick George 912-471-1315

Southern Garden History Society
Flora Ann Bynum
Old Salem Inc.
Drawer F Salem Station
Winston Salem, NC 27108

CLASSES AND SEMINARS

The following institutions and organizations host classes and symposia. Call for information.

Barnsley Gardens 770-773-7480

Callaway Gardens, Southern Gardening
Symposium (Winter) 800-282-8181

The Cloister Hotel, Sea Island (Spring) 912-
638-3611

Coastal Gardens, Savannah 912-921-5461

Dekalb College 404-244-2957

Georgia Perennial Plant Association and the
Atlanta History Center (Fall) 404-393-3451

Gwinett Tech (Fall and Spring) 770-962-7580

North Georgia Tech 770-975-4077

Olmsted Garden, Columbus (Spring)
706-649-0713

State Botanical Garden, Athens 706-542-1244

Vines Botanical Garden, Loganville
770-466-7532

FLOWER SHOWS

Southeastern Flower Show, winter: 404-888-
5638

Atlanta Garden and Patio Show, winter:
404-998-9800

PLANT SOURCES

There are many, many good, reliable nurseries
and garden centers throughout the state. The
following were included because they specialize in hard-to-find perennials and annuals.

GardenSmith
231 Hogans Mill Road
Jefferson, GA 30549
706-367-9094

GardenSouth
950 Highway 20 South
Lawrenceville, GA 30246
770-963-2406

Goodness Grows, Inc.
P.O. Box 311, Highway 77 North
Lexington, GA 30648
706-743-5112

Heistaway Gardens, Inc.
1220 McDaniel Mill Road
Conyers, GA 30207

Lost Mountain Nursery
824 Poplar Springs Road
Dallas, GA 30132

Niche Gardens
1111 Dawson Road
Chapel Hill, NC 27516

Piccadilly Farm
1971 Whippoorwill Road
Bishop, GA 30621

Pike Family Nurseries (headquarters)
3935 Buford Highway
Atlanta, GA 30345
404-263-2633

Planters
3144 E. Shadowlawn Drive
Atlanta, GA 30305
404-261-6002

Saul Nurseries, Inc. (Wholesale only)
P.O. Box 190403
Atlanta, GA 31119
404-257-3339

Triple Creek Farm
8625 West Banks Mill Road
Winston, GA 30187
770-489-8022

Wayside Gardens
1 Garden Lane
Hodges, SC 29695-0001

Woodlanders, Inc.
1128 Colleton Avenue
Aiken, SC 29801

5

ROSES

ANNA DAVIS, ATLANTA

Anna Davis has combined a natural affinity for and interest in roses with love and support from her husband and lessons learned from her mother-in-law to transform her garden in northwest Atlanta into a rose lover's paradise.

Hundreds of roses climb, scamper, and twine over a myriad of trellises and arbors, while others sit and spread branches laden with colorful blooms. In spring Anna Davis' garden brings Brookhaven traffic to a standstill.

The garden, designed by Brooks Garcia, includes more than roses. Perennials and annuals of every height, color, and description blend and complement the rose show. From exquisitely scented sweet peas to common Queen Anne's lace, these plants combine to create a garden that delights the senses.

Growing roses has become a lifelong education for Anna. Not only has she learned to grow prize-winning plants, she has also learned to speak enough French so that the tongue-twisting names of cultivars and hybrids come rolling gracefully off her tongue.

Anna's skill and knowledge are in high demand. She spends much of her time consulting with other rosarians and lecturing to diverse groups who are fascinated with America's favorite flower.

I interviewed Anna on a typically muggy summer day. Though it was too hot for full bloom, individual blossoms shone fiercely, determined to have their moment in the sun. We sat in Anna's rustic twig porch swing and talked of roses, as their sweet scent and incomparable beauty cast their spell.

LCM: How long have you been growing roses?

ANNA: For years! Before we moved and built this house and garden in Brookhaven, we lived in Sandy Springs. My mother-in-law lived with us and helped me start my roses. We lived there twenty-two years and by the time we moved, I had three hundred rose bushes. I joined the Greater Atlanta Rose Society about twenty-eight years ago and really learned how to grow roses.

My mother-in-law was one of my great inspirations, though. She was very knowledgeable about gardening, and started the first garden club in Commerce, Georgia. Back then they didn't have master gardeners, but she was one anyway.

LCM: What advice do you have for people who want to begin growing roses?

ANNA: In the Rose Society we are always laughing because there are so many different opinions about growing roses. We all have different ways of taking care of them, but we do know that they need at least six hours of sun every day, preferably full morning sun.

Roses also need good drainage, so you must put them in soil that drains well. We had to install a drainage pipe underneath the beds here. We dug the bed out to about two and a half feet, then put gravel in the bottom, added a French drainage pipe with holes in the bottom, and put it on a slight decline so water drains away from the bed. Roses need at least an inch of water a week, but they don't like wet feet.

LCM: In Georgia, what is the blooming season for roses?

ANNA: Here in Atlanta we go from April until the first frost.

LCM: Can you walk me through the succession of blooms?

ANNA: My earliest is a yellow species rose called 'Lady Banks', Rosa banksia.

It's usually in bloom at Easter. After that, in late April and early May, come the old European roses: the Damask 'Selsiana', then the Alba rose, 'Madam Plantier'. Then a Bourbon rose 'Souvenir de la Malmaison' (the climber), which is one of the first repeat bloom roses.

Old European roses bloom one time in the spring over a long period, and then do not bloom again that season.

LCM: What is your peak bloom time?

ANNA: Generally around the middle of May. Summer is a time for repeat bloom. It's really hot, and the roses are smaller and won't last as long on the bush. Some bloom cycles are faster than others. Some plants may bloom again in two or three weeks, some won't bloom again for six weeks.

As the weather cools in late September and October, you'll have another beautiful bloom period. Sometimes the roses are bigger in the fall, especially the hybrid teas, or the David Austin English roses. The color also seems more vibrant and prettier in fall.

LCM: For a real novice, the different names are confusing. How are roses divided into classes or groups?

ANNA: The species roses are those which grew naturally. They are known to have grown thirty-two million years ago.

LCM: Do all species roses have a single-petaled bloom?

ANNA: Most of them do. Most have five petals and a beautiful stamen, but not all. Rosa multiflora carnea is not a single. It blooms in clusters and has a small quartered center.

In about 1300, the apothecary roses were introduced. Rosa mundi was grown for its medicinal use, though it is known for its bright colors. After that, the Alba roses were introduced, and then the moss roses, which are called that because of the mosslike growth on the sepals and stem.

In the early 1800s, Portland roses were introduced. These were known for their small, compact growth and are often used with perennials. 'Comte de Chamborel' is probably the best one to grow today.

During Victorian times, they grew the hybrid perpetual roses, which were grown because the blossoms were so beautiful, even though the bushes are somewhat ungainly. From that group we still grow 'Mabel Morrison', 'Fran Karl Bruchki', and 'Baron Provost'.

COMPANION PLANTS FOR ROSES

Foxglove   Digitalis sp.
Snapdragon   Antirrhinum majus
Salvia   Salvia 'Indigo Spires'
Hollyhocks   Alcea rosea
Daisies   Chrysanthemum leucanthemum
Sweet peas   Lathyrus odoratus
Dianthus   Dianthus chinensis
Columbines   Aquilegia canadensis
Forget-me-nots   Myosotis scorpiodes

At one time the old garden roses were the only ones we had. These were introduced before 1867 and were known for intricate petal formation and fragrance. In 1867, the first hybrid tea rose, 'La France' was introduced, and it proved to be a big turning point. These were the first rose blooms with pointed centers and a long, single stem.

In the late 1800s, the Polyanthas were introduced. 'Margo Koster', 'Marie Pavie',

and 'The Fairy' are good ones to grow. These are hardy, low-growing roses that bloom in clusters.

In 1903, we had the first Floribundas.

Miniature roses are thought to have been introduced in the 1930s. Now we have hundreds of miniatures, and they are becoming more and more popular as people move into apartments or smaller homes. They are also good for flower arrangements and containers.

The last group, the David Austin English roses, were introduced in 1961. 'Constance Spry' was the first. These mix the charm, fragrance, and petal formation of the old roses with the beauty and diverse color of the new roses to get repeat bloom and wonderful fragrance. These are superb roses and are beautiful in flower arrangements.

We're still learning how to grow these. The first ones were really big—five to six feet tall and six feet wide. I put them into corrals, using crape myrtle wood stakes to lift them from the ground so they can grow like a climber. David Austin recommends growing them in groups of three and allowing them to support each other.

LCM: Do you have a favorite category of roses?

ANNA: Probably the Hybrid Musks. They are repeat climbing roses and I like them because I have so many trellises for them to climb over. They are good for the type of garden I have. 'Prosperity' and 'Felicia' are both good Hybrid Musk roses, as well as 'Ballerina', 'Cornellia', and 'Buff Beauty'.

LCM: When do you plant your new roses?

ANNA: We order in the fall to be sure to get what we want, and plant in February.

LCM: What planting technique do you use?

ANNA: It's really best to do it by the bed rather than by the hole. The best way is to dig the bed and replace the soil with something more porous: mushroom compost, topsoil, shredded pine bark, and lime. The pH needs to be about 6.5, and you should really check the pH every year. I generally put a cup of lime around each bush every year.

LCM: What else do you add to the soil?

ANNA: In the spring, I put one cup of alfalfa pellets around each bush, and do it again in midsummer. It's one of the best things you can put on roses for growth. I also add half a cup Epsom salts per bush twice a year, in spring and again in midsummer.

LCM: Your garden looks beautiful for so much of the year. Which perennials and annuals do you use with the roses?

ANNA: I like foxglove, snapdragon, pink lythrum, Salvia 'Indigo Spires', hollyhocks and daisies. For the smaller roses, I like to use plants that aren't too aggressive, like columbines, forget-me-nots, and dianthus; and sweet peas with the climbing roses. I also use Queen Anne's lace because I love it in arrangements.

LCM: Which are the easiest roses to care for?

ANNA: Probably the Rugosa roses. They are big, tough roses with thorns and thick green leaves and are not usually bothered by blackspot or mildew. Something like the hybrid 'Dr. Eckner' is good.

LCM: What do you like best about growing roses?

ANNA: The friends I've made. You'd be surprised at what interesting people you meet through gardening. To grow roses, you really have to have a love of it.

People say that it takes so much time, but if you really love it, it's something you're almost born with. When you're disciplined and keep on top of things, it's not difficult. You reap what you sow.

OLINE REYNOLDS, BAINBRIDGE

Oline Reynolds comes from a long line of school teachers and rose growers. Her maternal grandmother studied and taught Latin, and used the Gallic roses in her garden to teach Oline about history and horticulture. It was here that Oline first heard stories of the Gallic wars and Napoleon.

Oline grew up on a farm in Climax, Georgia. After teaching for several years, she married and then moved to Bainbridge.

"I never wanted to live in town, but here I am," she says. "We raised three sons here, and I worked each one of those boys like a hired hand because I was determined that they would know how to work and that they would have a feel for the soil.

"When one of my boys left home, he told me he would never put another shovel in the dirt as long as he lived. But he did, and now all three boys have their own rose gardens."

❦

For me roses bring a touch of history—with my own family, and with the history of the world.

❦

Oline shared her knowledge and love of roses not only with her boys, but with the community, and later the region. Always active in the Rose Society, Oline served as Deep South District Director from 1991 until 1997.

I interviewed Oline toward the end of May, which she said was "down time" in the rose garden. "Down time" here would be very "up time" anywhere else, for there were still hundreds of blossoms of every color in the garden of this gracious, rose-loving lady.

LCM: Why do you love roses?

OLINE: I've always loved roses. My mother had roses and she used to send me out with a butcher knife to trim them. I think it's an inherited ability to enjoy the plants and watch them grow. Those of us who grew up on a farm probably have a little bit of an advantage because we know what it means to feed the plants and keep them growing.

My mother came from north Georgia where her mother grew only Gallica roses. She had studied and taught Latin,

and she would go out into the garden and quote "All Gaul is divided into three parts." I had no idea what she was talking about, but later on I found out that Gaul was made up of the French, German, and lower Italian parts, and she would show me which rose came from which part of Gaul.

Now I'd give anything for just one hour with her. I never paid much attention to what she was trying to tell me, but enough soaked in so that now I grow roses too.

I won a first prize at the Thomasville Rose Show with the 'Dowager Queen', which I grew from a little root I'd gotten from her garden.

LCM: What is it about roses that has such an enormous appeal?

OLINE: For me, it's a touch of history—with my own family and with the history of the world. Roses tie it all together.

For example, Gallica roses don't have black spot like so many of the more recent introductions. That's because when Napoleon was marching to Prussia, he went across Austria and came across the Austrian rose, R. foetida. He took those roses back [even though] they had blackspot. But the color was so magnificent; they had no such thing in their part of Europe. [The French] crossbred them, and they came out with yellows and oranges—and blackspot.

LCM: How long have you been growing roses at this house?

OLINE: About twenty-five years. At first I only grew a few roses, but then I found out about the Rose Society and started taking their publications. Then I wanted to do everything they were doing. I started with the roses I got from my mother, then added the Hybrid Teas because that's what everyone had, and then I added a few Floribundas. For the past ten years, I've been concentrating on the old garden roses.

LCM: How did you start your rose garden here?

OLINE: The back part of the property was a horse pasture for our boys. Then we put a rose bush back there and built a little fence around it.

It's not hard to get started. Most garden centers carry the ones that are easiest to grow. These are the most common because they are the easiest. The roses you see at discount stores are not patented, but if they haven't been waxed, they are as good as plants you can find anywhere else.

LCM: Hold it. How long is a rose patented, and what's waxing?

OLINE: Patents stay on a rose for about fifteen years, and once a rose is out of patent, the price goes down by about half.

Waxing means that wholesale companies literally dip the entire plant into hot wax to preserve it. It feels like a candle—you can rub your finger down the stem and feel the wax. I have used waxed plants before, but I soak them in warm water first to get all the wax off. If you don't, they won't do well.

If you're going to put in six or eight roses, it's best to prepare a whole bed rather than individual holes. I prepare a bed two feet deep, about two shovels down, and then English double dig it. That just means that I [remove] the bottom soil, mix the top soil with enough humus or compost to fill the bed, and put it back into the [bed].

Be sure you do a soil sample when you're preparing beds. The soil should be at a pH between 6.4 and 6.5. Create the beds at least six weeks before you're going to plant. I like to do it two to three months ahead. You're adding so much stuff, it needs to settle before you plant. I try to get it done at least by November if I'm going to plant in February.

At the bottom of the planting hole I put Milorgonite™, which is sludge from the Milwaukee water system. It is high in iron but has no heavy metal content. You can buy it almost anywhere. Other than that, I don't add any other fertilizer until after the first bloom.

After you have filled the bed up again, dig a trench where you want to plant the bush. Put the roots down on top of that, spread them out, and water them in. Then take the bud union, raise it just a little bit, and water again. Do this a total of four times. Finally, you should have

STEPS FOR PLANTING ROSES

1. Double dig the bed at least six weeks before planting.
2. Add Milorganite™, mushroom compost, cow manure, lime (if needed), compost, perlite, or pine bark.
3. Dig a trench in the bed and place bare roots down in this. Water, then lift bud union slightly.
4. Repeat this step three more times until roots are down in the soil, and the bud union is just above soil level.
5. Spray bare stump with strong bleach solution.
6. Pile loose dirt around the bud union and leave until leaves have appeared on top.
7. Remove dirt and wash off stem.
8. Mulch heavily with pine straw or shredded pine bark.

your roots well down into the hole, and the bud union just about at ground level.

When I'm through, I pile dirt up around the bud union. [Leave it] until the plant puts out leaves on the top, then take the hose and wash it off. You have all these little green sprouts coming out from around the bottom, and it makes you feel so good to see them. If you're not careful, a late frost will come and kill those new little sprouts, and you'll say, "Lord, why did you do that to my rose?"

LCM: How susceptible are they to the cold?

OLINE: Frost will kill the new growth, but the plant itself should be okay. In fact, you'll be better off with a little cold because the roots will [continue to] grow and the top part won't.

LCM: What and when do you spray?

PRUNING

1. Prune by mid-February or the first of March.
2. Cut out dead canes.
3. Take off all leaves, which harbor insects.
4. Prune shoots to outside eye, encouraging the bush to grow out instead of up.

OLINE: I never use a spray which says "includes insecticides" because then I think I've taken care of everything. You still have to spray for specific problems. When you first put bare-root roses into the dirt, they need to be sprayed right then. Spray that bare stub with double strength bleach solution—two tablespoons per gallon. You can use double strength because there are no leaves on the plant. It will kill any insects on there.

You can use an Orthonex™ spray once the leaves start coming out. The more leaves you have, the weaker the solution should be.

I keep to a pretty tight schedule. During rose season, Monday mornings I prune and Tuesday mornings I spray. I spray every week for downy mildew, which is just devastating to roses.

Orthonex™ takes care of most everything except mites, which can be taken care of by washing the plants everyday with a water wand.

A solution of soap, like Ivory, not detergent, will take care of aphids. When I was a child, my mother used to have me throw the dishwater out over the flowers. The water would have grease in it, and it acted like the oil sprays we use today.

LCM: How do you spray?

OLINE: I have a set pattern that I try to teach. I'm what they call a consulting rosarian, and we have taken an oath that we will go anywhere within our range and help people with their roses. Wherever I go, I take my little sprayer.

I start at the bottom of the plant and go up, then come down. You can do the entire plant in about four sweeps up and four sweeps down, but you have to cover the leaves top and bottom.

LCM: How about fertilizing?

OLINE: I add mushroom compost, cow manure, and alfalfa pellets when I prepare the soil, and then I feed with a balanced fertilizer (10-10-10).

Sometimes I make a fertilizer tea by putting alfalfa pellets in a thirty-gallon container and adding water. I might also add fertilizer and iron to put on sick roses. Just be sure to cover it because it smells really terrible.

My mother used to do something similar. She'd pick up cow patties from the pasture, put them in a grocery sack and then bring them back to soak in water. We called it cow tea and put it on all the perennials.

Another thing people used to use is gypsum. Back during the War, I remember coming to town with my daddy on a wagon. He'd go to where they were building government housing, and he got all the wallboard scraps he could find. We'd take them home in the wagon. He'd take that old drywall, which is only gypsum, beat it to a powder, and then he'd put it on his peanut fields to sweeten the soil. Now you can buy agricultural gypsum by the ton, which does the same thing to the soil.

I feed the roses every two weeks until the middle of September alternating an organic fertilizer, such as cottonseed meal, with an inorganic such as 10-10-10. Frequent light feedings are much better than occasional heavy ones.

LCM: What about pruning?

OLINE: I prune everything except the old garden roses. They used to tell us to prune by Valentine's Day, but our weather has changed so much that I wait and prune by the first of March. I take all the leaves off. Over the winter they've been harboring mites and insects and if you take off all the leaves, you've done seventy-five percent of your insect control.

Most of the shrubs I leave about knee-high. The Floribundas, I prune a little higher. I cut any dead canes back to the bud union. Prune to an outside eye, making the bush come out instead of coming up. Every week during the growing season, I dead-head.

LCM: Do you leave hips on any of them?

OLINE: On the Gallicas, which are a once-blooming variety, and on 'Champney's Pink Cluster'. But if you use any insecticides, you can't eat or cook with them. They still look pretty in potpourris, though.

LCM: What do you do after you prune?

OLINE: After spring pruning, I remove all the mulch and start over with the organics, not just in a ring around the bush, but throughout the entire bed, because the roots will cross. You have to have organics because that's what keeps your soil loose and friable. I add a little Epsom salts to give them a spurt.

I cultivate around the plants, then I don't let anyone walk on the beds until I put the mulch down and let it settle. Here in Bainbridge, I have roses from the second week of April to heavy frost. This year, I had roses all year. We only had one freeze, and I put beach umbrellas over some of them to save them.

LCM: What is it about growing roses that you love best?

OLINE: Just the intrigue of walking through the garden in the morning to see what's new that day, how the dew looks, how it changes from one day to the next. I enjoy cutting buckets of roses and taking them to the hospital. I have met marvelous people—it's just a fever with me.

RESOURCES FOR ROSES

BOOKS

Austin, David. The Heritage of the Rose. United Kingdom: Antique Collector's Club, 1988.

———. Old Roses and English Roses. United Kingdom: Antique Collector's Club, 1993.

———. Shrub Roses and Climbing Roses with Hybrid Teas and Floribunda Roses. United Kingdom: Antique Collector's Club, 1993.

Druitt, Liz, and G. Michael Shoup. Landscaping with Antique Roses. Newtown, Connecticut: Taunton Press, 1992.

Handbook for Selecting Roses. American Rose
Society. Shreveport, Louisiana.

McCann, Sean. Miniature Roses—Their Care
and Cultivation. Mechanicsburg,
Pennsylvania: Stackpole Books, 1991.

McNair, James. All About Roses. San Francisco:
Ortho Information Books, 1990.

Welch, William C. Antique Roses for the
South. Dallas: Taylor Publishing Co., 1991.

PAMPHLETS, NEWSLETTERS

American Rose Society Bulletin
Deep South District
205 Donna Road
Savannah, GA 31410-2325

Antique Rose Emporium
80-page catalog, color illustrations ($5.00)
Route 1 Box 630
Dahlonega, GA 30533
706-864-5884

ORGANIZATIONS

American Rose Society
P.O. Box 30000
Shreveport, LA 71130-0030
318-938-5402
Publishes the American Rose, a monthly maga-
zine free with membership.

Local Georgia Chapters
Augusta Rose Society
Bill Bird, President
2506 Henry Street
Augusta, GA 30904-4677
706-738-7204

Columbus Georgia Rose Society
Richard Ramey, President
453 Cheyenne Road
Columbus, GA 31904-1239
706-323-3925

Golden Isle Rose Society
Jack S. Parker, President

510 Postrell Drive
St. Simons Island, GA 31522-1842
912-638-2327

Greater Atlanta Rose Society
Anna Davis, President
931 Club Station
Atlanta, GA 30319
404-233-7883

Middle Georgia Rose Society
Stephen Hoy, President
223 Sentry Oak Drive
Warner Robins, GA 31093-2969
912-953-7705

Millen Rose Society
Betty H. Black
RR 2 Box 279
Millen, GA 30442-9540
912-982-4981

North East Georgia Rose Society
P.O. Box 272
Watkinsville, GA 30677
706-769-5185

Savannah Rose Society
Robert H. Farrow, President
15 Chattahoochee Crossing
Savannah, GA 31411

South Metro Rose Society
Nelson Williams, President
360 North Avenue
Fairburn, GA 30291

Thomasville Rose Society
Rick Thomas, President
Thomas Drugs
Thomasville, GA 31792-5563
912-228-1411

Thomson Rose Society
Jerald W. Nicholson, President
418 Anderson Avenue
Thomson, GA 30824-1603
706-595-1032

PLANT SOURCES

Antique Rose Emporium
Route 1 Box 630
Dahlonega, GA 30533
706-864-5884

Edmonds Roses
6235 S.W. Kahle Road
Wilsonville, OR 97070

Giles Roses
2968 State Road
710 Okeechobee, FL 34974

Heirloom Roses
24062 Riverside Drive, N.E.
St. Paul, OR 97137

Jackson and Perkins
One Rose Lane
Medford, OR 97501-0702

Taylors Roses
P.O. Box 11272
Chicksaw, AL 36671-0272

DISPLAY GARDENS

Antique Rose Emporium, Dahlonega
    706-864-5884

Atlanta Botanical Garden 404-876-5858

State Botanic Garden, Athens 706-542-1244

6

COASTAL GARDENING

ROG AND ANNE DITMER, SEA ISLAND

In the magical way of the gardening world, two Midwesterners who found their way to Georgia have been instrumental in transforming the way people garden in the beautiful coastal community of Sea Island, Georgia. Rog Ditmer, a former farm boy from Ohio, and his wife, Anne, a former avid Girl Scout, met through their mutual love of plants at

Ohio State University. They now work for the Sea Island Company, Anne as a naturalist, and Rog in the landscaping division.

When asked if she came from a family of gardeners, Anne says, "No, but I spent all my time outdoors. Fun for me was taking wildflower books through the Teton Mountains. I couldn't fathom a job where I sat inside all day."

Anne got her wish. As naturalist for the Sea Island Company, she spends her days leading marsh and beach walks, and teaching visitors and locals about the plants and animals found in the myriad of ecosystems here. In addition, she teaches elderhostel classes and writes a gardening column for the local newspaper, the "Coastal Illustrated."

Rog's degree is in landscape horticulture. Before coming to Sea Island, he worked as resort grounds manager at Caneel Bay and Little Dix Bay, two Rockefeller resort properties in the British and U.S. Virgin Islands.

Although Rog's primary job is to keep Sea Island "green and beautiful twelve months a year," he has also created a series of test and display gardens to help educate both The Cloister's staff and visitors about horticulture.

Both Rog and Anne are staunch environmentalists and are happy to be working for the Sea Island Company, which they consider pro-active in wildlife preservation.

LCM: The gardens here on Sea Island are beautiful. Is gardening here quite different from gardening in other parts of the state?

ROG: When people think about gardening here, they think [of] a great growing climate with plenty of sun. If you have the right conditions, you can grow a wide variety of plants along the coast, but our climate is quite different from that of Atlanta. It is more like that of Orlando, Florida, even though we're in Georgia. Often what is applicable in Atlanta or Athens is not [applicable] here.

An essential element of coastal gardening is the concept of growing in microclimates. For example, we find that some plants won't grow well right along the coast, but they will grow thirty to forty miles inland.

LCM: What are some of the major differences? Salinity, soil composition?

ROG: A combination of those. We're finding that we can use many of the same plants that gardeners in other parts of the state use, only we use them at different times of the year. For instance, we have five planting seasons. We have two winter crops of annuals. The first crop, which lasts from late October through Christmas, includes violas, pansies, dianthus, alyssum, snapdragons, and ornamental kale. After Christmas, we plant a second crop of the same plants because the first has already reached a peak and is dying out. We can't afford to have a crop down for very long because we need to have something to show all

year long. Instead of cutting a crop back, knowing we could get another flowering from it in another four to five weeks, we take it out and replant.

This second crop carries us over to what we call our "shoulder season," which begins the middle of March.

LCM: So for the homeowner, it might not be necessary to replant?

ANNE: Right. Most homeowners keep plants in the ground from November until March, but they may run into some problems. Because the weather is so warm, we generally have a lot of problems like leaf spot on the dianthus, and fungus on the snapdragons and pansies. Also, it's never cold enough to knock off the insects, and we have problems with the plants year round here. It makes gardening a real challenge.

SEASON-BY-SEASON ANNUALS

Winter: violas, pansies, snapdragons, dianthus, ornamental cabbage and kale, ranunculus, Icelandic poppies, and calendula.

Spring and fall: marigolds, red and blue salvias, petunias, zinnia, celosia, and scaevola.

Summer: torenia, gomphrena, melampodium, blue daze, hypoestes, coleus, and portulaca

---

LCM: What do you plant during the shoulder seasons?

ROG: We have two shoulder seasons. The first is from middle of March until the heat comes on in the middle of May, and the next is from September until early November. This is when we plant

GARDEN-WORTHY NATIVE
(OR NATURALIZED) COASTAL
PLANTS

Goldenrods   Solidago sp.

Gaillardia   Gaillardia pulchella

Spiderwort   Tradescantia virginiana

Lantana   Lantana camara

Wax myrtle   Myrica cerifera

Yaupon holly   Ilex vomitoria

Cabbage palm   Sabal Palmetto

Carolina jessamine   Gelsemium
   sempervirens

Trumpet creeper   Campsis radicans

Virginia creeper   Parthenocissus
   quinquefolia

marigolds, red and blue salvias, and petunias. Many plants that are considered
summer annuals do not really thrive here
in the summer because of the combination of heat and humidity. We use many
of these during the shoulder seasons,
because they are only in for six to seven
weeks.

During the summer months, we use
torenia, gomphrena, melampodium,
blue daze—a somewhat different collection of plants from what Atlantans typically use.

ANNE: We also use a lot of perennials
such as salvias; Cuphea llaevia 'Georgia
Scarlet'; Cuphea hyssopifolia (Mexican
false heather); rudbeckias, and gaillardias.
We also use a lot of pentas, which are
great butterfly plants. We've been using
them for years, but now the breeders are
coming up with different colors and
heights, so we're using more of them.
Here it's considered a tender perennial.
If we have a bad winter, it won't come

back, or it will be slow to come back in
spring.

LCM: How about lantana?

ANNE: Even here it dies to the
ground and you won't see it in winter,
but it's a great plant for us.

ROG: Of course, Goodness Grows
introduced 'Miss Huff', which is a great
plant, as long as you like orange.

LCM: What do you suggest for shade-
loving plants?

ANNE: Hosta, astilbe, and bleeding
heart are good examples of microclimate
plants that will not do well here unless
you give them just the right conditions.
We grow them in our garden at home,
and we know a gardener in Sea Palms
who grows them, but most gardeners just
don't have the right conditions. We have
created the right conditions by combining
the shade of the live oaks, copious quanti-
ties of organic matter in the soil, and an
irrigation system which tends to keep
things cooler. With all those things, you
can coax along some of these plants,
though they are completely dormant all
summer. They just disappear and go
below the ground, but as it cools in fall,
they begin to put out new leaves. So we
see them in the fall until freeze and then
again in spring.

LCM: How about perennial plants?

ANNE: Perennial plants we use here
are totally different than those we used in
Ohio State. The basic perennials that we
were taught to use in the Midwest just
don't exist here. For example, we grow
neither peonies or chrysanthemums.

LCM: How about geraniums?

ANNE: No, they rarely thrive here.
Rog sometimes plants them in pots and
has good luck. We're working more and
more with them, and when we have a
successful crop, we're thrilled.

ROG: We use a lot of celosias, particularly the 'Century' series, which is good for us, and 'Purple Flamingo', which has potential. They become so large that we need to use them in the back of the border.

LCM: How about woody material?

ROG: That's one of the biggest frustrations we face here. Unlike Atlanta, we have a narrow range of northern selections of woody plants to use because many of these plants need a cold period. We have about several mainstay genera which we use in south Georgia coastal landscapes.

LCM: What kind of bulbs do you use?

ANNE: Many people come from the north and try hyacinths and tulips—which won't work here—and then think that you can't grow bulbs in this region. That's not true. You can grow some daffodil cultivars, as well as amaryllis, crinum lily, and agapanthus, which are members of the lily family. The true Easter lily does great here because it blooms twice a year. We also use zephryanthes, snow drops, and leucojum (summer snowflake).

LCM: The trial beds behind The Cloisters are really beautiful when they're in full bloom. Besides adding to the beauty of the landscape, what is their purpose?

ROG: My main mission at Sea Island is to make sure that this place is green and blooming twelve months out of the year. That's my bottom-line job. But we also are trying to do some testing and some display beds. We've seen that the guests who come here are interested in more than the beach and the food. They are also interested in the horticultural aspects. We've seen people with notepads and pencils taking notes out at the trial

beds. As a result, they introduce new things into their own landscapes.

LCM: Do you find a large population of gardeners here on the coast?

ROG: Yes. We have a lot of gardeners in the area. We lead garden and nature walks weekly, and they seem to be very popular.

FAVORITE COASTAL PERENNIALS

Cuphea   Cuphea 'Georgia Scarlet'

Mexican false heather   Cuphea hyssopifolia

Black-eyed Susan   Rudbeckia sp.

Gaillardia   Gaillardia grandiflora

Penta   Penta sp.

Lantana   Lantana camara

Lily of the Nile   Agapanthus sp.

Canna   Canna 'Tropica Rose'

Blue sage   Salvia guaranitica

Plumbago   Plumbago auriculata

Scarlet sage   Salvia coccinea

ANNE: And a lot of people seem to be interested in learning about gardening on the coast. Most people realize that if you're working underneath the live oaks, you have to use shade-tolerant plants. Most of our yards are equipped with irrigation systems because that's the only way we can get enough moisture to the plants, given our sandy soils. A lot of gardeners are composting now because they finally realize what a valuable resource they've been carrying to the landfill for years.

You can garden in coastal Georgia without an irrigation system, but you can't have, for example, a St. Augustine lawn. It's just not natural. We're caught in between because the plants people want to grow require fertilization, irrigation, and massive amounts of compost. And yet, if they would just look around, they could see that you need little extra water to grow beautiful native plants.

What is not yet fully accepted here is the use of wildflowers and native plants in the landscape. These plants are just not seen as beautiful for the garden. Goldenrod, gaillardia, and spiderwort (Tradescantia) are all native and beautiful, but you rarely see anyone putting them into the garden. You always see them pulling them out of the garden.

LCM: What are some other garden-worthy native plants?

ANNE: Wax myrtle, yaupon holly, grasses—bunch grass and pink muhly grass, cabbage palms or sabal palms, which are sister plants to palmettos, and are worthy of the landscape. As for vines on fences and trellises, we have Carolina jessamine, trumpet creeper, wisteria, and Virginia creeper.

LCM: These are all plants that I have to pay good money for in Atlanta.

ANNE: But they're wild here, and beautiful. Another is the loblolly bay, which is a pine land plant. We have it on the property at The Cloisters, but it's difficult to transplant it. Cercis canadensis, redbud, is a small flowering native tree which does well. Dogwood is not native, and it struggles.

ROG: There is a dogwood native 20 miles inland, but I've never seen it used in the landscape. We're dealing with distinctly different ecosystems here. When you get into the pine lands off the coast you'll see fetterbush (Leucothoe axillaris), sparkleberry (Vaccinium), and low-bush blueberry. It's totally different than what you'll find under the live oaks, which is yaupon holly, bay trees (Persea borbonia), cabbage palms, palmettos, and grasses.

ANNE: There's not a huge diversity of native plant material, but there are certainly plants that would be great for the landscape.

LCM: How about tropical plants—bananas, elephant ears, taro?

ROG: They'll die to the ground because we do not have a tropical climate. We had 9 degrees in 1983 followed by 17 degrees in 1985, and it wiped out many of the tropical plants. We lost plants like date palms and oleander. In 1985, they changed our horticultural zone from 9 to 8. Tropical plants grow in zone 10.

LCM: So, in a nutshell, what are the challenges and difficulties of gardening in the area?

ROG: Lack of sustained cold, so that insects are a problem year round. The soil—anything remotely coastal, even up to twenty or thirty miles away—is pure sand. We have a shallow water table. If you dig down three feet, you hit fresh water. Imagine having just that much ground to work with, and it's all sand. Most people do not amend the soil. We fertilize at half rates, but twice as often because it just leaches right through.

LCM: Are there some predictable soil imbalances here?

ROG: All of our soil samples have come back very high, or completely off the scale with phosphorous. So, we rarely put any phosphorous in our fertilizer mixes.

LCM: Is that true in all coastal areas?

ANNE: Salt marshes are known for their phosphorous content, so I think the answer would be yes, throughout coastal Georgia. We always tell people to take soil samples. People from the North come here and automatically begin to add lime because someone has told them that Southern soils are acidic. But it's not always necessary or beneficial.

ROG: Most of our soils range from 6.5 to 8.0 pH.

ANNE: Two of our big nutrient deficiencies are manganese and magnesium. Iron is a factor as well, so we have to make sure that our fertilizers have these in them.

ROG: People often ask me what I use as fertilizer, and I have to answer "Whatever the soil analysis shows is necessary," because it is very site specific.

LCM: So with the fertilizer here, it's not so much what you're planting as where you're planting it?

ROG: It's really both.

LCM: What kind of lawn grass do you use here?

ROG: Bermuda and St. Augustine are the best choices of the grasses we can grow. The other grasses are terrible here because we have so much shade from the live oaks. We end up having thin grass beset with numerous problems—year round.

ANNE: We have leaching soil so we have to use a lot of fertilizer, we don't get enough rain so we have to irrigate all the time, it's shady so it stays wet, and with the fog we can't get by without putting fungicide down on the lawns.

The conclusion we've come to is that coastal gardening is challenging. We're just now beginning to learn to garden correctly.

LCM: How do you "garden correctly" here?

ANNE: Use more native plants, get away from using lawns, and if you do want to garden with the more traditional flowers, then know that you must add compost to your beds, or plant in pots. We're big promoters of container planting here because it's much more cost effective to add spots of color to a garden rather than to a whole bed.

RESOURCES FOR COASTAL GARDENING

BOOKS

Gardening in the Lower South. Trustees Garden Club, Savannah, Georgia: 1991.

Marshall, David W. Tallahassee Gardening, Design and Care of the Southern Landscape. Tallahassee Democrat Publishing, 1994.

BULLETINS

Plants for Coastal Dunes of the Gulf and South Atlantic Coasts and Puerto Rico. USDA Soil Conservation Service Agriculture Information Bulletin 460.

Salt Tolerance of Landscape Plants for North Florida. Gary W. Knox and Robert J. Black. University of Florida Cooperative Extension Service.

Salt Tolerant Plants for Florida Landscapes. Florida Sea Grant College Report #28, August 1979.

NEWSLETTERS

The Coastal Gardener, Carol A. Krawczyk, Editor, P.O. Box 1694, Savannah, GA 31402

CONTAINER GARDENING

JEREMY SMEARMAN, ATLANTA: PLANTERS

Tucked into the heart of Buckhead is Planters, a little shop which offers all the necessary ingredients for creating minia-ture landscapes in the form of container gardens. Under the ownership and cre-ative influence of Jeremy Smearman, Planters offers plant material, information, advice, and inspiration.

Jeremy grew up in North Carolina, adjacent to a 100-acre tract of land.

Although neither parent gardened, both his grandmothers were avid gardeners. "I don't think that's unique; I think it often skips a generation," Jeremy says. "If your parents made you get out and weed and work in the garden, sometimes you don't want to do it yourself.

"I don't think I spent much time inside while I was growing up. I was always in the woods. When I was in high school, trying to think what I would do with the rest of my life, I knew I wanted to combine a love of plants and my artis-tic inclinations. I also wanted to indulge in my desire to be outdoors."

After receiving his degree in horticul-ture and landscape architecture from North Carolina State University, Jeremy worked for a gardening company in Nantucket, where the gardening commu-nity was fairly sophisticated but seasonally oriented.

It was his first exposure to the kind of gardening geared around a single event, such as a wedding or party. "We tried to go past that though, and employ sound horticultural principles that gave clients a peak of bloom, but also good plant mater-ial throughout the season."

From Nantucket Jeremy moved to Atlanta and found the same level of sophisticated gardener with which he had previously worked. He first worked as a landscaper and then opened Planters. The shop became progressively specialized in several types of gardening, one of which was container gardening.

I interviewed Jeremy at Planters in late June, with the bright purple pods of hyacinth bean vine hanging in clusters from the vines that wove a magical canopy over our heads.

LCM: You have said that since you moved to Atlanta, you have both gardened and landscaped in the Buckhead area. You seem to make a distinction between these two. Why is that?

JEREMY: Gardening is inherently more detailed and meticulous than landscaping, and requires more participation from the owner. A fine garden is not something I could design for you, plop down on your property, and say, "Okay, here it is, take care of it." Even if you paid someone to maintain it, it would not be a successful garden. A real garden has to have some input from the owner. This can be on many different levels—color preference, seasonal preference, likes, and dislikes.

The goals of landscaping are more utilitarian. They involve practicality and durability. It has an important role, however, in that it provides structure for the garden.

LCM: Planters is well known for container gardening work. How did that come about?

JEREMY: When I opened Planters, I did garden renovations for several people and I saw a changing trend in how people were gardening. They seemed to have less time and less space. Many of our clients were moving from big homes and gardens into high rise apartments with a

defined, small space, which was more challenging to work with.

In small gardens like these, you don't have an excess of space to hide a multitude of sins. Everything you do needs to be important and successful and it has to work because it is all right there in front of you. This led us into doing more container gardening. Although this wasn't clearly articulated in my original plans for Planters, it evolved with my clientele and their needs. We had to become more familiar with, and knowledgeable about, container gardening.

LCM: What are the most important aspects of container gardening?

JEREMY: The most important thing is scale. If I had to pick one area where people tend to err, it is with size and scale: too small a pot in too large an area, for example, or the wrong size plant in the pot.

A CONTAINER FOR FALL

Foxglove   Digitalis sp.
Russian Red kale   Brassica sp.
Red mustard   Brassica juncea
Hardy Ferns
Wallflower   Cheiranthus cheiri
Johnny-jump-ups   Viola tricolor
Violas   Viola cornuta

This is important not only aesthetically, but also from a horticultural aspect. The heat of Georgia summers, when it is 95 degrees for days on end, tends to dry out little pots very quickly. With a limited amount of time to spend in the garden, you need to have something durable. Our goal is to give them that—and not sacrifice aesthetics.

We suggest that people choose fewer, larger pots and group them to make a show. In any kind of design, you need to make an overall assessment of what you have, then decide what you need and group things accordingly.

LCM: If someone was starting with a bare patio, what are some of the first things to consider?

JEREMY: Decide what are the prominent views and how the space is going to be used. Will you actually spend time there, or view it through a window? If it is an area where you will be eating, reading, or using in other ways, how large is the area? How much room can you spare for the plants? What is the space's orientation to the sun? How much sunlight will you receive? Will the plants be under an overhang or will they receive rainfall?

❧

We try to water less often and more thoroughly. When you plant containers, it's important to remember that you don't have an entire planet underneath the plants from which to draw water and nutrients.

❧

What is the general feel and degree of formality of the patio? What are the paving materials? Brick? Slate? Containers need to reflect that, too. Continuity is too often ignored in gardening and landscaping. The style and formality of space are important factors because they will dictate the style and number of containers.

For example, if you have a Cape Cod style home, the plantings and containers need to reflect that.

After these general considerations, we begin to narrow it down and start to think of the function of each container. Will it anchor the corner of the building? Screen an undesirable view? Will you use the containers on either side of the door to provide or reinforce horticulturally some kind of symmetry or formality given to us architecturally? Will you use containers to force a traffic pattern? As a safety wall for a dangerous corner, which perhaps might drop off? Very seldom do we use a container for a single purpose. People tend to think of a container as a vessel to hold flowers and look pretty. In actuality, it should be many more things.

So, the decisions that need to be made are: number of containers, how large, the type and function, and where to put them.

Container gardening is vastly different from perennial gardening, where ebb and flow is expected and it never looks the same at any two-week interval.

A container needs to be maintained at a certain level throughout the season. When you take a container and place it, you're essentially saying, "This is a focal point." You are bringing nature into an artificial environment, and when you manipulate something so thoroughly, you have to reward the viewer with something pleasing to look at. That's why I believe you should not use many perennials in containers. Something that only blooms for two weeks should not be placed in a place of prominence. There are, of course, exceptions to the rule. You could, for example, have a pot full of lilies, which you would only remove from the greenhouse and display while they were in bloom. That puts you into a

94

❧

whole different level of container gardening, where you have a whole array of different potted plants that you shuttle back and forth.

For basic container gardening, the containers should always look good. We tend to like to use evergreens—sometimes clipped sometimes not—and combinations of annuals to form what we call a seasonal composition. This is where different colors are employed to attain a desired effect.

We group small pots together and anchor them with a permanent planting, such as an evergreen boxwood, hemlock, or ligustrum in a large container. The effect is that the sum is greater than its parts—a massed grouping gives a more dramatic effect than individual pots.

LCM: Can you give me specific examples of combinations that you like and use a lot?

JEREMY: For a terrace that receives good light—six to seven hours daily—you could use a combination of two big pots. A larger pot with an evergreen, and a smaller one that contains something like blue salvia in the center, pale pink geranium around that, white petunias around that, and white verbena and English ivy trailing over the edge. Each plant has a specific function in the container: not only color, but texture and [height].

The blue salvia gives you a royal blue color and a tall spike. It is fairly self-supportive, though it can get floppy over time. The geraniums are sturdy, self-supportive, beefy, and give a nice massed look. The petunias knit themselves around other things and fill in the gaps that the geranium does not. It gives additional intermediate height. The verbena has a fine, lacy texture, and the ivy provides a foliage foil for color. From a func-

tional aspect, you don't have to change out everything. The ivy can stay season after season.

If you want a higher degree of formality for this same combination, you can swag the ivy or braid it together to form bands that go around the pot.

POSSIBLE USES FOR A PLANTED CONTAINER

To anchor an area.

To screen an undesirable view.

To add symmetry.

To force a traffic pattern.

As a safety wall for a dangerous corner or wall.

LCM: What about a fall container?

JEREMY: In fall, we would have similar or better light because the deciduous trees have lost their leaves. You might now have eight hours of light. A difficulty in fall and winter is height. You might use foxglove and treat it as an annual. Include red mustard, Russian red kale, and hardy ferns such as autumn, tassel, or holly to give height. You could use Cheiranthus, wallflower, combined with Johnny-jump-ups and violas instead of pansies. Violas are a little more durable, take heat better, and start blooming sooner in fall. Johnny-jump-ups are more graceful than pansies because they trail down [over the container's edge] and curl back up. Also, their blooms are a little smaller and better-suited for residential situations.

Although pansies are a good plant, they have been overused because our winter palette is so limited. They've also been so highly hybridized that a number of pansies are not particularly strong. They may give you just the right color, but they have lost hardiness.

Containers planted for winter generally go well into June and still look good.

LCM: What about a summer container in a shady area?

JEREMY: Just as with a shady garden, the focus shifts from color to texture. For texture we use the plumosa fern, which is related to the asparagus fern. It has the same fine texture but a simpler growth habit. It branches laterally, but the foliage stays in a single plane, giving it a graceful look, almost like a bonsai.

For a bit of color we use the pink angel wing begonia, which is both sun- and shade-tolerant, with a mounding, arching habit and greenish-bronze leaves. The less light it has, the greener the leaf will be. It serves the same function as the geranium in that it is self-supportive and provides [mass].

For additional color we might use browallia, cape primrose, or monkey flower—the latter has bluish-purple blooms that last all summer if you keep it dead-headed. If you don't keep the flowers picked off, it forms attractive lime-green seed pods. We sometimes use impatiens too, though they've been a little overdone.

For permanency, we might use English ivy or maybe variegated Swedish ivy. For containers in the shade, we often use variegated foliage. For example, we might use evergreen boxwood, cherry laurel, or ligustrum underplanted with variegated ivy. If we have no light, we'll use cast iron plant (Aspidistra), hosta, or a collection of ivy and ferns such as Japanese silver-painted fern and the tassel fern,

which give you interesting textural combinations.

LCM: How about planting and maintenance techniques?

JEREMY: In the sun, we use a heavier soil mix than we would in the shade because the heat and sun will dry it out more quickly. The heavier soil will be more moisture retentive.

With all pots, drainage is very important. We seldom plant a container without a drainage hole, which must be adequately sized. We cover the hole with a piece of terra cotta or Styrofoam peanuts or whatever so it won't become clogged with soil.

LCM: When you use a deep pot, do you need to plant all the way to the bottom?

JEREMY: It depends on what you plant. If it is an evergreen with a large, deep root system, you will need a lot of soil. If you use the same kind of container and use only annuals, the roots will not go as deep. You can fill the bottom of the container with [foam] packaging peanuts. It's a good use for them.

A rule of thumb—though not etched in stone—is that the volume of planting needs to be equal to or greater than the volume of the planter. Basically, the shape of the plant needs to reflect the shape of the container. A flat bowl should have plants that mound and spill over. It should be generously planted because you have a lot of surface area.

LCM: Do you need to keep on a rigid maintenance and fertilization schedule?

JEREMY: No, it's more on an as-needed basis. We try to water less often and more thoroughly. When you plant containers, it's important to remember that you don't have an entire planet underneath the plants from which to draw water and nutrients.

We also don't depend on rain, because 80 percent of the rainwater rolls off the foliage and over the side of the pot. An appropriately planted pot is very full and rain won't get into the root system.

Before you water, check to make sure that you need to. Actually poke your finger down into the soil a couple of inches. If it's dry, use the hose to soak the soil until you see water freely coming out of the bottom of the pot.

It's important to use plants with the same moisture and light requirements.

As for fertilization, evergreens need less fertilizers than colorful plants. Use a water soluble fertilizer because it is less caustic and easier to use than granulars. To get started, use one high in nitrogen, and later in the season, use one high in phosphorous to stimulate bloom. We use Peter's Fertilizer, and base the amounts on what is recommended on the package.

LCM: How often do you fertilize?

JEREMY: We feed a pot of colorful annuals at most every two weeks. Usually, more like once a month.

LCM: What other maintenance chores are necessary?

JEREMY: Dead-heading spent blooms is very important. If you spend a little bit of time [every day pinching off dead blooms, a container] will look better, stay fresher, and give you a more continuous show of color than if you let it go and try to catch up all at once.

LCM: Do you have some general advice for people who want to garden in containers?

JEREMY: Go slowly, even if it is a small space that you want to fill quickly. Consider how you will use the space and choose each container thoughtfully. Good containers are expensive, so don't rush into buying something you don't really like. Choose a simple container and let the plants do the talking.

RESOURCES FOR CONTAINER GARDENING

BOOKS

Colborn, Nigel. The Container Garden. New York: Little Brown, 1990.

Wilson, Jim. Landscaping with Container Plants. Boston: Houghton Mifflin, 1990.

Yang, Linda. The Terrace Gardener's Handbook, Revised Edition. New York: Random House, 1990.

————. The City Gardener's Handbook: From Balcony to Backyard. New York: Random House, 1990.

8

HERBS

ASHBY ANGELL, SAVANNAH

Born and raised in Savannah, Ashby grew up in a family of gardeners, then contin- ued this tradition when she married a man with a passion for digging in the earth. After they were married, she and her husband continued to live in the city, but also bought a farm eighty miles inland. Her husband raised vegetables and hay, and she started an herb business,

selling cut herbs to gourmet restaurants in the area.

Twelve years ago, however, they decided to leave the city and buy a piece of property south of Savannah. Today, Ashby's home overlooks acres of salt marsh, and the smell of the sea is heavy in the air. The wide expanse of lawn is punctuated with hundreds of colorful flowers and pungent-smelling herbs.

"This is a wonderful place to garden," Ashby says. "The soil right here is great. It's different in the city, where it is worn out from generations of people using and abusing it. But here, the soil is rich from hundreds of years of oak leaves, which make a rich, dark, loamy soil so you don't even need to add much fertilizer.

"I've gardened all of my married life. I started with herbs and then got into blooming things, but really anything that grows interests me. I do flower arranging for my church chapel downtown and because of that, I got interested in year- round bloom, which we can certainly do in Savannah. In the dead of winter we have camellias. The rest of the year, I use annuals and perennials."

Ashby is now working to pass on her love of herbs and flowers to her four granddaughters. Not far from the house, almost completely hidden by low-hanging branches and Spanish moss, is a secret garden that Ashby has created for the little girls. Each granddaughter made a stepping stone for the garden and decorated it with her own footprint. Small animal statues and a table set for a garden tea complete the scene, making grandmother's garden the most special place on Earth.

LCM: I know that you have been involved in the herb business for a long time, first professionally and now for your own pleasure. Do you have favorite herbs that do well in the Savannah area?

ASHBY: Oh yes! Rosemary is hardy here and does wonderfully. We have it planted in the back, where the upright form grows shoulder high and blooms most of the year. I also have the creeping form planted by the pool, where it cascades over a brick wall. It grows in a handful of soil and takes very little care.

Because it's warmer here, we can grow more basil over a longer period of time. I like the small-leafed basil because I think it has better flavor. The bigger the leaf, the more chlorophyll, and the less taste. Purple basil is spicy, and cinnamon is also good.

Texas tarragon does well here, though we have to grow French tarragon as an annual. I also like to grow bronze fennel, which flower arrangers just love because of the texture. We can grow dill, winter chervil, and parsley from fall, through winter, and into spring.

We do have trouble during the summer because of the heat and humidity, however. We have a difficult time with thyme, and we often lose common culinary sage in the summer. The multicolored hybrid sages—the purple, tri-color,

and golden—seem to take the heat better. Actually, they are a good choice because the taste is the same and they are much prettier.

Because of our heat, many herbs, such as chives, parsley, lemon balm, chervil, and French sorrel, do better with filtered shade rather than full sun.

LCM: It's obvious from your lovely garden that you grow flowers as well as herbs. Do you have favorite flowers?

ASHBY: The herb business led me into decorative sages, and now I have over sixty different varieties of them. That might sound like a lot, but there are over seven hundred species worldwide, so it's really not. I'm fascinated with these plants because they are heat and drought tolerant and beautiful. You can't beat that.

Many of them make wonderful cut flowers. Just take a bucket of warm water out to the garden with you and put the stems right into the warm water. They'll

DECORATIVE HERBS

Alliums (all) *Allium* sp.

Artemisias (All) *Artemisia* sp.

Fennel, bronze *Foeniculum vulgare* 'Purpureum'

Ginger *Asarum* sp.

Geraniums, scented *Pelargonium* sp.

Santolina, grey and green *Santolina chamaecyparissus*

Southernwood *Artemisia abrotanum*

Sweet woodruff *Asperula odorata*

Wormwood *Artemisia Absinthium*

Yarrow *Achillea* sp.

Tansy *Tanacetum vulgare*

DECORATIVE SAGES

Salvia madrensis
S. karwenskii
S. Greggii
S. clevelandii
S. buchanani
S. blepharophylla
S. Farinacea × longispicata
S. koyamae
S. miniata
S. rutilans
S. uliginosa
S. vanhoutti

hold up for a week in a vase, and many of them dry well, too.

And, since they're in the mint family, they're very easy to propagate. They will root within about two weeks.

LCM: Are there *Salvias* that you are particularly fond of?

HERBS FOR SHADE

Chives   *Allium schoenaprasum*
Parsley   *Petroselinum crispum*
Lemon balm   *Melissa officinalis*
Chervil   *Anthriscus cerefolium*
Sorrel, French   *Rumex acetosa*

ASHBY: Quite a few. One of my favorites is forsythia sage, *Salvia madranthus*, which has large yellow flowers. Two years ago I began with a four-inch pot, and now the plant is six feet wide and fifteen feet tall. I had it in the perennial bed and had to move it because it was eating up the whole bed.

Another is *S. karwenskii*, which has huge, fragrant leaves and blooms at Christmas with red spikes eighteen inches long. It gets about fifteen to sixteen feet tall and five to six feet wide. They're just amazing plants. You have to have space for them, though; they don't belong in a small, enclosed garden.

LCM: Are there *Salvias* that are more suitable for smaller gardens?

ASHBY: Yes, *S. Greggii* gets to be about hip high. It blooms from March to frost and comes in almost every color of the rainbow. *S. buchanani* and *S. blepharophylla* both grow about two and a half feet tall and will take some shade. *S. coccinea* is also satisfactory. It comes in scarlet, white, and a lovely pink-and-white bi-color form.

LCM: Are these easily found in nurseries and garden centers?

ASHBY: Not as much as I would like to see, although you can find many of them at specialty nurseries. I'm really excited about sages. I read in the *American Horticulturist* magazine that they are the plants of the twenty-first century.

I'm interested in promoting something that I think is so neat and successful. They bloom over a long period of time—much longer than daylilies—[and they are far less work].

LCM: How adaptable are they to other environments, such as Atlanta and north Georgia?

ASHBY: I tried to grow some in western North Carolina, but didn't have much luck. The smaller ones, such as *S. Greggii* will survive north of zone 8, but the larger ones probably won't.

LCM: Do you use a lot of native plants?

ASHBY: Yes, they're tried and true. My interest in them has been sparked by the fact that my youngest son, who is a landscape architect, has made quite a study of them. We have so many beautiful native plants. Wax myrtle makes a wonderful hedge, although ten years ago, no one would have thought of using it in a garden. The Florida anise tree is great, as well as leucothoe.

LCM: Are there other flowers that you really like?

ASHBY: Columbine does well in the shade here, both the species and the cultivars. Although it's not native, foxglove does well in the shade too. I've also had good luck with the old-fashioned single hollyhock, which needs more sun. People down here rarely think about growing either of these plants, but they make a nice addition to the garden. Pentas do wonderfully well and make a good cut flower. The red pentas come back year after year here, but not in Atlanta.

The gloriosa lily, *Rothchildiana*, is almost a weed here. There are several different types of gloriosas—one called green-eye, and another called little brown basket and one with spiral petals. The cultivars seem to be as hardy as the species.

The shrub, *Cassia corymbosa*, which blooms in summer and *Cassia* 'Superba', which blooms in fall, are wonderful plants for our climate.

LCM: Do you have any hints for gardening in the Savannah area?

ASHBY: We have to plant things farther apart for better air circulation, and we encourage people to use raised beds to improve drainage. The soil should be routinely tested. Generally, we have acidic soils, and most of the herbs like a pH between 6 and 7.

LCM: Since you have such a long growing season, do you try to keep all the beds going year round?

ASHBY: No. The perennials will go dormant in fall, and I clean up the beds, and treat them to a blanket of horse manure, compost, or Milorganite™. Everything needs to rest sometime.

DENISE SMITH, JEFFERSON: GARDENSMITH

Born in south Georgia, raised in Pennsylvania, inspired by a love of plants, and sustained by unfailing energy, humor, and determination, Denise Smith has created a nursery—GardenSmith—which is now a mecca to herb lovers throughout the Southeast.

"I first discovered herbs during my hippy-dippy flower child days and I really loved them. They had so many textures and scents. And then I became fascinated with the mythology of the herbs—the stories behind their names and uses."

Although Denise confesses that she killed more herbs than she grew for a while, education and experience transformed her from herb-killer to herb-guru in a short amount of time. In addition to culinary, medicinal, and fragrant herb plants, GardenSmith carries a wonderful assortment of unusual annuals and perennial bedding plants.

GardenSmith is not a mail-order business, but the trip to Jefferson is well worth the effort. Go ahead and spend the thyme to search out Denise for a little sage advice. It's a decision you will not rue.

LCM: How did you happen to start GardenSmith at this site?

DENISE: Two sisters had a little business growing flowers here. When one of the sisters died, the other sister just lost heart and sold it. When I bought this, I inherited three dilapidated greenhouses, and I must have had more attitude than brains. I knew about plants, but I was clueless about buildings, heaters, and fan motors.

The first year I had a huge compost pile because I composted everything I killed. I worked hard making little raised beds in the vegetable garden. One day my neighbor was driving his tractor down the road and stopped to tell me he could knock down those hills in my garden, and not to worry, it wouldn't take him any time. When I told him I'd just spent four days digging those hills, he shook his head and said he would pray for me.

LCM: So you began working the soil and planting. How did you become interested in herbs?

DENISE: When I was in high school we moved from south Georgia to Pennsylvania. Every year they had a huge two-week craft festival close to where I lived. One year Bertha Reppert from the Rosemary House in Mechanicsburg, Pennsylvania, had a little card table set up with herbs and books, and I just loved it. I bought some plants and a book, took them home, and killed the herbs in four days.

But the show was still going on, so I went back and got some more herbs and another book and I killed those, and I thought, "There's something to this," and I really became interested.

I was studying pre-med in college at that time, but I knew that I could never be a doctor, because I'm basically a hypochondriac and every time I listened to symptoms, I got them. I couldn't even read books or magazines about diseases or I'd get sick.

Herbs sounded better, so I went to Temple University and started taking classes on herbs.

LCM: What brought you back to Georgia?

DENISE: Well, I'm from here, and the growing season is great. Growers can grow and sell all year long, and people are starting to see plants as a necessity.

LCM: What do you mean, that plants are becoming a necessity for people?

DENISE: I think they are necessary for both aesthetics and psychology. Not only are they beautiful, they are also soothing. Post Properties was the first to have apartment complexes that looked like gardens. Then gas stations and fast food places started planting flowers, and now everyone in Atlanta is doing it. It makes people feel welcome.

As the world becomes faster-paced and increasingly dependent on technology, people need plants more and more.

There's something wonderful about planting plants, watching them grow and bloom, and enjoying the flower. It grounds people and puts them back in touch with the earth.

No one works forty-hour weeks anymore. Most people work sixty, and then still have things to do. When you have five minutes to putter in the garden, it really relaxes you—unless gardening becomes an obsession. Then you get stressed about that, and have to go to a shrink to get over the garden.

LCM: It seems that people are becoming more and more interested in gardening. I know that in Georgia, we have many people who have moved here from different regions and want to begin gardening. How do you advise people about gardening in the South?

DENISE: It's a matter of educating people. In the North, no one planted before Memorial Day. Here, we plant on Good Friday.

LCM: What else makes gardening in the South so different?

DENISE: All of it. Plants that are not perennial up north, such as rosemary, usually are perennial here. Gardeners will find that the limiting factor here is not the higher temperatures as much as it is the poorly drained soils.

Gardeners in the North add fine peat moss and well-rotted compost to the soil, which is not effective here. It's too hot and humid, and the material burns away too quickly. Gardeners need to understand about building [raised] beds and creating good drainage. Drainage here is much more of an issue than in the North because of the heavy clay soils.

When we first began gardening here, we did soil tests and found that the pH in our fields was about 3.5. We created raised beds and limed like crazy. Most herbs, especially those that are Mediterranean in origin, should have a neutral pH.

LCM: Do you lime every year?

DENISE: I should.

LCM: How do you recommend improving drainage?

DENISE: If you can, mound the beds, or berm them. Or, if you have to, just plant a little higher, leaving the root crown exposed an inch or two above soil level, and covering the roots with loose soil or mulch.

This is especially good for plants like rosemary and thyme, which need good [air] circulation. If the plant is lifted, you get a little better air flow and better drainage. Sometimes it makes the difference between surviving the winter or not.

☙

As the world becomes more fast-paced and increasingly dependent on technology, people need plants more and more. There's something satisfying about planting plants, watching them grow and bloom, and then enjoying the flower. People feel that it grounds them and puts them back in touch with the earth.

☙

LCM: What most frustrates northern gardeners when they come south?

DENISE: Names are different. I'd been back down here a couple of years when people started asking for 'toad bellies.' I finally figured out that they were asking for sedum: the epidermis on the leaves separate, and kids blow on it and it looks like a toad belly. Or 'Tommytoes.' I had no idea what they were talking about. Turned out to be cherry tomatoes.

Plant names can be frustrating. In Pennsylvania, my mother kept asking for 'Sultanas' and they sent her to the grocery store for raisins. Finally, someone realized that she meant impatiens.

UNUSUAL— BUT WONDERFUL— GARDENSMITH PLANTS

Spanish lavender   *Lavandula stoechas*
Dutch lavender   *Lavandula × intermedia*
Long-leaf grey thyme   *Thymus glabrascens*
Salpiglossis   *Salpiglossis sinuata*
Four o'clocks   *Mirabilis jalapa*
Sweet peas   *Lathyrus odoratus*

LCM: Other than learning the local names of all these plants, what are your goals here?

DENISE: I love herbs, but I'm also getting into perennials and ornamental grasses. I just like plants. We try to introduce new herbs to people, and to reintroduce herbs that have come around again.

LCM: Are there plants that you find to be stunning and wonderful, but which don't seem to have caught on yet?

DENISE: Spanish lavender. It blooms from late March into May. The flowers are not as fragrant as English lavender, and it blooms earlier, but it makes a great perennial plant. It's loose and open and it mounds. It's just wonderful.

Dutch lavender is also good. We have it growing under a pine tree, and it's lived there for five years and bloomed wonderfully well. If you dead-head it, it will bloom on and off throughout the summer. The lavenders you see in catalogs look great in the pictures, but they're just too [compact] for our climate. They'll smother themselves out in the sun.

Another great plant is long-leaf grey thyme, *Thymus glabrescens*, which is bigger than wooly thyme. In a pot it's nothing special, but in the ground, it grows quickly. Don't put it between stepping stones, because it will just cover them in no time. It doesn't have [problems with] the heat and humidity that some other thymes do. The light purple flowers are small, but it blooms for six weeks from the last of March into May.

For bedding plants, we grow *Salpiglossis,* an old plant that's coming back, and four o'clocks, the old-fashioned varieties that actually open up in late afternoon and smell sweet. People remember these plants growing in their grandmother's gardens, and now they want them in their own gardens.

We sell a ton of sweet peas in pots. It seems as if a lot of men buy this. They'll walk up and smell the sweet peas and invariably say, "My grandmother had those growing on a fence at her farm when I was a kid." He'll buy it. He may have no place to put it, but it reminds him of a happy childhood memory, and it touches him emotionally.

LCM: People buy plants for all kinds of reasons. From a practical standpoint, are there certain herbs which you consider "must-haves"?

DENISE: It depends on what you want to do with them. If someone likes to cook, then we suggest rosemary, thyme, oregano, basil, dill, and fennel.

If someone wants to make potpourris, we suggest lavenders, scented geraniums, lemon balm, lemon verbena, some of the thymes, and eucalyptus, which does fine here. We don't sell eucalyptus as a hardy plant but as a long-season annual, and suggest that people bring it indoors about Christmas time.

LCM: Are there herbs people can grow in the shade?

DENISE: Yes, quite a few. Chives do better with a little shade, and comfrey. We don't sell a lot of comfrey because it's kind of coarse looking, but it's a useful herb, and a good bee plant. And the leaves have an activating enzyme, which is good for the compost pile. We also grow mints and lemon balm in the shade, and valerian, which has a strong, heavy fragrance, like gardenias, where a little can go a long way.

Many people say that you have to have full sun to grow herbs. It's true that the oil content will be higher and the flavor more potent when grown in the sun, but most people season to taste anyway. If you use shade-grown herbs, just use a little more of it for seasoning. And in cooking, the rule of thumb for seasoning with herbs is to use three times as much fresh material as you would dried. It's like the difference between a slice of bread and a saltine cracker.

LCM: Do you have any other suggestions for successful herb growing?

DENISE: Just follow good gardening practices. Amend the soil, allow for good air circulation and good drainage, and enjoy yourself.

PENNY MELTON, MOUNTAIN CITY: PENNY'S GARDEN

Penny Melton and her husband Don have made herbs an "event" in Georgia. More than an event, they've made herbs a celebration!

Former antiques dealers, Penny and Don moved in 1974 from their home in Florida to take up permanent residency at their summer home in Mountain City. Here Penny indulged in her love of gardening and began to share not only the herbs and flowers she grew, but also the information and knowledge that she had acquired. People became so interested in learning about all aspects of herbs— crafts, cooking, growing—that she began inviting other herbal experts to come and share their knowledge as well. The result is an annual series of workshops and classes at Penny's Garden, which draws enthusiastic herb lovers from Georgia, Tennessee, and the Carolinas.

Although the official name of the shop is "Penny's Garden," anyone who visits knows that a more accurate name is "Penny and Don's Garden," for Don is as enthusiastic and knowledgeable about the herbs as his wife.

DON'S PESTO

2 cups packed fresh basil
$1/2$ cup extra virgin olive oil
$1/2$ cup Parmesan cheese
$1/4$ to $1/2$ cup pine nuts or walnuts
3 garlic cloves

Blend all ingredients in food processor or blender until purée is formed. Serve over pasta or as a pizza sauce.

In their cozy cottage on Blacks Creek Road, Penny and Don offer a wonderful array of plants, dried flower crafts, books, and herbal supplies. In addition, they are hosts for the North Georgia Herbal Faire, held annually on the second Saturday in August. The 1995 Faire included thirty dealers and attracted over 1,100 visitors.

I interviewed Penny on the porch of the cottage shop where cats rolled in ecstasy in the catmint, and neighborhood dogs sighed in the cool shade and slowly wagged droopy tails.

LCM: Do you come from a family of gardeners?

PENNY: My mother really liked to garden. She didn't grow herbs, but she loved flowers. I think back now and know we had scented geraniums, but I didn't know what they were then. My background is in elementary education, not horticulture.

We always had a summer house in Mountain City, so when we decided to move from Florida, we came here.

LCM: How did "Penny's Garden" evolve?

PENNY: We had been in the antiques business for many years and wanted out. Don suggested that we do something with plants since I have always liked to garden. So, in 1987, I started selling fresh cut flowers. We discovered that the people who came were more interested in the herbs and the vegetables we were growing out back than they were the flowers we were selling in the front. They were full of questions. They wanted to know how we grew them and how to use them. Now the herb plants we sell, and the classes and workshops we offer, are a big part of our business. People are interested in learning, and they seem to love a hands-on seminar.

LCM: Maybe that's because you have such a beautiful garden here. It's natural that people would want to go back home and do the same thing. What is it about herbs that attracts you so?

PENNY: I can't think of anything that I don't like about herbs. I love their fragrance, and I love to cook with them. I like the way they look, and I like their simple flowers. And I love the fact that if you know what you're doing, they are easy to grow.

LCM: How do you teach someone to "know what they're doing?"

PENNY: First, they need to ask themselves what they want from their herbs. Do they want to use them for cooking? For dried flowers? For their fragrance? Or for their medicinal properties? The use of herbs for medicines and beauty products is becoming increasingly popular.

LCM: What are some of the most useful medicinal herbs?

PENNY: Comfrey is used to make a salve or poultice, though people are advised against taking it internally. A salve made from comfrey leaves is good for cuts and bruises.

Another good medicinal herb is *Echinacea*, or purple coneflower. We grow it, but don't harvest our own plants, because you have to use the root and we don't want to lose our plants. Instead, we purchase the tincture. It has a somewhat unpleasant taste, but it is supposed to be really good for you.

Many people use feverfew, which is also really bitter, although I think it's beautiful to look at. And of course, ginseng is an extremely important medicinal plant. We don't grow ginseng because it is a shade plant, and we don't have a suitable spot for it. Unfortunately, we think it's almost all gone from the mountains where it grows wild. People do grow it commercially, but it is said that the potency of the root is not nearly as strong as that which you get from the wild roots. To help protect it, ginseng diggers, called "sang diggers," are only supposed to harvest it in fall after the berries have formed.

LCM: I know that ginseng tea is supposed to be beneficial. Do you make teas from other herbs as well?

PENNY: I make a mint tea, but mostly I cook with the herbs.

LCM: Which are your favorite culinary herbs?

PENNY: Rosemary and basil. And French tarragon, which I've grown for years and years—although I almost lost it this year. French tarragon is difficult to grow in the South, because it needs a period of dormancy during winter, and our winters for the past few years have not been cold enough. It's even more difficult the farther south you go. Many people grow Texas tarragon instead, because it has a similar taste. It's never wintered over for me here, so I grow it as an annual, but it might last the winter even as close as Atlanta.

Our growing conditions are really different from Atlanta. It's hotter here in the summer and about four degrees colder in the winter. We are very aware of microclimates here. Our own house is right across the road in an area surrounded by trees and a stone wall. It presents us with a more protected growing area. We can grow plants there, such as pineapple sage, which we can't grow here [near the cottage shop] where it's more exposed.

TIPS FOR FREEZING HERBS

Do not wash herbs (water dilutes flavor); brush dirt off with paintbrush. For tough-stemmed plants like rosemary, tarragon, or sage, remove leaves for freezing. Freeze leaves on a cookie sheet and then store in a sealed plastic bag in the freezer. This allows you to remove individual leaves as needed. Herbs can be stored up to six months in the freezer.

LCM: What are some other herbs you enjoy growing and that do well in north Georgia?

PENNY: I love to grow thymes, particularly lemon thyme and creeping thyme, and chives. And although I can't cook with it, I love catmint, especially the 'Six Hills Giant', which begins blooming early spring and continues until late summer.

HERBS TO FREEZE

Chives (chopped) *Allium schoenoprasum*
French tarragon *Artemisia dracunculus*
Rosemary *Rosmarinus officinalis*
Lemon balm *Melissa officinalis*
Oregano *Origanum vulgare*
Basil (blanch first) *Ocimum basilicum*
Sage *Salvia officinalis*
Thyme *Thymus praecox*
Parsley, flat *Petroselinum neapolitanum*
Dill *Anethum graveolens*

The best time to harvest the leaves is later in the morning after the dew has dried but before the sun gets too hot.

I have not had much success with artemisias, but we can grow southernwood, which is evergreen with a greyish green foliage. It has a pungent odor, almost like camphor, which some people don't like. We rub it on us to keep the gnats away. There's a tangerine southernwood that smells a little better.

We've done well with Spanish lavender, which is easier to grow in the South than English lavender. It takes the heat better, although it doesn't smell quite as good.

We also grow dill, and fennel, which was the 1995 International Herb Association herb of the year. *Monarda*, or beebalm, is the 1996 herb of the year. Each different color of *Monarda* has a different flavor, and wild varieties taste different from the cultivated varieties.

LCM: Do you have trouble with mildew on *Monarda?*

PENNY: Not a lot. There are several cultivars that are more mildew resistant than others, such as 'Gardenview Scarlett' and 'Marshall's Delight'. We find that if you keep plants well watered, they are less likely to get powdery mildew. When they get really stressed, then they are more susceptible.

LCM: How do you use *Monardas?*

PENNY: They're wonderful for attracting hummingbirds to the garden. Though I've never tried it, I understand some people have included it in salsa because of its spicy taste. I've sprinkled the blossoms on a fruit salad because it looks so pretty.

LCM: Do you grow sage?

PENNY: I cannot grow sage anywhere in this garden. I've been told that it's because of the fusarian wilt in the soil. Sage does fine for a while, but then it's gone. Without the wilt in the ground, it's a long-lived plant. It grows well at our house across the road or in a pot, but I cannot put it in the ground at this location.

LCM: Could you tell me how you harvest and preserve herbs?

PENNY: The best time to harvest the leaves is after the dew has dried but before the sun gets too hot. The oil content in the leaves is highest then and should yield the most pungent flavor.

We freeze a lot of herbs and make pesto base from basil, which we also freeze. You can make pesto many different ways, with just plain basil, or with opal basil and sundried tomatoes, or with a parsley base.

We freeze chives whole, or chop them up. When I'm chopping chives for a recipe, I do some extra ones and put them in the freezer in a sealed plastic bag.

You can freeze tarragon by putting a few sprigs in a freezer bag. They don't look particularly pretty, but they taste good. You can also freeze—or dry—parsley, or bring it indoors to grow on the windowsill.

I air-dry rosemary, thyme, and oregano by hanging a few sprigs in a cool, dry place. You can do it in the microwave; just be sure not to leave them in too long. When they are crisp, take them out.

You can also dry basil. It doesn't have a lot of taste, but if you dry it yourself, it certainly has more taste than what you buy in the store.

LCM: How do you use lemon balm?

PENNY: We chop it up, freeze it, and then use it in cookies or lemon bread.

LCM: You seem to have quite a variety of uses for these plants. What is your definition of an herb?

PENNY: It's fairly broad. I consider an herb to be any plant that is of use to man—medicinal, fragrant, or culinary. Under that definition, even roses are considered herbal.

LCM: Do you have any further advice to give to people who want to grow herbs?

PENNY: Don't be intimidated. It's easy and fun to grow herbs, and you can do so in a small space, particularly if you also use containers. People who are intimidated by the thought of herb gardening should begin by growing a few herbs in a tub or pot. It's an easy and fun way to begin something that might become a lifelong passion.

RESOURCES FOR HERBS

BOOKS

Adams, James. *Landscaping with Herbs*. Portland, Oregon: Timber Press, 1987.

Brown, Deni. *Herb Society of America's Encyclopedia of Herbs and Their Uses*. New York: Dorling Kindersely Publishers, 1995.

Garden Guide to the Lower South, 2nd Edition. Savannah, Georgia: Trustees Garden Club, P.O. Box 22215, Savannah, Georgia 31403-4215, 1991.

Hill, Madalene, and Gwen Barclay. *Southern Herb Growing*. Fredricksburg, Texas: Shearer, 1987.

Oliver, Paula. *The Herb Gardener's Resource Guide*. Northwind Farm, Rte. 2, Box 246, Shelvin, Minnesota 56676.

The Organic Gardener's Complete Guide to Vegetables and Fruits. Emmaus, Pennsylvania: Rodale, 1982.

Rodale's Illustrated Encyclopedia of Herbs. Emmaus, Pennsylvania: Rodale, 1987.

Simmons, Adelma Grenier. *Herb Gardening in Five Seasons*. New York: Hawthorne Books, 1964.

PERIODICALS

The Bu$iness of Herbs
Northwind Farm Publication
Route 2, Box 246
Shevin, MN 56676

The Herb Companion
Interweave Press
306 N. Washington Avenue
Loveland, CO 80537

The Herb Quarterly
P.O. Box 689
San Anselmo, CA 94960-0689

DISPLAY GARDENS

Atlanta Botanical Garden Herb Garden

Botanical Gardens and Garden Center, 1388 Eisenhower Drive, Savannah

Penny's Garden, Mountain City

Vines Botanical Garden, Loganville

SOURCES

The Cook's Garden
P.O. Box 535
Londonderry, VT 05148

GardenSmith
231 Hogan's Mill Road
Jefferson, GA 30549

Goodness Grows Nursery
P.O. Box 322
Highway 77 N
Lexington, GA 30648

Penny's Garden
P.O. Box 305
Blacks Creek Road
Mountain City, GA 30562

Sandy Mush Herb Farm
316 Surrett Cove Road
Leicester, NC 28748

Shepherd's Garden Seeds
30 Irene Street
Torrington, CN 06790

Wayside Gardens
Hodges, SC 29695-0001

ASSOCIATIONS

American Herb Association
P.O. Box 353
Rescue, CA 95672

Georgia Coastal Herb Society
Don Bass, 912-354-7299

Herb Society of America
9019 Kirtland Chardon Road
Mentor, OH 44060

Chattahoochee Herb Chapter of the
Herb Society
Chris Adams
P.O. Box 434
Lilburn 30247
770-921-0358

CLASSES AND WORKSHOPS

Atlanta Botanical Garden, Atlanta

Coastal Georgia Herb Society, Savannah

Penny's Garden, Mountain City

State Botanical Garden, Athens

Vines Botanical Garden, Logansville

9

WATER GARDENING

CRAIG LUNA, RIVERDALE: LUNA'S LILLIES

Craig Luna, owner of Luna's Lillies, is an enthusiastic and knowledgeable water gardener. Although his formal education and training had little to do with horticulture—or water—he feels that with Luna's Lillies, he has found his niche.

I asked Craig how he got into pond-scaping and water gardening.

"I am a therapeutic specialist for multi-handicapped children and taught

recreation therapy for ten years. I always loved plants so I had a little horticulture program with my kids, and we built a little two-by-two-foot in-ground fish tank. It was so much fun that I went home and built a larger pond. Then my parents went on vacation and we built a huge water pond at their house, and it escalated from there."

Today Luna's Lillies specializes in the installation and maintenance of water gardens. Although Craig no longer works with handicapped children, he continues to do therapeutic work—now by creating a space of peace and tranquillity for over 500 clients.

LCM: This garden looks as if it has been here forever. When did you put in the ponds?

CRAIG: Only five years ago. As you can see, it has matured quickly. I think that this is a unique characteristic of our business; we can put in a water garden and have it look well-established almost immediately.

LCM: How long have you been interested in water gardens?

CRAIG: We've been doing this a long time. We started the business in 1987, just before the boom in water gardening really hit.

LCM: To what do you attribute this great interest in water gardening?

CRAIG: People are now focusing more on their homes and back yards. We have clients who would much rather spend money on their garden instead of going on vacation.

MAINTENANCE SCHEDULE

In spring, from February to mid-March:

✧ Empty the pond and clean thoroughly.

✧ Check all fish for disease.

✧ Raise potted plants closer to the surface to stimulate growth.

✧ Prune and begin fertilizing all plants.

During the growing season:

✧ Analyze water once a month to be sure filtration system works properly.

✧ Continue to fertilize plants.

✧ Continue to check fish for disease.

After the first frost:

✧ Cut plants back and place on bottom of pond.

✧ Cover ponds with translucent netting.

LCM: What, specifically, about water gardening has caught people's attention?

CRAIG: I think it's the tranquillity and the mesmerizing feeling of the water and watching the fish and plants flourish. After an eight-hour work day, our clients don't go in to watch television. They go right out to their back yards because they find it to be therapeutic. The sound of water calms you. We put on a garden show two weeks ago and had over 1,500 people attend. The comment most often heard was that the water sounded peaceful.

LCM: Do you think that it's easier to get an established look faster with a water garden than with a perennial border?

CRAIG: Yes, I do, because so many of the water garden plants establish quickly. We have groundcovers that are already flourishing a month after we install them.

LCM: What kind of groundcovers do you use?

CRAIG: Mosses, creeping jennie (*Lysimachia nummularia*), gold moss sedum *(Sedum acre)*, and walking fern (*Camptosorous rhizophyllus*), which grows laterally and then cascades down. Garden ponds are basically liners bordered with stone. In order to soften that, you need to plant immediately. We use mosses and groundcovers to make it look as if the pond has always been there.

LCM: Is it hard to establish mosses?

CRAIG: We leave a half- to one-inch layer of earth attached to the moss, and then we place it wherever it's needed. It must be watered every day for six weeks, and then it will spread.

LCM: Do you try to use a lot of natives or do you just use what is hardy and does well?

CRAIG: We try to use the natives. The best is the evergreen Christmas fern because it stays green during winter. We also use maidenhair fern, walking, and ostrich ferns, all of which are native. We also use plants such as golden club and spider lily.

LCM: Do you plant bog gardens as well, or just ponds?

CRAIG: Both. We use a lot of plants in run-off areas and these become a simulated boggy creek bed. We use a wide variety of cattails, such as the variegated cattail, a hybrid that has been out for two years. It has absolutely beautiful texture.

Another variety is the 'Whispering Cattail', which is known for its long slender swords. I love it because it is so graceful. Both the leaves and the blossoms are tall and thin. So many of the aquatic plants tend to be invasive that we plant everything in containers.

LCM: What other plants do you use?

CRAIG: The Louisiana iris grows in the water; as well as white and purple pickerel, which comes in either broadleafed or narrow-leafed varieties; and lizard tail, *Saururus cernuus*, which is native to Florida. It has a broad, heart-shaped leaf and a wonderful white, fuzzy bloom. In the back of the ponds we often use a big plant like green-stemmed taro (*Colocasia esculenta*), which is like an aquatic elephant ear.

Another of our favorites is powdery thalia (*Thalia dealbata*), which is known for its beautiful long oval leaves. I like the blossoms as well, though some people think they're boring. It shoots up a long vertical bloom and then produces seed pods which later turn purple. Hummingbirds and dragonflies love it.

The pink 'Ellen Longwood' hybridized water cannas were probably our most popular this year. We also use a lot of ginger lilies in bog areas because they like to get their feet wet.

LCM: Do you grow pitcher plants?

CRAIG: Caterpillars love the pitcher plant, and literally destroyed it this year. This has been a bad year (1995) for bugs, because it's been so dry and because the winter was so mild we didn't have enough cold weather to kill them off.

LCM: How about lotus and water lilies?

CRAIG: The Asiatic white lotus has great seed pods. Ours has been blooming since late June and it will continue until

People love water gardening because of the tranquillity and the mesmerizing feeling of the water. After an eight-hour work day, our clients don't go in to watch television; they go right out to their gardens. I think it's because the sound of water calms you.

early September. The bloom only lasts three days, but we've had about twenty-five blooms throughout the season. This is its third year in this container, so I'll repot it next spring. The more crowded the roots, the fewer blooms you get.

GROUNDCOVERS TO USE AROUND PONDS

Creeping jenny   *Lysimachia nummularia*
Mosses   *Selaginella* sp.
Gold moss sedum   *Sedum acre*
Walking fern   *Camptosorus rhizophyllus*

We have seven tropical lilies—native Floridians—which will survive throughout Georgia. These include 'Tropical Tina', 'White Knight', 'Blue Danduben' and 'American Beauty', known for its large, glossy pad, which is about ten to twelve inches across. The pink bloom is not vibrant unless the plant receives full sun. I love the hybrid 'Charlene Strawn', which is probably the most prolific bloomer in Georgia. It has double yellow blooms in clusters and is just phenomenal.

During the growing season, from mid-March through August, we fertilize all the aquatic plants to get maximum growth and bloom.

LCM: What will overwinter in water gardens here?

CRAIG: Everything in this garden is winter hardy in Georgia and stays in the pond year round.

LCM: How do you keep the water clean and healthy?

CRAIG: We use a little white-flowered plant, anacharis (*Elodea canadensis*). If you choose to install a pond, you should grow this plant to help make your water ecologically sound. It is a submerged, oxygenating and filtration plant and is also great for fish spawning. As the season progresses, it will rise to the surface and grow across the surface of the water. We say that when this plant begins to produce white blooms, your pond is ecologi-cally healthy. This, along with organic treatments and a biological filtration system, should keep the pond healthy.

LCM: Could you tell me about the process of installing a pond?

CRAIG: After we excavate, and if it's in a heavily wooded area, we put news-papers down first because the ink helps divert the root mass. Then we install an underliner, which is a superthick felt. It's expensive, but it adds extra protection. Next we install a thick, 45 millimeter durable rubber lining. We've never had problems with punctures or a single leak. Finally, we place the stone.

LCM: So it's a pliable rubber, free-form pool, rather than something rigid, like a child's swimming pool?

CRAIG: Right. We like a free-form shape, not a contrived shape.

LCM: What kind of maintenance is required to keep a water garden healthy?

CRAIG: The lower pond here is 17 × 23 × 33 feet and holds about 18,000 gallons. The top one measures 18 × 26 × 30 feet. In spring, from February to mid-March, we empty the ponds, clean them thoroughly, and check the fish for disease. We raise the potted plants to the surface to stimulate growth, repot any that need it, and begin fertilizing them.

During the growing season, we make a monthly water analysis to make sure the filtration system is functioning properly and check the fish for bacteria or disease.

After the first frost, we cover our ponds with a translucent netting, cut the plants back, and place them on the bottom of the pond for the off season.

LCM: What is the correct terminology for what you do?

CRAIG: We call our work "pondscaping," which means placing plants correctly—artistically and ecologically. We do

---

POND PLANTS

Parrot's feather *Myriophyllum aquaticum*

Cattails *Typha* sp.

Louisiana iris *Iris virginica*

Pickerel *Pontederia cordata*

Lizard tail *Saururus cernuus*

Thalia *Thalia dealbata*

Water canna *Canna* hybrids 'Ellen Longwood'

Lotus, Asiatic *Nelumbo* sp.

Anacharis *Elodea canadensis*

Australian water poppy *Hydrocleys nymphoides*

the entire set, from design and installation to the lily pads, fish, frogs, tadpoles, snails, and newts. We really set up an entire ecosystem.

LCM: What mistakes do you find people make in putting in and maintaining water gardens?

CRAIG: Not setting the pond up so that it is ecologically sound—with the proper number of aquatic plants. Setting up the pond so that the water doesn't filter properly. Another problem that we see is water loss because the sides of the pond are not built up high enough and they begin to erode and settle, resulting in leakage.

RESOURCES FOR WATER GARDENING

DISPLAY GARDENS
Atlanta Home and Garden Show, February

Luna's Lillies, Inc. Pond Tour, August, free admission

BOOKS
Garden Pools and Fountains. Susan A. Roth, Editor. San Ramon, California: Ortho Books, 1988.

Post, George. *Textbook of Fish Health.* Neptune City, New Jersey: TFH Publishers, 1987.

Schimana, Walter. *Garden Ponds for Everyone.* Neptune City, New Jersey: TFH Publishers, 1993.

Thomas, Charles B. *Water Gardens for Plants and Fish.* Neptune City, New Jersey: TFH Publishers, 1988.

Vrbova, Vuza. *Koi for Ponds.* Junior Pet Care Series. Neptune City, New Jersey: TFH Publishers, 1990.

Wieser, K.H., and P.V. Loiselle. *Your Garden Pond.* Melle, West Germany: Tetra Press, 1986.

PERIODICALS
Atlanta Koi Club Newsletter
Erik I. Johnson, Editor
302 Hamilton Trace, S.E.
Marietta, GA 30068

Fish Stories
Harvey L. Feller, Publisher
300 East 55th Street, Suite 1
New York, NY 10022

The Lily Pad
c/o LilyPad Publications
J. Sullivan
P.O. Box 3309
Brentwood, TN 37024-3309
625-370-0932

Pondkeeper Magazine
c/o Vivicon Productions, Inc.
1000 Whitetail Court
Duncansville, PA 16635
814-695-4325

SOCIETIES AND ORGANIZATIONS
The Goldfish Society of America
P.O. Box 851282
Richardson, TX 75085-1282

International Water Lily Society, Georgia Chapter
Anne and Bill Anderson
2932 Happy Hollow Drive S.E.
Conyers, GA 30208

National Pond Society
P.O. Box 449
Acworth, GA 30101
800-742-4701

PLANT AND FISH RESOURCES

Harp's Farmer's Market and Nursery
1692 Highway 92 South
Fayetteville, GA 30214
(*On-site sale.*)

Lilypons Water Gardens
Box 10
Lilypons, MD 21717-0010

Paradise Water Gardens
62 May Street
Whitman, MA 02382

Slocum Water Gardens
1101 Cypress Gardens Boulevard
Winter Haven, FL 33880-6099

10

❦

NATIVE PLANTS

GEORGE SANKO, ATLANTA: DEKALB COLLEGE NATIVE PLANT GARDEN

George Sanko is a chemist by training, but soon after he began to teach at Dekalb College, where he has now been for over thirty years, he was asked to teach botany instead. It is fortunate for gardeners throughout the Southeast that George was asked to make this switch

early in his career, because the energy and enthusiasm of this gifted man has resulted in an herbarium at Dekalb College with over 5,000 species represented, and a botanical garden that now boasts over 1300 different species.

"We are the native plant center of Georgia," George admits proudly. "If you want to know about growing native plants in this state, we can tell you." It is far from an idle boast. In addition to the botanical garden, which is a treasure for anyone interested in gardening with native plants, George also offers eleven different classes on native plants through the college's continuing education program.

George's determination and drive were perhaps best exemplified the summer after he began teaching at Dekalb College. During these months, he took a 12,000 mile plant-collecting trip to the Arctic Circle. "It was a magnificent experience. I was supposed to have someone go with me, but that fell through, so I just went by myself."

Although George was fascinated by the plants of Alaska and the Yukon, it is the plants of Georgia that he really knows and loves. I interviewed George in late summer at the botanical garden located on the south campus of Dekalb College.

LCM: How long have you been at Dekalb College?

GEORGE: I'm starting my thirtieth year. I am now the senior faculty member, although I don't teach full time.

LCM: Do you teach just horticulture and gardening?

GEORGE: No. first of all, I'm not a gardener.

LCM: Not a gardener! You must be! Look around you.

GEORGE: I'm a chemist by training, and did graduate school in biology. I got into botany because the school needed a botany professor. Frankly, I wasn't very happy about it. But I felt that I should give these kids some field experience, so in 1970 I started an herbarium.

LCM: Are you still working on the herbarium?

GEORGE: We are still adding to it, but not with the same vengeance. For a while I was spending my summers traveling all over the United States collecting plants. We have over 5,000 species—I doubt that another junior college in the country even approaches that.

The summer after I came here I took a 12,000-mile field trip and drove to the Arctic Circle, collecting plants. Alaska and the Yukon are incredible, and it was amazing to see all those plants in their habitat.

I teach a lot of continuing education courses now, and I try to teach the students about plant family characteristics. After the first year, some of my students said, why don't we have some of these plants growing outside? So we started the garden. We were only going to plant fifty, and now we're up to about 1,300. It is the largest native plant garden in the state, probably one of the largest collections of natives in the South.

LCM: Are all these plants native to Georgia?

GEORGE: Not necessarily. Out of the 1,300, most of them are native to Georgia, but quite a few are native to other parts of the Southeast, especially the Florida panhandle. Our goal at this garden is to determine which native plants have ornamental value.

I've been from California to Alaska, and for unusual and beautiful native plants, as far as I'm concerned, the best place to botanize is the Florida panhandle. They have a wonderful diversity of ecosystems—pine woods, hardwoods, and roadside.

LCM: Your thrust now is really finding native plants suitable for the garden?

GEORGE: Yes. I collect everything. If it's native, hopefully it will find its way into this garden for us to test. We have a lot of roadside plants, plants you wouldn't even consider using in the garden. But we're finding some wonderful plants. People just don't know what they're missing. There are some incredible, incredible native plants.

For example, we're looking at the *Sabatias*, marsh pinks, which are magnificent, gorgeous little plants. A couple of species look very promising, and we're going to work with those.

LCM: Do a lot of commercial growers come here to see what you've found?

GEORGE: Yes, two weeks ago at our fern sale, the landscapers almost wiped us out because we had plants they could not find anywhere else.

I'll show you one of the rare penstemons, which is a Georgia endangered species. It's been in the same spot for three years and finally it's started to run.

LCM: How is the garden funded?

GEORGE: In part with the money we raise through the plant sales. We have two sales in spring—one in early April and another in May, and two in the fall—a fern sale and a fall plant sale. One of the biggest sellers this year were the *Marshallias*. We offered seven or eight different kinds. People did not know much about them, but they're beginning to learn now.

We try to educate people with our Sunday walks during spring and fall. And I teach eleven different classes on native plants in the continuing education program. This is the state center for native plant gardening. For spring blooming plants, I doubt that you could pick up a plant catalog anywhere and find a native plant that we are not already growing.

Probably one of our biggest introductions has been the Florida wood fern, *Dryopteris ludoviciana*. It's magnificent. It creeps and spreads rapidly, so every twelve months, I go out, dig up the entire plant, divide, and replant it. If you're careful and know what you are doing, you can dig the garden like a farm.

LCM: Do you find that you sell to an educated public?

GEORGE: Not necessarily. But even when people don't know what they're doing, most of these plants are so hardy, they survive anyway.

At the garden we try to put plants in areas that resemble their native habitat, but it's hard to do because we deal with so many different kinds of plants. Many native plants are quite adaptable. For example, *Penstemon digitalis* is one of the hardiest plants out here. We grow it everywhere—full sun, semishade, and full shade—so people can see what difference the habitat makes. This penstemon

grows in all three locations, but blooms less with deeper shade. It's a teaching garden, so we want to show and educate people as much as we can.

Baptisias are one of the up and coming plants, and we've grown all ours from seed. The public is just starting to recognize baptisias, but they are definitely garden-worthy plants. They come in yellow, white, and blue. In about two years, everyone will be clamoring for it.

LCM: Are they all perennial?

GEORGE: Yes. The only plant we sell that is not perennial is the *Silene armeria*, which reseeds everywhere.

We have some plants that are very common. The odorless wax myrtle, *Myrica odora*, is one of the nicest shrubs we grow. It looks exactly the same, summer or winter. We've also introduced some strange plants, such as this yellow

---

UNUSUAL NATIVE PLANTS FOR SHADE

Ginger, Harper's wild   *Hexastylis speciosum*

Ginger, variegated wild   *Hexastylis shuttleworthii*

Vase's trillium   *Trillium vaseyi*

Bleeding heart   *Dicentra eximia*

Jacob's ladder   *Polemonium reptans*

Monkshood   *Aconitum uncinatum*

Gentian   *Gentiana villosa, G. saponaria*

Irises   *Iris versicolor, I. fulva, I. virginica, I. primatica, I. cristata, I. verna*

Woodland phlox   *Phlox maculata*

Cardinal flower   *Lobelia cardinalis*

UNUSUAL NATIVE PLANTS FOR SUN

Baptisia   *Baptisia australis, B. minor,*
B. megacarpa

Seashore mallow   *Kosteletzkya*
virginica

Barbara's button   *Marshallia obovata,*
M. trinerva, M. morhii

Red-flowered black-eyed Susan
Rudbeckia graminifolia

Narrow-leafed aster   *Aster lineari-*
folius

Milkweed, pink swamp   *Asclepias*
incarnata

St.-Johns-wort   *Hypericum densiflo-*
rum; H. frondosum

Amsonia   *Amsonia hubrectii*

Frog fruit   *Lippia nodiflora*

Cranberry   *Vaccinium macrocarpon*

Joe-Pye weed   *Eupatorium*
maculatum

Queen of the prairie   *Filipendula*
rubra

Scutellaria   *Scutellaria incana*

Marsh pink   *Sabatia bartrami*

rattle box, *Daubentonia drummondii,* and the red rattlebox, *Daubentonoia punicea.* These need full sun, and will die back to the ground in winter.

Seashore mallow, *Kosteletzkya virginica* grows right in the sand on the coast, but also does well in this garden. When you deal with mallows, you usually have to deal with insect damage, but not on that one.

The *Marshallia* called "Barbara's button" has a head with all white disk flowers. We also have the federally endangered species, *Marshallia morhii,*

which is the least attractive because it has such a tiny flowering head. *M. obovata,* which is native to Dekalb County, also has a big white head of disk flowers in spring. We also have *M. gramifolia,* which blooms late summer into fall. The others bloom from late April into May.

LCM: Don't you feel like you're sitting on a treasure house? Look at all these great plants!

GEORGE: Oh yes. This is it. We started this *Rudbeckia graminifolia* from seed. It's from the Florida panhandle, has grasslike foliage, and produces a reddish flower. There's nothing like it, but the first question I have to answer is, will it survive here?

LCM: Do you find that a lot of the Florida panhandle plants survive here?

GEORGE: More make it than not. Many south Georgia and Florida plants do well here.

LCM: What is this plant that looks like a rosemary?

GEORGE: It's narrow-leafed aster, *Aster linearifolius.* It's a beautiful, beautiful aster. Beside it is *Vernonia arkansana,* which is also beautiful. It reseeds easily, and now it's taking over the garden.

Asclepias incarnata, swamp milkweed, is one of the most beautiful plants we have. Another is *Hypericum densiflorum,* St.-John's-wort, which has hundreds and hun-dreds of small yellow flowers. Another species, *H. frondosum,* grows on top of Stone Mountain and has giant yellow flowers. If you climb Stone Mountain in May and see a shrub with big yellow flowers, that's it. We also have tons and tons of the swamp sunflower, *Helianthus simulans.*

This is *Amsonia hubrectii,* Arkansas blue star. It is interesting all year long with pretty blue flowers in spring and attractive foliage in fall.

This is called frog fruit, *Lippia nodiflora*. It is from south Georgia, where it grows along the beach in the sand, but it seems to like the rich soil of north Georgia as well. It's flourishing here. In the sand, it stays flat and makes a wonderful groundcover and while it will bloom there, it doesn't look as lush as it does here. This is cranberry, *Vaccinium macrocarpon*, which we got out of the pine barrens of New Jersey.

LCM: I thought cranberries only grew in bogs or swamps.

GEORGE: You're correct, but no one ever bothered to find out if it would grow anywhere else. And it does. It fruits and spreads, but it is not evergreen. Even so, it's magnificent.

Seashore mallow, *Kosteletzkya virginica*, started blooming back in late May and has given us continuous bloom all summer. It grows easily from seed.

LCM: It looks so pretty growing with the blue salvia.

GEORGE: Better than that, we have some growing with the Joe Pye weed and it looks magnificent.

A really nice plant is this *Silene* hybrid, a cross between the federally endangered *Silene polypetala*, the campion, and the old red fire pink, *Silene virginica*. You end up with a silene that grows in full sun. The foliage doesn't melt away and it blooms most of the spring. This started blooming March 15, bloomed into May, and intermittently into December.

LCM: You're talking about eight months of bloom?

GEORGE: We're not really sure how long it will bloom in any given year, but it's pretty good. It's sterile, which means it won't set seed. It's not available for sale yet, but it will be eventually.

One of my favorites is Queen of the Prairie, *Filipendula rubra*. It does not have a long bloom time, but it is one of the most stunning plants in the garden. It blooms in July for about two weeks, and produces a panicle of flowers that looks like red smoke. It's native to the Midwest, but it does really well here.

Scutellaria incana is surprisingly beautiful. We'll try to propagate it for next year because it is an excellent plant. Cumberland rosemary, *Conradina verticillata* is federally endangered; it has typical rosemary flowers and attractive evergreen foliage.

This is a little red sage, *Clinopodium coccinium*, which is short-lived but very hardy, and loves pure sand.

LCM: All the plants we've seen so far are sun plants?

GEORGE: Yes, though some will grow in shade as well. Peak bloom for the sun beds is August, when the place just lights up like a firecracker.

LCM: Obviously you have plants grouped according to their sun needs. How else are they divided?

GEORGE: We have many beds planted according to family. We have a sunflower family bed, *Asteraceae*; a mint family bed, *Lamiaceae*; and a bean family bed, *Fabaceae*, and we have a federally endangered plant bed.

In that bed you'll find hairy sumac, which is one of our rarest plants. It gives you beautiful fall color. Sumacs are generally runners. In this case we will allow it to run, then dig it up, and sell the divisions. Another plant in this bed is *Helianthus schweinitzii*, which is the ugliest sunflower I've ever seen, but it is rare, so we grow it.

This is pygmy fringe tree, *Chionanthus pygmea*, which is probably the rarest plant in the garden. It's rare because fringe trees are so difficult to propagate. We have more federally endangered plants here than in any other garden in Georgia. Part of our objective is to get endangered plants, propagate them, and reintroduce them to the wild.

Peak bloom for the shade area is mid-April. The fern collection here has turned into a real specialty for us. The students planted this hairy lip fern, *Cheilanthes landsa,* right on the rocks. When moisture is not available, it shrivels up like the resurrection fern. The secret is to have some kind of moss like *Sellaginella* (spike moss) on the rock to maintain moisture.

FERNS FOR GEORGIA WOODS

Log fern   *Dryopteris celsa*

Autumn fern   *Dryopteris erythrosora*

Clover leaf fern   *Marsilea uncinata*

Interrupted fern   *Osmunda claytoniana*

Walking fern   *Camptosorous rhizophyllus*

Marginal wood fern   *Dryopteris marginalis*

Virginia chain fern   *Woodwardia virginica*

Southern wood fern   *Thelypteris kunthii*

Blunt lobed woodsia   *Woodsia obtusa*

Netted chain   *Woodwardia areolata*

Christmas fern   *Polystichum acrostichoides*

New York fern   *Thelypteris noveboracensis*

Royal fern   *Osmunda regalis*

Florida wood fern   *Dryopteris ludoviciana*

We only sell four plants that are not native; autumn fern is one of them and we sell it because it is such a good plant. Clover leaf fern, *Marsilea uncinata* grows in water or on land and spreads everywhere.

LCM: Does it need moist conditions?

GEORGE: No, it will do fine if you give it shade and water it occasionally. It is native to south Florida and every book will tell you that it will not live out of south Florida, but it's been thriving in our garden for about four years.

Log fern is probably the nicest native fern we have. It is incredible. It is a natural hybrid between Florida woodfern, *Dryopteris ludoviciana,* which is hardy, and Goldie's fern, *Dryopteris goldiana.*

LCM: Which of the ferns are evergreen?

GEORGE: The log, goldies, and Florida wood fern, walking ferns, and the marginal wood fern, and a deer tongue fern out of the redwood forest, *Blechnum spicant.* It is low growing, deep green, and evergreen.

We have over ninety species of ferns here. It is the largest collection of native ferns and fern allies in the South.

Along with the ferns we have some beautiful woodland flowers. *Hexastylis speciosa,* Harper's wild ginger, has a large flower. One year we had one hundred-fifty flowers on a single plant. The species with a more variegated leaf is *H. shuttleworthii,* which is found mostly in north Georgia. That's a premium plant and is considered one of our finest wild gingers.

We have fourteen species of trilliums. You can transplant these very easily, but to grow them from seed it takes seven years for them to bloom.

LCM: Do you have a favorite trillium?

GEORGE: Probably *Trillium vaseyi,* Vase's trillium. It has a nice big flower and big foliage.

LCM: What other woodland plants do you like?

GEORGE: You can't beat bleeding heart, *Dicentra eximia*, and we grow a lot of Jacob's ladder, *Polemonium reptans*, which is easy to grow from seed. I also like monkshood, *Aconitum uncinatum*, which is a neat little plant.

We grow a few gentians, *Gentiana villosa* and *G. saponaria*. We don't grow the fringed gentian because it is an annual, doesn't spread, and doesn't grow well here because we're a little too far south for it.

We have *Lobelias* in the stream area, both the blue, *Lobelia siphilitica*, and the red cardinal flower *L. cardinalis*.

The phlox, *Phlox maculata*, is also an excellent plant for the woodlands.

LCM: Do you grow any of the lady's slippers?

GEORGE: Not really. The problem is that they are just too difficult to grow. We are, however, increasing our iris collection. We have *Iris versicolor*, *I. fulva*, *I. virginica*, and *I. prismatica*. This bed is nothing but ferns and iris, and it is spectacular in spring.

LCM: What do you do about soil preparation?

GEORGE: We work the beds every three years. We dig up every single plant, add organic material to the soil and replant.

LCM: What are your goals for this garden?

GEORGE: I'd like to see more people garden with natives. If people continue to move in that direction, then I feel that we have done our job. We don't have a lot of money, staff, or space, but what we do have is plants that no one else has, and we can make people aware of these plants. They are such a treasure for the South.

TERRY TATUM, MADISON: WILDWOOD FARMS

Think of persimmons and think of—who else?—Terry Tatum! Although Terry's expertise goes way beyond that puckering fruit, the Persimmon Festival, which she hosts every fall, has brought visitors from all over the state to Wildwood Farms, the nursery she started in 1985.

Although Terry has always been interested in nature, she admits that she took a roundabout way to arrive at her present state. "Once I discovered plants, I knew that this was what I wanted to do," she told me. "It just took a long time to get here."

Today Wildwood Farms, located near Madison, is a marvelous combination of retail and wholesale nursery, display beds, a natural Georgia wildflower meadow and trail, and a cattail pond.

Although the emphasis at Wildwood Farms is on plants native to Georgia and the Southeast, Terry also includes non-native ornamental plants in the wonderful collection of plants she grows and sells.

Plants in the display bed are grouped either by some common theme or by family, and generally include both native and non-native species, making for wonderful educational displays.

LCM: How did you first become interested in plants?

TERRY: I have an undergraduate degree in biology from West Georgia College and I thought that I wanted to be a vet. When that didn't work out, I took a job with the Department of Natural Resources, cataloging the vegetation on one of the Georgia barrier islands. I had to teach myself everything—about the plants, how to collect them, and how to set up an herbarium—but I was very much taken with botany. After two years I realized that this was it. This was what I wanted to do with my life.

The people I worked with were great. I worked with Jerry McCollum, and we eventually got married. He now works with the Georgia Wildlife Federation, the state affiliate of the National Wildlife Federation.

One of the most inspiring people that I met there is Wilbur Duncan, who taught botany at the University of Georgia. He is just crazy about plants and his enthusiasm is infectious.

Once we were riding down a dirt road in a jeep. All of a sudden he started yelling, and then he leapt out of the jeep before it even stopped. He ran over to this palm tree which had turned over and started describing how the palm had anchored itself to the soil with a hook mechanism. I'm sure that his enthusiasm, and the way he explained things, contributed to my love of plants today.

At first I thought that I would teach, but eventually I went to the University of Georgia and earned a degree in horticulture and started this business. I never wanted to do design, I was always more interested in growing.

LCM: When you started the nursery, was it your goal to grow and sell only native plants?

TERRY: No, not really. At the University I worked with Dr. Allan Armitage, and I thought maybe I would do cut flowers. I also studied with Dr. Michael Dirr and became interested in woody plant propagation. When I received a contract to propagate magnolias and a couple of contracts to propagate red maples, I began seriously working with woody plants.

My real education about growing and gardening has come in the last ten years in working with the nursery. I'm still very interested in cut flowers, but not the traditional greenhouse cut flowers. I'm more interested in finding nontraditional uses for the native plants: using them as cut flowers, as edible plants, or for gardening for wildlife. I like looking at native plants and trying to figure out what else I can do with them.

For example, the Dutch have been using *Liatris* for years as a cut flower, and florists almost always use *Liatris spicata*. But we found that some other native liatris also make wonderful cut flowers. Something like *L. squarrosa* or *L. aspera* is much looser and more graceful. There's more space between each inflorescence, and it has a more open look.

LCM: What other natives do you use for cut flowers?

TERRY: Goldenrods, of course. They're great but we have to keep educating people about using them and assuring them that goldenrods do not cause hay fever. One of my favorites is *Solidago caesia*, wreath goldenrod. It has a beautiful sulfur yellow color. I also like *S. rugosa*, or wrinkle-leaf goldenrod.

The flowering and fruiting branches of woody natives also make great cut flowers, particularly plants such as native chickasaw plum, *Prunus angustifolia*, and the deciduous hollies. I also like to use the dried native grasses like broomsedge.

Natives also make great edible ornamentals. I've made bread and cookies out of pawpaws, *Asimina triloba*, chinquapin, *Castanea pumila*; and I make jams and jellies from mayhaws, *Crataegus*.

I even use persimmons and chokeberry. I had a good crop of chokeberries one year and wasn't about to let them go to waste. I knew they were bitter—that's how they got their name. But I also knew they weren't poisonous, so I tried anyway and made twenty to thirty jars of the best jelly in the world.[1]

LCM: Do you ever use the fruit of the passionflower?

TERRY: Sometimes. I usually save some of the seeds to replant. I use it in the garden for the caterpillar of the fritillary butterflies. The plants often look munched on and not particularly attractive, but if I can educate people that these wormy caterpillars need the plants to become beautiful butterflies, I feel that I've helped.

LCM: What is it about the native plants that attracts you so much?

TERRY: I guess that's where I started. But I'm not a purist. There are other plants that are not native that are absolutely fabulous. Maybe I have a certain fondness for them because they've been ignored. It seems that if it's not exotic or imported, some people see little value in it.

NATIVE PLANTS FOR CUT FLOWERS

Liatris   *Liatris squarrosa, L. aspera*
Goldenrod   *Solidago caesia*
Plum, chickasaw   *Prunus angustifolia*
Holly, deciduous   *Ilex verticillata*
Black-eyed Susan   *Rudbeckia* sp.
Purple coneflower   *Echinacea purpurea*
Viburnum   *Viburnum* sp.
Hydrangea, oakleaf   *Hydrangea quercifolia*
Beautyberry   *Callicarpa americana*
Aster   *Aster* sp.
Beebalm   *Monarda* sp.
Sumac   *Sumac* sp.
Obedient plant   *Physostegia virginiana*
Baptisia   *Baptisia australis*

I don't tell people that a plant will be hardier or more adaptable just because it's native, because that's not always the case. Plants are native to particular habitats within a region. If you provide a plant conditions similar to their native habitat, then they won't suffer so much from bugs and disease.

I don't spray much for bugs or weeds here, and I don't have a huge irrigation system. The plants pretty much have to fend for themselves.

---

[1] In using edible native plants, be careful. Make sure that you have positively identified the plants, that they have not been sprayed with insecticides or herbicides, or have been subjected to heavy doses of car exhaust.

See that big oak tree? It's full of mistletoe and people keep telling me that it's going to kill the tree, but when the berries are on, the tree is full of bluebirds. So I think that mistletoe has its place, too, and if I can sit and watch fifty bluebirds eating lunch, then I think that's pretty fabulous.

It's the same with the box elder growing across the marsh. I know it's considered a trash tree, but it has a nice shape and cedar waxwings love the little seeds. So there are trade-offs.

LCM: Were there other people who influenced you along the way?

TERRY: Some of my favorite books were written by Geneva Stratton Porter. She was a feminist, nature writer, and photographer from Indiana who lived from 1863 to 1924. She wrote many books about nature, but my favorite is called *Music of the Wild*. It has become my bible. It's all about the different habitats, the animals, and the sounds of nature that really are music if you listen closely enough.

RESOURCES FOR NATIVE PLANTS

BOOKS

Druse, Ken. *The Natural Garden.* New York: Clarkson Potter, 1989.

Foote, Leonard E., and Samuel B. Jones. *Native Shrubs and Woody Vines of the Southeast: Landscaping Uses and Identification.* Portland, Oregon: Timber Press, 1989.

Jones, Samuel, and Leonard Foote. *Gardening with Native Wildflowers.* Portland, Oregon: Timber Press, 1990.

Martin, Laura C. *The Wildflower Meadow Book.* Old Saybrook, Connecticut: Globe Pequot Press, 1986.

Merilees, William J. *Attracting Backyard Wildlife.* Stillwater, Minnesota: Voyageur Press, 1989.

Phillips, Harry. *Growing and Propagating Wildflowers.* Chapel Hill, North Carolina: University of North Carolina Press, 1985.

Pope, Thomas; Neil Odenwald; and Charles Fryling. *Attracting Birds to Southern Gardens.* Dallas: Taylor Publishing Co., 1993.

Wasowski, Sally, and Andy Wasowski. *Gardening with Native Plants of the South.* Dallas: Taylor Publishing Co., 1994.

PLANT SOURCES

Goodness Grows
P.O. Box 311
Highway 77 North
Lexington, GA 30648
706-743-5055

Niche Gardens
1111 Dawson Road
Chapel Hill, NC 27516
919-967-0078

Southern Perennials and Herbs
98 Bridges Road
Tylertown, MS 39667-9338

Wildwood Farms
5231 Seven Islands Road
Madison, GA 30650
706-342-4912

Wilkerson Mill Gardens
9595 Wilkerson Mill Road
Palmetto, GA 30268
770-463-9717

Woodlanders, Inc.
1128 Colleton Avenue
Aiken, SC 29801
803-648-7522

SOCIETIES

Georgia Botanical Society
2490 F. Windson Wood Lane
Norcross, GA 30071-2336
770-448-7613

Georgia Native Plant Society
Jim Harrington
4004 Dover Avenue
Alpharetta, GA 30201

Georgia Wildlife Federation
1930 Iris Drive
Conyers, GA 30207
770-929-3350

DISPLAY GARDENS

Barnsley Gardens, (ferneries, woodland garden),
  Adiarsville

Dekalb College Botanical Garden

Wild Wood Farms, Madison

Wilkerson Mill Gardens, Palmetto

11

SHRUBS AND TREES

MICHAEL DIRR, ATHENS: UNIVERSITY OF GEORGIA

It was hot—one of the hottest Augusts Georgia had seen in many years, with temperatures soaring past 100 degrees several days in a row. Plants dropped, and most gardeners were weary of watering and distressed at the toll that the heat had taken.

All except Michael Dirr. Michael was undaunted, ready for action, and eager to get into the garden in spite of the heat.

For three hours, I jogged after Michael as he strode through his home garden in Athens and ran through the University of Georgia field test plantings and green-houses. Mike never stopped talking and never stopped to take a breath; obviously the Dirr philosophy is that life is just too short to do things like walk and breathe. My initial intimidation was soon lost in the sheer effort of keeping up with him and recording as much as possible of the fountain of information that spewed forth.

Michael Dirr is one of Georgia's great natural resources. Born in Kentucky and raised in Ohio, he received his B.S. and M.S. degree from Ohio State University, and then received his Ph.D. from the University of Massachusetts. After teach-ing at the University of Illinois for seven years, and spending a one-year sabbatical at the Arnold Arboretum, he came to Georgia, originally as associate professor of horticulture and director of the State Botanical Garden in Athens. He now serves as professor of horticulture at the University of Georgia.

Michael's knowledge of plants has made an indelible mark on the plant industry, not only in Georgia, but nation-wide. Many plants on the market today are the result of his work. His publications include hundreds of articles and papers, and several books, including the *Manual of Woody Landscape Plants*.

Although his knowledge and expertise have been tremendously influential, it is his passion for plants that has touched hearts and gardening spirits throughout the world. It is impossible to spend time with this man and not come away with fingers itching to take up a spade, plant something, and watch it grow.

Michael admits that gardening has been the love of his life. His home garden is full of the plants he loves, and teeming with the memories of the nurserymen and friends with whom he has shared plants through the years. I was privileged to walk through this garden with Michael—and his dog, Dusty.

LCM: Your garden is amazing, even in the middle of August.

MICHAEL: My wife, Bonnie, and I are passionate about it. No one else has ever worked this garden and no one ever will, until I can no longer hold a spade.

The excitement that people feel about plants really comes from the heart, but it also comes from observation. People need to garden based on their own experiences, not what they read in gardening books. Many gardening books are written about the northeastern quadrant of the country. If you bring some of those plants down here, they won't last a week. I think if people are going to try to teach others about gardening, they have to garden themselves.

It's been the love of my life. My dad was an avid gardener, and hope springs eternal. He died at the age of 83, and in his last year, he was still planting his vegetable garden.

LCM: Where did you grow up?
MICHAEL: In Cincinnati.

LCM: Was your mother a gardener as well?

MICHAEL: No. my mom loved [gardens], but she didn't particularly like to dig.

❦

It's the memories that go with the plants that make them really special. I think a lot of people become emotionally attached, not just to the plant, but also who and where they came from.

❦

We'll take a quick trip through the garden. This is my dog Dusty. She's my gardening buddy—ten years old and still digging up plants. We're always trying something new. We just put this bed in this spring and took the lower limbs off these trees to create high shade.

This plant, *Plectranthus amboinicus* 'Variegatus', has been terrific. We have it growing in semishade, but I've also grown it in full sun, and it's done well. It makes a great annual edging plant, though the first frost will knock it down. It's extremely easy to root. I pruned off a few stalks and threw them in a pile and even in the heat this summer, they took root.

The great thing about this plant is that it doesn't wilt, and we should know, because the temperatures this summer [1995] were in the 100s. Al [Armitage] found a sport off this plant that's variegated—lime green with just a little yellow in the center. It's beautiful too.

Another plant that I have here in the high shade is *Magnolia ashei,* which will put out beautiful, fragrant flowers when it gets about five feet tall.

Magnolia 'Pristine' was developed by J.C. McDaniel. The foliage is wonderful, but when it flowers, it's something special. The flowers have fifteen milk-white petals (sepals) held upright like little chalices. The fragrance is absolutely magnificent.

This new magnolia is called 'Greenback'™ and it's outstanding. Look how green the leaves are on both sides. Without pruning, it makes a nice, dense pyramid. I'm using it as a screen along the property line, to frame and separate our garden.

Here, where we have a little more sun, we planted an herb garden this year. The reality is that a lot of these things melt out in the heat. We found out that the golden oregano does well here, although it isn't very golden in the heat. We also had terrific luck with rosemary, but none of the other herbs did very well.

You learn by doing. People are always saying, "Plant an herb garden, it's easy!" This is great soil, but no matter what the books say, plants don't read the books, and sometimes they die.

I always wanted a red garden like the one at Hidcote. Then I decided that I would never achieve that, so we created a fall border instead, which is spectacular from September through November when *Rudbeckia triloba* and *R. laciniata,* are blooming.

I also included an old-fashioned mum that I found on campus next to one of the old buildings. I have no idea what it is, but I propagated it, and it has beautiful double white flowers. It sort of flops over, but the Sedum 'Autumn Joy' helps hold it up.

Aster tartaricus is a big aster with light blue flowers and a yellow center. I like the asters. Some of the best are 'Hella Lacy', a purple that blooms in September and October, *A. lateriflorus* 'Purple Prince', *A. carolinianus*, climbing aster, and *A. oblongifolius*. Everything melds together in the fall. I won't say it's a Monet, but I will say that it's beautiful.

LCM: Maybe not a Monet, but definitely a Michael Dirr, right?

MICHAEL: That's right.

A FEW DIRR FAVORITES

Magnolia   *Magnolia ashei,*
  M. 'Pristine'

Bottlebrush buckeye   *Aesculus parviflora*

Japanese apricot   *Prunus mume*

Yellow-fruiting yaupon holly   *Ilex vomitoria* 'Katherine'

Florida anise tree   *Illicium floridanum*

Japanese anise   *Illicium anisatum*

Yellow anise   *Illicium parviflorum*

Henry anise   *Illicium henryii*

Mexican anise   *Illicium mexicanum*

Oak-leaf hydrangea, compact   *Hydrangea quercifolia* 'Peewee'

Sweet pepperbush   *Clethra alnifolia* 'Fern Valley Pink', 'Ruby Spice'

Seven-Son flower   *Heptocodium miconioides*

Yellowrim   *Serissa foetida*

Loropetalum   *Loropetalum chinense* var. *rubrum* 'Fire Dance', 'Plum Delight', 'Zhuzhou'

Fuchsia   *Fuchsia* 'Burgundy', 'Blush'

Stewartia   *Stewartia monadelpha*

This is what we call our eclectic bed, and it looks eclectic. I'm tired of beebalm (*Monarda*). I have eight different kinds, but I'm pulling most of them out because they don't do well for me. The only one that I've had luck with is a purple form—and it hasn't flowered yet.

This is one of the best ajugas for the sun. It's called 'Catlin's Giant'. I've had 'Metallica Crispa', and 'Burgundy Glow', and neither worked well in the sun. This, though, has spread from just a little piece, and even though I'm not much of a groundcover person, I think it looks great. It has a bigger leaf and more purple color than most of the others and as long as you water it, it will hold up in the sun.

These are my "disease-free" roses 'Carefree Wonder' and 'Carefree Beauty', which I just cut back because they had a phenomenal amount of black spot on them. What may be disease free in New England isn't necessarily going to be disease free here.

This is a double pink form of *Prunus mume*, Japanese apricot, which flowers in January and February. The leaves don't hang down and look drought stressed like so many of the others. It is robust and just beautiful.

This is one of my favorites—bottle-brush buckeye, *Aesculus parviflora.* I can never get enough of this plant. Both the summer and fall foliage are great. It has flowers about eighteen inches long, which open all at once in June, making it look like a big white bottlebrush.

This holly, *Ilex vomitoria* 'Katherine' is one I named for our oldest daughter. It's a yellow fruiting form, which is beautiful, and the birds don't bother the yellow berries as much as they do the red. They'll only eat them when the red berries are all gone. It's an incredibly adaptable plant. I planted it almost on bedrock, digging as far as I could with my pick, then put it upright, and mounded soil around it. Obviously, it looks great now, so it must be pretty hard to kill.

This has become a little trial area. I have butterfly bushes and bottlebrush buckeyes popping up everywhere. I also grow a lot of Japanese and Siberian iris from seed in this bed. We'll try just about anything here, and if it pans out, we'll move it out into the garden. I think every garden needs a little test or nursery area. Otherwise, you put plants in, and if they die, you get discouraged.

LCM: I know that people from all over send you plants to test for our region. Have you met some interesting people through your work?

MICHAEL: I've been fortunate through the years to have interacted with some of the greats in the horticultural world, such as J.C. McDaniel, a former professor at the University of Illinois. He was originally from Alabama and was a complete iconoclast. He never taught a class, but the guy was brilliant when it came to plants. He bred many, many great plants.

It's the memories that go with the plants that makes them really special. I think a lot of people become emotionally attached, not just to the plant, but also to the thought of who and where it came from.

LCM: You seem to have many different kinds of growing conditions here in the garden, from full sun to full shade. Do you test for sun or shade tolerance for some of these plants?

MICHAEL: We try to work with the microclimates we have here in the garden. You don't fight nature, you just learn to work with it. Here in the shade of the oaks we have *Fothergilla major* 'Mt. Airy'. Planting in this much shade is causing the plant to stretch a bit, and flowering is not as good, but the fall color is magnificent. When grown in full sun, the plant is much more compact, but it's very adaptable. I've seen this growing in both the North and the South, and I've read that they even grow it in Iowa.

We have several anise trees hiding in the shadows. This is Florida anise tree, *Illicium floridanum*; these are *I. anisatum*, Japanese anise tree, with dark glossy green leaves and creamy flowers; and *I. parviflorum*, small anise tree, which has a really strong smell.

Illicium henryi, is one of the greats. It has a rose-pink flower, and though it's not well known yet, it will be. I suggest that people use *Illiciums* instead of trying to grow rhododendrons in heavy, wet soils. These have rhododendron type foliage with a pink flower. They actually grow in the swamps, so they can take the wet soils better.

Hydrangea quercifolia 'Peewee' is a compact form that everyone is trying to get their hands on. This will be a big seller in the trade.

LCM: What do you do about spraying for bugs, or feeding the plants?

MICHAEL: I don't spray, I really don't. I buy the cheapest fertilizer I can get, something like 10-10-10, and I sort of eyeball it, because I don't take the time to measure it out. But I don't put out too much. I think the garden is a place where you don't necessarily want everything to grow ninety miles an hour. Rather than pushing a plant with excessive fertilizer, I try to simply maintain it in good visual condition. Anything more necessitates additional pruning and work.

I think that the balance of nature applies to the garden. There are butter-flies and bees in this garden, but there are also things that are chewing on the plants, and they should live in peaceful coexistence. For the most part, our garden stays pretty clean. If you have an equilibrium where there is not a dominance of one kind of pest, then I think the best advice is live and let live—for garden-making as well as in life.

LCM: What are some other favorite woody plants?

MICHAEL: We pruned back crape myrtle 'Nachez' to get the multistem character that is so beautiful in winter. I don't care if it ever flowers; I just love the cinnamon brown, exfoliating bark.

The new *Clethras*, or sweet pepperbush, are great. Some of the best are 'Fern Valley Pink', 'Hokie Pink', and a new one called 'Ruby Spice', which is a deep pink. They are attractive, put out fragrant flowers from July into August for about six weeks, and have lovely yellow fall color.

This is an unusual tree from China, *Heptocodium miconioides*, seven-son flower. The white flowers aren't spectacular, but the rose-colored sepals, which hang on until fall, are beautiful. The yellow-green fall foliage persists late, and the new leaves come out early in spring, about the time the fothergillas begin to flower.

The little shrub, yellowrim or *Serissa foetida,* is evergreen and very hardy. In Athens, it has gone through −3 degree F. temperatures. It has little white flowers in May and looks spectacular in the shade. It has nice texture, and if you have an herb garden, you can use this as a little hedge. It'll prune up and be a terrific plant. It's not well known, but is something to think about.

Another plant group that is going to be hot is the new cultivars of *Loropetalum chinense* var. *rubrum*. There are currently nine or ten different cultivars, including 'Fire Dance' and a new one introduced by Hines Nursery called 'Plum Delight'™. Even in the heat, it's phenomenal.

LCM: How tall will the *Loropetalums* get?

MICHAEL: No one knows, because we just haven't been growing them long enough to find out. They came in from China in about 1989.

A new one, called 'Zhuzhou Fuchsia', is actually used as a street shrub in China, and it's terrific. 'Ruby' has a more compact growth habit, with good ruby-red foliage. This is 'Blush', which leaf out bronze and then ages to a dark olive green. I see *Loropetalums* as replacements for nandina. They're heat and drought tolerant and insect resistant.

One of my favorite plants is *Stewartia monadelpha*, which is the most tolerant stewartia for the area. The flaky, exfoliating, brown bark is great.

LCM: What do you recommend for sunny areas?

MICHAEL: I have a whole collection of baptisias and even though they don't look great now, they were spectacular earlier.

Another thing about gardening is that you've got to be willing to accept that some things aren't going to look good all times during the year. Ideally, I would recommend designing beds or portions of the garden for specific groups of plants.

We have this meatball idea that if you plant cherry laurel and hollies, and stick a crape myrtle in between, that's a garden. That's not a garden. This is a garden! It has flavor and spice and seasonality and fragrance and color. This bed looks terrific in April and May and then it starts going down hill. There's not much I can do about it, but that's okay.

This is one of the Georgia Gold Medal Award winners, *Lantana* 'New Gold'. The butterflies just flock to it. *Lantana* 'Ms. Huff', which is fairly tolerant to cold is proving to be one of the great landscape plants for the South.

LCM: You've obviously had tremendous influence in the gardening community all over the United States, but particularly in this region. Why do you think gardening is so popular in the South now?

❧

I like to have a series of garden rooms. You don't want everything exposed to view when you first walk into the space. You frame it, or have something behind a fence so that you have pocket gardens and little areas of mystery where you walk from one to another.

❧

MICHAEL: Northerners were always leaders in gardening, but they're not pioneers anymore. We are. One factor that has changed this is the Southern flora. In Georgia alone we're looking at over 3,000 different taxa [species, varieties, and subspecies] native to the state. This native plant bounty is ripe for selection and breeding.

We have so many different climates and plant communities—the southern Appalachian mountains, the Piedmont, and the coastal plain. Many of the plants in this region are waiting to be investigated.

Another thing that has contributed to the popularity of gardening in the South is the influx of gardeners from the North who have moved here and want to continue to garden. Once they arrive, they are turned on to a whole new world of plants such as the broadleaf evergreens and flowering shrubs that you can't grow in many of the northern climates. So, we've opened up their eyes to a whole new cadre of plants.

Everywhere I go people are positive about the profession. I sense that people want to hear about new plants and new products. They want plants that look good in every season, and something that gives them a jump up on their neighbor's garden. They want what's new and hot. Robert King, the principal buyer for Pikes Family Nurseries in Atlanta, says that eighty percent of their customers want new items. The state-of-the-art customer doesn't ask what's old, they want to know what's new.

People are looking to North Carolina State University and the University of Georgia for leadership in plant material introductions. We don't find everything ourselves. We're more akin to evaluators, middlemen, and marketers. The red lorapetalums are a good example. They are magnificent plants that came from China; we got them to some of the growers, and now it's a multi-million dollar seller. Why? Because it's new, user-friendly, and has been easy for the nursery industry to propagate and produce.

LCM: You really seem to enjoy your garden. What is it about gardening that attracts you?

MICHAEL: Part of the fun of gardening is anticipating what's going to happen, whether you're planting a vegetable seed

or looking at a new shrub. I'm always trying to answer the questions, "What's the future going to hold for my garden? How is it going to look different?" You have to get out there and just play with plants. We'll put a plant in, and if we don't like it, we'll dig it up and throw it away. Our garden is never staid and traditional.

JEFF AND LISA BEASLEY, LAVONIA: TRANSPLANT NURSERY

Childhood sweethearts Jeff and Lisa Beasley have combined forces, not only to create a home and family, but to make a thriving business out of a mutual love of plants and growing things. Rhododendrons, evergreen and native azaleas, and other woody shrubs from their Transplant Nursery find their way to gardens throughout the Southeast.

When they first began growing these woody ornamentals, Jeff and Lisa were frustrated by their lack of success with many plants brought from the West Coast. They built up the small nursery, which Jeff's father had started many years earlier, and decided to offer unusual plants to the Southern homeowner. In addition to the camellias, azaleas, and rhododendrons that George Beasley, Jeff's father, had loved so dearly, Jeff and Lisa also offer such treasures as *Kalmia*, *Fothergilla*, deciduous hollies, unusual *Hydrangeas*, *Viburnums*, *Loropetalums*, and whatever is new, exciting, and easy to grow in Georgia gardens.

I walked through the nursery with Jeff and Lisa in late October, when the plants were settling in for a long winter's nap and the incredibly beautiful blossoms of which they spoke were but a dream that only spring could make a reality. Although keeping a nursery running and thriving is constant and often difficult work, Lisa and Jeff's passion for their work came through in every word they spoke.

LCM: How did you get into gardening, and how did Transplant Nursery come about?

JEFF: I grew up gardening here on this property. Lisa was born and raised in Red Hill, which is about eleven miles from here. This is my childhood home: mother's house is right across the fence.

Daddy started growing camellias and loved to show them. Certain camellia species aren't hardy here, so he had glass frame houses built and grew them just for his own pleasure. I can remember going down and cutting blooms for anyone who came. We always kept a good stand of chickweed on the floor of the greenhouse to pull and put in the boxes. Daddy would cut the blooms, and I would fill the boxes up with chickweed and send beautiful blossoms home with people.

Then he became interested in rhododendrons and native azaleas. He was an avid trout fisherman and had always spent time in the woods. That's where he fell in love with native plants.

Lisa and I both studied horticulture at North Georgia Tech, and began seriously expanding the nursery in 1982, though I think we really started defining our focus in 1988.

LCM: What is your focus?

JEFF: We want to make available to the gardener evergreen and native azaleas and rhododendrons, which are difficult to find in the trade.

The key is to test and evaluate them. It doesn't matter how well things grow here if they don't live in someone else's garden. We want to make plants available that will live and grow, and offer them to the customer at a price they can afford. That's what being in the nursery business is all about.

LCM: Do you have a favorite plant?

LISA: If I had my choice, I would just grow native azaleas. But I can't make a living that way because we can only sell so many native azaleas per year.

LCM: What is it about the native azaleas that you love?

LISA: I think I like them because they are so beautiful and yet so tough.

JEFF: Can you name me another group of woody ornamentals that start blooming before the last frost in spring and go all the way to frost in the fall? Fourteen of the sixteen deciduous azaleas that we sell are native to the South, and all are native to the United States. The reason they grow so well is because they occur here naturally.

LCM: Where do you find new species to introduce to the trade?

JEFF: We sometimes take cuttings from wild species, although any time we find plants in the woods, we're very careful not to destroy or deface that plant. If it is on National Forest land or state land we get a permit to take cuttings. We do not remove plants from the wild, although a lot of people do that. It's only hurting generations down the road.

LISA: We try to find the best species, although sometimes the "best" might not always be the best one to grow for commercial use because it may be difficult to propagate and grow. However, we look every year to see what's good.

JEFF: I think our main job is to produce plants that will grow in people's gardens. I love yellow rhododendron, but I can't get it to live here. They come from the West Coast.

LCM: Is the West Coast a good source of plants for you?

JEFF: Growers on the West Coast do a lot of work with rhododendrons, but they have a totally different climate than we do, and that makes a big difference. There's an old saying, "A plant starts dying when it crosses the Mississippi River," which originated because people have a lot of trouble with West Coast rhododendrons. There's nothing wrong with their plant material, and there's nothing wrong with the way they grow it, but they're in a different climate. The plants don't have to work as hard to live on the West Coast as they do here. For example, the transpiration rate is greater here because of our heat and humidity.

LISA: We're right at the edge of the Georgia foothills. We get extreme heat at times and sudden, extreme temperature changes.

JEFF: That's why so many West Coast varieties won't do well here.

LCM: So the West Coast may have the same range of temperatures, but the change is not as drastic, and the climate is not as difficult?

JEFF: Well, think about it. Their heat comes during a dry period, so they don't have the heat and the humidity at the same time like we do. They don't have to deal with our soils, either.

LISA: On the West Coast, they can grow rhodies out in the full sun, which we cannot do.

JEFF: They can have a bigger top on a plant with less root, and that's fine out there. But when you try to place the same size plant here, you'll have trouble because we lose moisture at a faster rate. That's why in the past, rhododendrons have received a bad name, because they're grown on the West Coast, many of them die [when transported here].

People buy plants from us, and six months later they come back and say, "I can't believe it. They're still alive." The fact that they are Georgia-grown plants is important.

LCM: Do you feel that part of your job is educating the public about these plants?

JEFF: It's a continuous battle. Educating people about gardening is sort of like being a Christian. You can talk about it, or you can do it. It's best just to do it. We try to lead by example.

LCM: Could you walk me through the sequence of bloom for the evergreen and native azaleas?

LISA: Starting in the end of March, the evergreen azaleas 'Dayspring', 'Festive', and 'Mike Bullard' are the first. By the first of April, the native azaleas *Rhododendron canescens, R. periclymenoides,* and *R. vaseyi* begin to bloom, and then the Kurume azaleas 'Coral Bells', 'Hino', and 'Snow'.

During the second week of April, 'Margaret Douglas' and 'Martha Hitchcock', and then the Harris hybrids will bloom.

The first of May the Robin Hill azaleas and the early rhododendrons will bloom, followed by more rhododendrons. Native azaleas that bloom during early summer include *R. calendulaceum*. In June, the Dexters [rhododendrons], the Satsukis, and later blooming native azaleas such as *R. arborescens* and *R. viscosum* will begin.

We offer a group of plants that are groundcover azaleas called the North Tisbury azaleas. These bloom in late May or early June.

R. serrulatum is the last native azalea to bloom, from August into September. With good planning, you can have bloom from late March into September.

LCM: Are there any shrubs that you sell that can't be grown in other parts of the state?

JEFF: We don't recommend most of the rhododendrons south of Macon. There are people who grow them—we even have customers who grow them in Florida—but they pamper them and really have to work at it. Azaleas will do fine in south Georgia—natives as well as evergreen.

LCM: What are some common mistakes you see people make with these plants?

JEFF: With rhododendrons, planting too deep is the most common mistake. In Georgia, the correct planting depth is completely *above* the ground.

To plant a bed of rhododendrons, till the ground to a depth of ten inches, or as deep as you can, then put on a four-inch layer of aged bark. Make sure that whatever you put on does not have lime in it, because these plants like an acidic soil with a low pH.

Till the bark in, put four more inches on, and plow that in. Then plant the plants with your hands. Plant the root crown level or slightly elevated. That kind of bed needs a lot of water. We don't rec-

ommend any fertilization for the first six weeks, for the beds need to settle a bit.

If you plant rhododendrons [singly], take a wheelbarrow and a shovel and dig a hole about three times as wide and as deep as the plant's container. If it's decent soil save it; if it's packed red clay, throw it away. Estimate the volume of soil in the wheelbarrow. Add equal amounts of bark and mix it well. [Use this to] fill the hole back up, but don't pack it or stomp it.

☙

Can you name me another group of woody ornamentals that start blooming before the last frost in spring and go all the way to frost in the fall? Fourteen of the sixteen native azaleas that we sell are native to the South, and all are native to the United States. The reason they grow so well is because they're here naturally.

☙

Take the plant out of the container, tickle the roots, and set it right on top of the dirt in the hole. It will be setting right up on top of the ground. Keep adding bark, mixing it with the remaining soil, and mounding it around the plant. Remember that you have soft fill dirt in this hole. When all that settles, the plant will be at the right depth.

When you're mounding the dirt, don't make a cone shape. If you do, the soil will settle more than the root ball; the root ball will protrude and act just like a wick—you won't be able to keep it wet.

In about three years, the plant will have had a chance to put out a good root system and will be well-established. The roots of rhododendrons are close to the surface, so using a groundcover sometimes helps keep roots cool.

LCM: How about fertilization?

JEFF: We recommend a slow release fertilizer like Osmacote™ or 18-6-12. Wait until after the plants bloom, before you fertilize them. Or, in spring, wait until all danger of frost has passed. Here, we consider May 1 the last frost date.

LCM: How about pruning?

JEFF: The best time to prune rhododendrons is when they're young. You might have to sacrifice a bloom or two early on to build a good foundation, but it's worth it in the long run.

❦

The most common mistake with rhododendrons is planting them too deep. Rhododendrons are really particular about good drainage.

❦

If the plant does get out of hand, selectively prune out bigger limbs after they bloom, but don't try to take them all out at the same time. These plants set their bloom buds on mature wood, not on new wood like a crape myrtle. Rhododendrons are difficult to prune. You can sheer azaleas any way you want—native azaleas respond really well to pruning—but you have to be careful with rhododendrons.

LISA: For the early evergreen azaleas, my cut-off date for pruning is July 1. We

try to do all the cuttings during the month of June. The best time to prune azaleas or rhododendrons is right after they bloom.

LCM: How about water and light requirements?

JEFF: Most of the plants we grow have the same cultural requirements. You need to water heavily, but only when they need it. Dig down and feel around the roots; if it's dry, then water them again. Watering just a little bit and never saturating them won't do any good.

Our nursery will never be on automatic irrigation; we have to come out and see what's happening. Watering depends on so many things: how hot the sun is, if we've had rain or mist that day, or if the wind is blowing, which dries out the plants more quickly than anything else.

LISA: We've had some really dry winters. People call and ask what's wrong with their "rhodies" and Jeff will ask, "Have you thought to water this winter?" The azaleas are usually okay, but the rhododendrons need that extra water.

JEFF: As for light, these plants will grow just fine in the shade, but they won't set buds as well. I always tell people that you can give these plants as much light as possible, but they need to be kept out of the hot afternoon sun. That sun from about 3:00 P.M. is tough on them.

LISA: We find that with the early blooming azaleas, those that bloom until the first of May can go in full sun. Those that bloom after May need shade, because the sun is so hot, the blooms won't last.

LCM: Are there any native evergreen azaleas?

LISA: Most species of evergreen azaleas are from Japan. The sixteen species of azaleas native to the United States are deciduous.

LCM: Any other bit of advice?

JEFF: When you start gardening with azaleas and rhododendrons, stay with varieties that are tried and true for the South. Read as much as possible, and try to learn the specific needs of the plants.

LCM: What do you like best about what you do?

JEFF: One of the best things is the people we meet. We belong to the American Rhododendron Society and go to the meetings, not only to learn things, but to see the people. It's the people you meet and the friendships you cultivate that makes it all worthwhile. People open up to you and offer so much knowledge and friendship. If you're willing to try, and you show some interest, these people will bend over backwards to help you.

ELIZABETH DEAN AND GENE GRIFFITH, PALMETTO: WILKERSON MILL GARDENS

What are an ex-lawyer and a former college art major doing running a nursery? In the case of Gene Griffith and Elizabeth Dean, they're making magic at Wilkerson Mill Gardens, their retail nursery located just thirty-five minutes south of Atlanta.

❦

The more you garden, the less important blossoms become. What you really look for is interesting foliage.

❦

In 1983 this husband and wife team fell in love with, and subsequently bought, thirty acres of land near Palmetto. "The nursery came about as a vehicle to allow us to garden thirty acres," Elizabeth says. "I was tired of trying to garden on a third of an acre in Atlanta and I wanted more land. When we bought the Mill property, we realized that we could never "own" a site this special, we could only act as stewards of this land. We thought about all kinds of ways of working with the land, and growing woody plants seemed to make the most sense."

Their original plan was to grow trees and shrubs as a source of cut flower material, but it quickly became apparent that it would take fifteen to twenty years of maturation for a cut flower farm of woody plants to provide enough income to make a difference. Gradually, Elizabeth and Gene shifted their energies to propagating and selling a wonderful variety of hard-to-find trees and shrubs. In doing so, they began to influence gardeners and their gardens throughout the Southeast.

Today Wilkerson Mill Gardens offers a variety of plant material including small trees, distinctive shrubs, and unusual groundcovers and vines.

LCM: The grounds here at Wilkerson Mill Gardens are filled with some of the most beautiful woody plant material I've ever seen. In spite of your obvious expertise, neither of you had formal training in horticulture. Is that right?

GENE: That is true. Had we known more about plants and the nursery business, we probably would have had serious doubts that we could ever start a nursery from scratch and hope to make a living at it. In this case, ignorance was a blessing that allowed us to risk changing the focus of our lives to growing plants. Now we love it.

❦

I believe that there's magic in the world. But I believe that you have to go to the magic. It just doesn't happen when you're sitting at your desk. You have to go out to find it.

❦

Like all ventures, we've learned from both our mistakes and successes. We've tried to spend more time finding answers to the problems in front of us, rather than worrying about the ones behind us.

ELIZABETH: It's exciting to be so engaged with something and to have so many challenges, and it's wonderful to have to be learning so much all the time.

This land deeply moves us, and we like to think that we can share some of our wonder with other people. They come out here and will hopefully trip across a little something outside of their regular world. We are working hard to landscape the property so that people can see what these plants look like in a garden setting.

We're fortunate that we have so many different microclimates and mini-environments that can landscape. The old mill building is still here under those huge, spreading white oak trees and this gives us an area of deciduous shade. Paths along the creek and through the woods are planted as naturalized areas. Closer to the house, where we have full sun, we've included a more formal garden area with views out to the "flower orchard."

GENE: We believe that display areas are important so people can see these plants in the ground. For us, the emphasis is always on the plants, for we are not a garden store, we are a nursery and we grow plants.

ELIZABETH: The concept of growing is essential to what we are about. We are growers of plants, and growers of beauty. I believe that there's magic in the world, but you don't often find it sitting at your desk. You have to go to where the magic happens, which for me is outdoors. We hope to share this magic with others through our plants and through the site itself. Our goal is to help Southern gardeners learn that there are three seasons besides spring, and each has magic in it.

GENE: Most people buy plants in spring and end up purchasing whatever is in bloom. This results in a lack of diversity in our gardens. The kinds of plants we're interested in are the ones that can bloom through the summer, or look good in fall or even the dead of winter. We encourage people to think ahead, which is particularly important with shrubs and trees.

ELIZABETH: We're all limited in our view of what woody plants are. Too often we think of them as foundation plants, and we don't have a good idea of how to use them.

GENE: We encourage people to use trees and shrubs, not only for their beauty, but because they take less time and maintenance in the garden.

ELIZABETH: People often ask how to reduce the size of their lawn, or how to cut back on intensive labor. We suggest ways of using shrubs and groundcovers in place of grass. They still take some work, but then what's the point of gardening if you don't want to garden?

When I garden, I want the most effect for the time I have to put into it. And the best way I know how to do this is to use shrub material. Woody plants take up more space than annuals and perennials and they offer good texture.

GENE: We suggest that people put in a small tree here or there to create shade for the plants underneath. Or we tell them to use shrubs or a grouping of shrubs to go behind perennials, annuals, and bulbs, to really make it a mixed border.

LCM: What mistakes do you see people making?

GENE: Educating the public is sometimes a long process. People want instant gratification. They want full-sized shrubs, but then they begin to realize some of the problems involved. First, they realize that they don't have a vehicle big enough to carry a full-grown tree, and then they realize that these plants don't come with holes already dug—and big plants need big holes.

SHRUBS AND TREES

Purple smoketree *Cotinus coggygria* 'Velvet Cloak', part shade to sun

Grancy gray-beard *Chionanthus virginicus,* part shade to sun

Japanese barberry *Berberis thunbergii* 'Royal Cloak', full sun

Lilac daphne *Daphne genkwa,* full sun

Spiraea *Spiraea* × *bumalda* 'Froebelii', 'Limemound', sun to part shade

Beautyberry *Callicarpa americana,* part shade

Clethra *Clethra alnifolia,* full sun to part shade

Fothergilla *Fothergilla gardenii,* full sun to part shade

Hydrangea *Hydrangea paniculata,* full sun

Hydrangea *Hydrangea macrophylla* and *H. quercifolia,* part shade

Winterberry (deciduous holly) *Ilex verticillata,* full sun to part shade

Florida anise-tree *Illicium floridanum,* full shade

Florida leucothoe *Leucothoe populifolia,* full shade

Japanese pieris *Pieris japonica,* full shade

Leatherleaf mahonia *Mahonia bealei,* full shade

Sweet box *Sarcococca confusa,* full shade

People love the way a well-established garden looks, but they don't like to admit that it takes a long time to achieve that look. We suggest that they take plants in one-gallon containers, put them in with good spacing to allow the roots to grow, and let them get established.

LCM: What kinds of plants do you recommend for beginner gardeners?

ELIZABETH: We like plants that have multiple seasons of interest. The more you garden, the less important the blossoms become. What you really look for is interesting foliage.

There are several plants that I used to look down my nose at because I thought they were too common—plants like nandina, spiraea, and mahonia—but now I think they're just incredible plants because they have such great foliage. Mahonia is one of the handsomest plants around. It's wonderful how you get new eyes as you go into this.

Another one that I've grown to love is Japanese barberry, (*Berberis thungergii*). It's tough and adaptable, and will grow in any soils except really soggy ones. The cultivar 'Royal Cloak' grows to about six feet tall and has deep purple-red leaves and gracefully arching branches. It's a wonderful color foil in the garden, looking rather like a small purple smoke tree.

Some of my favorites are not very well known, such as sweet box, *Sarcococca hookerana humilis*. This small evergreen groundcover only grows eighteen to twenty-four inches tall and produces blooms in February that smell like heaven. It's a great filler in deep shade and is particularly nice near a path or doorway. The shrub form grows three to four feet. Both the shrub and the low-growing form produce berries which turn a deep blue-black color, making this plant attractive during much of the year. It likes a shady spot with moist, acidic soil.

There's a redbud cultivar, 'Forest Pansy', which has pink flowers in early spring, followed by red-toned leaves. As it

gets hot in summer, the leaves turn green with only flushes of red on new growth. It grows well in full sun or partial shade, but it tends to keep the red color better in the shade.

LCM: What are some of your other favorite vines and groundcovers?

ELIZABETH: *Acorus*, which looks almost like a grass, and American pachysandra or Allegheny spurge, *Pachysandra procumbens*. Also a little vinca, 'Gertrude Jekyll', which has a beautiful little white flower.

Another of my favorite groundcovers is autumn leadwort, *Ceratostigma plumbaginoides*. It is a perennial with beautiful blue flowers late in the growing season. As the weather cools in the fall, the foliage turns red.

As for vines, *Clematis armandii* is a wonderful evergreen shade plant, and I'm hot for a collection of noninvasive honeysuckles we're trying out. And climbing hydrangeas. Hydrangeas have become a "thing" for us. We offer many different varieties, including the native oak-leaf *Hydrangea quercifolia*, as well as the more familiar big leaf forms, both mopheads and lacecaps. We also have a variety of *H. paniculata* for full sun.

LCM: Can you tell me a little bit about growing hydrangeas?

GENE: *Hydrangea macrophyllas* need part shade and adequate moisture. They're not shy about letting you know when they need water: the big leaves wilt and droop when the plants get thirsty.

We suggest pruning these hydrangeas by cutting out the old, woody canes and dead wood in early spring. Flowers are produced on growth from the previous year, so know that if you shorten the stems or cut the entire plant back, you'll be cutting off flowers for that season.

We also recommend that you do not feed hydrangeas during summer months. The soft new growth is slow to harden off and can be easily damaged by early cold weather.

LCM: Why do you think you enjoy working with plants so much?

ELIZABETH: Because it is very life-affirming and life-confirming. When I walk into the propagation hut, I know it is filled with a life force, which is transforming sticks into new plants. It is thrilling. We know it is magic.

BETTY HOTCHKISS, FORT VALLEY: AMERICAN CAMELLIA SOCIETY

Betty Hotchkiss is a woman supremely suited for her job. Originally from the little town of Attapulgus in south Georgia, this soft spoken, pretty lady with a perfect Southern drawl is now queen of that quintessential Southern plant, the camellia.

Betty comes from generations of gardeners, as both her parents and grandmother loved growing things. "I grew up on a farm. I think many people who work with gardening today had farming or gardening parents. My mother was a teacher and while she enjoyed growing flowers, it was really not a big deal for her."

Not so her daughter, who received a Master's Degree in plant pathology from Clemson University. In 1983, Betty became the first full time horticulturist for the American Camellia Society, a job which she still enjoys. "Since I was the first person to have this job, I have been able to develop it to fit my skills. I primarily work with the gardens here at Massee Lane, do some educational programs, and a little research."

LCM: Of all the plants in the world, why do you think you chose to work with camellias?

BETTY: I think a lot of it had to do with luck in getting this job with the Camellia Society, and then I stayed with it because I enjoy it.

LCM: What can you tell me about the American Camellia Society?

BETTY: In 1995 we celebrated the fiftieth anniversary of the founding of the Society. At first the headquarters were located at the University of Florida, and then they moved to Tifton, Georgia. We were always in a borrowed space, and we wanted permanent home. Finally, in 1968, we moved to Fort Valley and built the permanent headquarters building.

The grounds at Fort Valley were originally a private garden, which was donated by one of the founding members of the Society, Dave Strother, who owned the Fort Valley Oil Company. Even after he built the gardens, he never lived here, but used the property as a farm. He did have a caretaker on the property, and the gardens, which were well known to camellia people, were eventually opened to the public. In that era, people would drive out on Sunday afternoons just to walk around and see the gardens.

WHAT TO LOOK FOR IN A NURSERY-GROWN PLANT

✧ Good, healthy foliage—not too light, which indicates too much sunshine or lack of nutrients.

✧ Smooth stems without disease cankers.

✧ White roots. Brown roots are caused by root rot.

Mr. Strother did not marry, and had no children, so when he died, he left the farm to the Camellia Society. He donated ten acres of gardens and 160 acres of farmland, which was to be left as a buffer for the formal garden. In addition, he gave money for the founding of a head-quarters building.

LCM: What is on the property now?

BETTY: We have a wonderful head-quarters building and ten acres of fairly formal gardens—primarily camellias. We also have a large educational museum, built in 1989. The gardens are still plant-ed in basically the same design used by Mr. Strother, with straight brick walks and pine trees planted for shading the camellias.

LCM: Have the gardens changed much since Strother's time?

BETTY: Yes, but mostly through no fault of our own. In December 1983 and January 1985, we suffered from the worst freezes in many years. Everything froze, and it looked as if someone had taken a blowtorch to the garden. There were no green leaves. Some of the camellias were totally killed; others came back from the roots.

Some of the shrubs that we cut back had a [trunk] diameter of twelve inches or more. For months, we pruned with chain saws. Mr. Strother never had a planting list or an inventory for the original gar-den, so we don't know exactly what we lost.

LCM: What do you do with the camellias when you have a cold like that?

BETTY: Hopefully, it was a once in a lifetime experience. At the time we thought it best to cut the shrubs partially back. Now we recommend cutting the shrubs low to the ground. The roots are pretty tough.

Before you cut, you need to know if the plant is grafted, or on its own roots. If it's grafted, you can't cut below the graft-ing point. If it's on its own roots, you can cut back farther.

LCM: Camellias are considered an old-fashioned plant, aren't they?

BETTY: Yes. Camellias are ancient flowers. The Chinese used *Camellia sinensis*, the tea plant, back in 500 B.C. Their use as an ornamental plant is much more recent—the early eighteenth centu-ry. It wasn't until the early nineteenth century that camellia collections in the South came into popularity.

Camellias have historically been a man's flower, and the Society was found-ed mostly by men. I think that some types of gardening have been more social-ly acceptable for men than others, and this is one of them.

Many of the men were wealthy. These were doctors and professional people who wanted to do some gardening for relaxation. They also seemed to enjoy the social aspects; camellia shows were a big part of the social scene.

Even today, people join the Society not only to learn more about camellias, but also because of the people they meet and the shows. There are currently over sixty shows a year. It's nothing for a judge to travel six hundred miles to participate in a show.

LCM: Are there still more men involved than women?

BETTY: There are still a lot of men, but now there are probably just as many women. I only know of one men's-only chapter, in Opelika, Alabama.

LCM: How many members are in the Camellia Society now?

BETTY: Nationwide, we probably have between 4,000 and 5,000 members.

LCM: Are camellias grown only in the South?

BETTY: Basically, you can grow camellias along any coast, Gulf, East or West. Inland, it's too cold. If temperatures regularly drop below ten degrees, you shouldn't try to grow camellias.

In some of the western states, the climate is too dry. Camellias like warm temperatures and high humidity. They never go completely dormant.

LCM: Can you grow camellias throughout the state of Georgia?

BETTY: You'll run into problems in the north Georgia mountains. Really, anywhere north of Atlanta is marginal. But researchers are working on cold hardy varieties. During the 1970s, Washington, D.C. experienced a series of cold winters that essentially wiped out all the camel-

lias at the National Arboretum except for one species, *Camellia olifera.*

A breeder took that plant and developed other cultivars. Among these new hybrids were some fall-blooming *C. sasanqua* hybrids and some spring-blooming *C. japonica* hybrids that can be grown to zone 6.

Another hybridizer from Chapel Hill, North Carolina, has been to China on numerous occasions and found *Camellia japonicas* growing in naturally cold habitats, such as mountaintops. He worked at hybridizing these and developed some varieties that are good for many North Carolina areas.

LCM: What is the southern range for camellias?

BETTY: Probably central Florida. Camellias are not tropical plants, but temperate ones. In south Florida, the heat may be a limiting factor. If it is 80 degrees when the flowers bloom, they won't last. They really hold up much better when it's cooler. Also the alkalinity of the soils in Florida are not conducive to good growth. Camellias like acidic soils. The collection at Bok Tower Gardens in Lake Wales, Florida is probably the most southern collection of camellias. Camellias really are plants well suited for the south Georgia climate.

LCM: What is the blooming season?

BETTY: Out of the 3,000 varieties to choose from, you can have series of blooms from September to April, depending on where you live. For this part of the state [just south of Macon] the main blooming season is November to March, with the peak in late January to early February.

LCM: What is ideal weather for these plants?

BETTY: Cool weather, but not much below freezing.

LCM: At the gardens at Massee Lane, did Dave Strother plant according to group or bloom type?

BETTY: He planted according to *whim.* He was a man who always wanted the finest of everything, and this included camellias. He wanted to plant the latest and best varieties and was known to travel hundreds of miles to get the newest varieties.

And although I love new varieties, I haven't followed this same principle. I think what we need to do is preserve some of the older historical varieties, but also have on display as many of the newer ones as we can.

❦

A big drawback to growing camellias is that they're very slow growing. You have to have a lot of patience to establish and nurture them until they are large enough to reward you with the beautiful blooms.

❦

When people think about camellias, mostly they think of *Camellia japonica*, which is still the standard, even though many hybrids have been introduced.

LCM: Are all species from the Orient?

BETTY: Every camellia is from the Orient. The closest relatives are *Stewartia, Gordonia*, and *Franklinia*, which are native to North America.

LCM: What do you recommend as companion plants to the camellias?

BETTY: In its native habitat, as a mature plant, camellias are small trees getting up to twenty to thirty feet in height, so you have to consider carefully how you want to include them in the landscape.

Most people keep their camellias pruned as a large shrub, from five to eight feet tall. Combined with azaleas or rhododendrons, camellias make good background plants. Their growth habits and cultural needs are similar. They all prefer shade and slightly acid soil.

Although camellias form a deep root, the majority of the roots tend to be close to the surface, so people don't use a lot of groundcovers around them. I've read that if nothing is planted over them, the roots can get more oxygen.

LCM: Should you mulch?

BETTY: Yes. We recommend two to four inches of something like pinestraw mulch because it helps moderate temperature extremes and conserves moisture.

LCM: How do you choose a good camellia from a nursery, plant, and maintain it?

BETTY: Before you buy a plant, select a location. Make sure you have shade, preferably filtered shade from pine trees or a building. If you use it as a foundation plant, remember that it will get large, so don't put it in front of a window where it would block the view. North and west exposures are best as they avoid the early morning sun, which causes the bark to split.

Prepare your hole as you would for any other plant. Dig a hole at least two feet wider than the root ball. We usually amend the soil with finely ground pine bark or compost. Mix this with the dirt and plant so that the root crown is slight-ly above the soil level.

If you are planting several shrubs, it's better to prepare an entire bed rather than plant hole by hole.

Good drainage is important, so don't plant at the bottom of a hill or the foot of a gutter.

LCM: How do you choose the best varieties?

BETTY: Read about the different char-acteristics of the cultivars. There will be some that are more cold hardy, which would be better suited for Atlanta than middle and southern Georgia. Unless it gets really cold—below five to ten degrees—the plants will survive, but you'll lose a lot of bloom.

When you grow camellias, you just have to be ready to live with a little bit of disappointment. Every year is not going to be a good year. You'll almost always have some blooms turn brown from the cold, so just consider the good years as a bonus. The years 1992 to 1995 were really good.

LCM: How long do individual bushes bloom?

BETTY: Many of them have a long period of bloom, from December through February. A mature bush might bloom for several months, but a young plant might not have more than three flower buds.

One of the drawbacks of growing camellias is that they're very slow grow-ing and you have to have a lot of patience to establish and nurture them until they are large enough to reward you with the beautiful blooms.

LCM: What size plants do you recom-mend?

BETTY: You can put in larger plants if you can supply enough moisture. These

---

COLD HARDY CAMELLIAS SUITABLE FOR THE ATLANTA AREA

❖ **Red**
  'Governor Mouton'
  'Mathotiana'
  'Miss Charleston'

❖ **Red and White**
  'Donckelarii'
  'Tricolor'
  'Ville de Nantes'

❖ **Pink**
  'High Hat'
  'Debutante'
  'Pink Perfection'

❖ **Pink and White**
  'China Doll'
  'Daikagura'
  'Mississippi Beauty'

❖ **White**
  'Leucantha'
  'Purity'
  'White Empress'

---

take a lot of water, particularly during hot, dry summer months. Once a camel-lia becomes established, moisture require-ments are not as stringent.

LCM: Can you transplant camellias?

BETTY: Yes, although it's difficult because they form a fibrous root system. It's hard to dig up a really good root ball.

LCM: When do you recommend planting?

BETTY: In the fall. People often want to plant a shrub while it is in bloom, so you can plant in winter, but fall is proba-bly best, especially in north Georgia.

LCM: How do you choose a healthy plant at the nursery?

BETTY: Look for good foliage. Make sure color is not too light, which can indicate too much sunshine or a lack of nutrients. But remember that new growth is a lighter color too, so it depends on what time of year you're looking.

You'll also want to check the stems. Disease causes cankers on stems, so look for smooth stems without cankers.

Pull the plant out off the pot and look at the roots to make sure they're white. Camellias are susceptible to root rot, so you don't want brown roots.

LCM: Will camellias bloom in deep shade?

BETTY: Filtered light is better. With deep shade you'll have fewer flowers.

LCM: How about diseases and blight?

BETTY: You shouldn't have too many problems. Tea scales are often found on the underside of the leaves. These look white and cottony. For this, you need to spray with a lightweight organic oil, which actually smothers the insects.

I highly recommend pruning to thin out older shrubs and allow for a little air circulation, which cuts down on disease problems. It's okay to cut off new growth, if you stop pruning by June. If you prune later in summer, know that you're cutting off next year's flower heads.

As for disease, root rot is often a problem. You can avoid that by planting in areas with good drainage. If the plant has root rot, it will have an overall unhealthy appearance and the leaves will droop. *Camellia sasanquas* are resistant to this disease, so many cultivars are grafted onto a *sasanqua* to avoid it. Grafting is fairly easy, though time consuming. It is a common practice among hobbyists, since it speeds up the propagation practice. Flower blight, dieback, and canker are other serious problems for camellia growers.

As for feeding, we fertilize with 10-10-10 in spring, around the first of March after the plants have flowered. This pushes new growth. We fertilize again at the end of May when flower buds are forming. If the plants are in containers, or in sandy soils, we fertilize more frequently. On established shrubs, I use one tablespoon for every foot of height, which works out to be about a cup for a good size shrub. We put the fertilizer on top of the mulch and let it wash in. If you pull the mulch back, surface roots might get fertilizer burn. I wait until after the first year to fertilize new shrubs.

LCM: Do you think that the popularity of camellias is cyclic?

BETTY: The bad years, when we have deep freezes, really scare people. But they always come back, and now more and more nurseries are carrying camellias again.

LCM: Do you have favorite varieties?

BETTY: I do, but it changes year to year because one year a particular variety will do really well. Some of my favorites are 'Debutante', which is pink; 'Governor Mouton', a red; 'Professor Charles S. Sargent', another red; and 'Betty Sheffield Supreme', which originated in South Georgia. It is beautiful, but it doesn't always hold true to color, and I don't recommend it for people who are easily disappointed.

'Mathotiana' is a good early bloomer, red to crimson. 'Daikagura' is a good pink and white for the Atlanta area. For the Atlanta area and north, we recommend all the early bloomers because they will probably be through blooming by the time really cold weather hits.

C. sasanqua varieties are especially good for fall bloom. They make good landscape plants, sometimes blooming from September through December. You can grow them in full sun or filtered shade.

RESOURCES FOR SHRUBS AND TREES

BOOKS

Camellias for Beginners. American Camellia Society. $2 or free to new members.

Dirr, Michael. *Manual of Woody Landscape Plants: Their Identification, Ornamental Characteristics, Culture, Propagation, and Uses.* Champaign, Illinois: Stipes Publishing Co., 1983.

Foote, Leonard E., and Samuel B. Jones. *Native Shrubs and Woody Vines of the Southeast: Landscaping Uses and Identification.* Portland, Oregon: Timber Press, 1989.

Gallee, Fred. *Azaleas.* Portland, Oregon: Timber Press, 1987.

Macoboy, Sterling. *The Colour Dictionary of Camellias.* 1985. Available through American Camellia Society.

PERIODICALS

American Rhododendron Society Journal
P.O. Box 1380
Gloucester, VA 23061
Fact Sheets from American Camellia Society

SOCIETIES

American Camellia Society
One Massee Lane
Fort Valley, GA 31030
912-967-2722

American Rhododendron Society
Mrs. Barbara Hall, Secretary
P.O. Box 1380
Gloucester, VA 23061
804-693-4433

Azalea Society of America
Ralph T. Bullard, Jr.
6159 Ridge Way
Douglasville, GA 30135
404-949-0494

Middle Georgia Camellia Society
Grady Stokes
P.O. Box 79
Marshallville, GA 31057

North Georgia Camellia Society
John Newsome
2405 Howell Mill Road, N.W.
Atlanta, GA 30318

Valdosta Camellia Society
Buford McRae
2212 Briarcliff Drive
Valdosta, GA 31601

DISPLAY GARDENS

Atlanta Botanical Garden, Atlanta
404-876-5858

Barnsley Gardens, Adairsville
770-773-7480

Hamilton Rhododendron Garden, Hiawasee
706-896-4191

Homeplace Garden, Commerce
706-335-2892

Massee Lane Gardens, Fort Valley
912-967-2358

Transplant Nursery, Lavonia
706-356-8947

Wilkerson Mill Gardens, Jonesboro
770-463-9717

PLANT SOURCES

Gerbing's Camellia Growers
7098 Old Nichols Highway
Millwood, GA 31552
912-283-1590

Homeplace Garden Nursery
P.O. Box 300
Commerce, GA 30529
706-335-2892

Massee Lane Gardens
One Massee Lane
Fort Valley, GA 31030
912-967-2358

Transplant Nursery
1586 Parkertown Road
Lavonia, GA 30553
706-356-8947

Valdosta Camellias
24436 Meadowbrook Drive
Valdosta, GA 31602
912-242-1390

Wilkerson Mill Gardens
9595 Wilkerson Mill Road
Palmetto, GA 30268
770-463-9717

12

LAWNS

GARY GLEASON, LAWRENCEVILLE: GARDENSOUTH

As manager of GardenSouth in Lawrenceville, a garden and nature store owned by the Gold Kist Company, Gary Gleason brings both love and knowledge of nature and plants to his job.

Gary came by his love of the outdoors, and the plants which inhabit it, through both his parents. His mother, who worked with the New York Conservation Department, inspired a love of nature at an early age. It was she who instigated family camping trips to state forests and nearby parks.

Gary's interest in plants came from his father's side of the family, for they owned greenhouses and a florist shop. "I used to ride my bike to the shop every day, and I can still remember the scent of the flowers. It was something very special."

Although Gary went to the University of Georgia in the school of landscape design, he feels that much of his education comes from working in the nursery business for over twenty years, first in Athens, then later as manager of Hastings Nature and Garden Center in Atlanta, and most recently at GardenSouth.

"I enjoy the people who come into the stores. I like showing them what they can do with plants, and I like knowing that I may have helped bring a little beauty to their lawns and gardens."

Gary could easily be considered an expert in many horticultural fields, from growing perennials and annuals to attracting wildlife to the garden, but he has found a special niche in sharing information about establishing lawns and grasses, in creating broad open areas for play, for entertaining, for making a quiet pool of green in an increasingly frantic world.

LCM: Why do people need lawns?

GARY: A lawn provides a carpet for an outside play area and complements planting beds and shrubbery.

LCM: How does a homeowner with a new construction site begin a lawn?

GARY: In this part of Georgia, there are basically two types of lawns: those with cool season grasses, and those with warm season grasses. Some geographic regions don't have the luxury of two kinds of lawns. As you go south of the Fall Line, you don't have the cool season grasses. As you go north, many of the warm season grasses aren't hardy.

LCM: What are the cool season grasses?

GARY: These are the fescues, blue-grasses, and creeping red fescues. Tall fescues have always been and are still a good basic grass. They are sometimes better known as pasture, or forage, grasses because they clump, grow quickly, and yet look great while growing. Even though the fescues are nice because they stay green year-round, they don't like hot weather. When summer temperatures reach one hundred degrees, it's tough to have a fescue lawn if you don't irrigate regularly.

We're shying away from using the tall fescues, and instead we promote the turf-type tall fescues. These are called turf-type because they don't clump as tightly; they look more like a true turf grass, such as bermuda. They've been tested nation-wide, including the experiment station in Griffin, Georgia, as to overall resistance to disease, insects, and heat.

There are a couple of key points to growing the new turf-type fescues. They don't run or spread like bermuda, but they do have a finer blade, which allows them to take more heat, and they don't have as many disease problems. They grow well in average shade but are also designed to take sun, so you can use them in a variety of conditions. In our area, these are the grasses to use if you want year-round green grass.

There are many trade names for these new turf-type grasses such as 'Rebel', 'Rebel II', and all the improved 'Rebels', 'Shenandoah','Winchester', 'Anthem', and so on. There are probably twenty good turf-type fescues with few differences among them. In tests they seem close, so any turf-type on the market is probably fine.

Another benefit of these turf-type fescues is that the seeds are smaller, so although it looks like it costs more, you actually get better coverage per pound of seed. They don't tend to die out as much. Although you had to replant the tall fescues almost every fall, these newer grasses shouldn't need replanting unless we have a really harsh summer.

Another cool season grass is creeping red fescue. I don't know why it is called that, because it doesn't creep and it isn't red. It is recommended for deep shade conditions. It's a difficult grass to grow, particularly when temperatures reach above 90 degrees. For best results, it should be kept tall and watered often.

LCM: Are the grasses packaged as single kinds, or do they come as a mixture?

GARY: They come both ways. Personally, I don't like the mixture theory. The idea is that you are putting something in for every situation. And in some gardens, some of it may do well, and in other areas, something else will, but in the long run, I feel like you're throwing away money. If you can find a good turf-type, you're probably better off just planting that.

LCM: What are some of the differences between the named varieties of turf-type fescues?

GARY: The main difference is height. Dwarf varieties are now available. These are shorter, should not need mowing as often, and ought to do better in dry conditions, but we don't really know because they have not been on the market long enough for good testing.

LCM: How about warm season grasses?

GARY: These are the true turf-type grasses, or southern grasses. These include bermuda, zoysia, centipede, and St. Augustine.

St. Augustine is sometimes used here, or in Athens. It's fine, but a hard frost below zero, or a sustained cold period could do a lot of damage. Like many things, it might be just fine in a protected area. It's not the sort of thing we consider reliable for a lawn in the Piedmont or the mountain areas of Georgia, though.

Centipede, zoysia, and bermuda are the three main grasses used in this area for turf grasses. Centipede probably takes more shade than the other two, although even it will not tolerate deep, heavy shade.

Zoysia will also take some shade, but only a little. Bermudagrass must have full sun to fill out properly.

Although there are many named varieties of bermuda on the market, you can also get a common or coastal bermuda. If you are planting a big yard, this is the one to use because the seed is less expensive. It takes a couple of pounds to plant a thousand square feet. It's not a particularly pretty grass, but it's solid coverage.

When you plant bermuda, it's like planting kudzu because you've got it and it's going to go everywhere. With edging, you can control it.

The hybrid bermudas such as 'Tift' are used around many new homes today where trees have been removed, and a well-kept lawn area is desired.

LCM: Are the bermudas as susceptible to the cold as the St. Augustine?

GARY: No. It should do fine as far north as Tennessee.

LCM: Which are your favorite lawn grasses?

Perhaps the best organic weed killer is a hoe and two hands.

GARY: I love centipede. It's the lazy man's lawn. It doesn't grow quickly, so you have fewer cuttings per year, it has fewer problems, and takes less care. It does not like areas that don't drain well, but that is solved with correct preparation.

Zoysia is the next best. It's a little harder to maintain and gets a little thicker, which makes it a little more susceptible to disease damage, and it doesn't have as much shade tolerance, but it can be cut with a regular lawn mower, as can the centipede.

When you get into the bermuda, you really need to cut it with a reel type mower or keep the blades of the lawn mower really sharp. Otherwise, it won't cut it cleanly and will look ragged.

Bermuda is a high maintenance lawn. If you're going to pamper it and take care of it every day, and you have full sun, then you want bermuda, because it will look great.

All the warm season grasses go dormant in the winter and turn to what we like to refer to as a "rich, golden hue," but which is actually brown or yellow. You can plant annual rye grass over the warm season grasses for the winter. That will come up and grow during the winter and stay green. It's a lighter green but it's a nice, pretty grass. When it starts to get warm, the warm season grass will push it out and the remainder will be compost.

LCM: What cultural conditions make it difficult to have a lawn?

❧

I think . . . the key is soil preparation. If you lay a good foundation, everything else will work better. It's imperative, with our soils, to do it right.

❧

GARY: Poorly drained soil; heavy, heavy shade; or an area under oaks or some of the nut trees that produce acids that create problems. In those cases, you might have to go to an ivy, vinca, or other shade-tolerant groundcover.

A lawn is not always the answer. If you have a steep bank or slope, rather than risking the mower falling over on you, you might choose to plant it with a groundcover. Just like everything else in life, you should have a balance. You should have just enough grass so that you can easily care for it. A nice vista in the back yard, a nice open area is great, but it

wants to be complemented by colorful flower beds.

LCM: What is the best way to plant the lawn?

GARY: Like any other kind of gardening, you want the right plant in the right place, and this goes for lawns as well. When you're designing your garden, the sun/shade factor is the most important one. If you have hot, hot sun, then you should definitely use one of the warm season grasses or a turf-type fescue.

Consider the overall design and look at what you want. I think you should let a lawn be a lawn without putting trees or bulbs throughout it. It should be open and easily maintained. Think about what you'll be doing with the mower. You need smooth curved edges that will be easy to cut.

The most important element in installing a lawn is soil preparation. It is well worth your time to till in organic matter at the very beginning. Ninety percent of the time our soils are extremely acidic and most of these grasses do not like acidic soil, so lime is generally necessary.

It is a good idea to do a soil test. Since you're investing a lot of time and money in establishing a lawn, it's best to know as much about the soil as possible. Nine times out of ten, you'll need lawn starter fertilizer and lime. You can either use powdered lime or pelletized. The advantage to the pelletized is that it goes through a spreader, which makes the application much easier.

When you begin to design the lawn, lay it out with a tape or garden hose, then till it to a depth of about twelve inches and get the rocks and big sticks out. Then go back and add some finely ground pine bark, compost, or anything that will improve the soil, and till that in. We use less and less peat moss because it is expensive, a nonrenewable resource, and not highly effective. The fine-ground bark, which goes by the trade name Nature's Helper™, works better.

As you till the composted material into the soil, put in your fertilizer and lime.

LCM: What kind of fertilizer do you recommend?

GARY: In the beginning, you want a fertilizer high in phosphorous (the middle number) to produce the quickest growth of roots to help get it established. Lawn starter fertilizer, or 18-24-12, is good.

Normally nitrogen (the first number) will be half slow-release, and half immediate-release. Potassium (the third number), helps produce strong stalks, so it's important in the beginning, too. Apply this based on the recommendations on the bag.

You need to lime, fertilize, and till it all into the top six inches of soil until it is well mixed. Then go back and rake over to get it as smooth as you can. A turf-type grass is going to show up any indentations that weren't raked smooth.

You can use seed to start almost any kind of lawn. Seed is, of course, the least expensive way to go, but if you can afford sod, then do it. It's faster and you don't have to worry about the seed washing away.

It's critical to sow grass seed based on the recommended rate. There's a tendency to want to put down too much, and it might look beautiful and lush right away, but it's going to crowd itself out and begin to die out. For seeding on bare ground, for common bermuda, you will need about two pounds per 1,000 square feet. A pound of centipede will do about

4,000 square feet because it is such tiny seed. For the turf-type fescue, you'll need about five to seven pounds per 1,000 square feet. I recommend shoulder-type spreaders for spreading the seed.

Put the seed out, and then rake it in with a good steel tooth rake; work it down into the soil. Put wheat straw [over the seed] in a salt-and-pepper fashion to prevent the seeds from washing away. Don't mulch too heavily, or the grass can't grow through it. You should be able to see the soil through the mulch.

I don't recommend rolling a lawn here. A lot of places it's necessary, but our soils are so heavy, and compact so quickly anyway, that it's not recommended here.

Watering should start right away. Start a sprinkler on the new lawn to help wash the seed down into the soil. No matter which type of grass you have used, you should water every day for a week, and then every other day for the next couple of weeks.

Most grasses will be up in about seven to fourteen days, except centipede which won't come up for about three weeks. Moisture is critical at this juncture.

Don't cut fescues until they are about two to three inches tall.

LCM: What is the optimum time to put in a lawn?

GARY: For the fescue and cool season grasses, fall is absolutely the best. For the cool season grasses, mid-September to mid-October is probably best. You can also plant in early spring after danger of frost. Something you need to watch out for in fall is falling leaves, which could smother the new grass. You need to get the grass up and growing before the leaves come down. The soil is warm in fall, but the air is cool enough so the grasses can grow comfortably.

Warm season grasses should ideally be planted when they start to show green in spring. Centipede is one of the last to green up, so it could be May or June before you plant it.

LCM: How about maintenance?

GARY: In general, fescue lawns should be left taller in summer months. It's important that they are not cut low during the hot weather. It's best to cut more often, but keep it high—around two to three inches.

Mulching mowers are excellent. These mowers chop up the grass and put the material back on the lawn.

LCM: How about fertilizing after the lawn is established?

GARY: Feed a fescue lawn when it is actively growing, in fall and maybe a little in winter (but not January and February), and again in spring. Once it gets hot, in July and August, don't do anything.

Lawn foods, such as those marked 27-4-8, are high in nitrogen, and once the lawn is established, you need that nitrogen to keep it green and growing. Do a soil test periodically to see if you're really low in something, and relime every couple of years.

LCM: What mistakes do people make with their lawns?

GARY: The two things I see most often are poor watering and mowing techniques. People let the grass get too high and then try to cut it all at once. With the fescue it just looks horrible because the blades are not green down below. I think by letting it get too long, you also let disease problems build up. Cut more often and cut less.

As for watering, if you water in the evening, you're asking for fungus problems. I feel that you should water when the dew is naturally on the lawn, in early morning. This is more efficient because you're not losing so much water to evaporation. When you water, try to put at least an inch on. Water fewer times, but more when you do water.

Irrigation systems are becoming less expensive and easier to install. In the long run, an irrigation system on a timer will save you a lot of money, particularly if you install it before the lawn is seeded.

LCM: How about weeds?

GARY: If you are going to be a plant, you really ought to be a weed because you *will* survive. If you're doing the proper fertilizing and watering, your lawn problems with weeds shouldn't be significant. It's the old adage: the best defense is a good offense. The more you can do to have a healthy lawn in the first place, the fewer weed problems you will have.

You should consider lawn treatments as you would medicine. Don't use them unless you have to. Many people spray on a regular basis, and you really don't need to do this. Although organic fertilizers are available, there are really no effective organic herbicides. Perhaps the best organic weed killer is a hoe and two hands.

RESOURCES FOR LAWNS

BOOKS AND PAMPHLETS

Pamphlets from University of Georgia Cooperative Extension Service

All About Lawns. Second Edition. San Ramon, California: Ortho Books, 1994.

Controlling Lawn and Garden Insects. San Ramon, California: Ortho Books.

Sombke, Laurence. *Easy Lawns and Landscapes.* Old Saybrook, Connecticut: Globe Pequot Press, 1994.

13

ORGANIC GARDENING

ANDREW AND BERNADETTE GOLDSTEIN, DAWSONVILLE: WILD-FLOWER ORGANICS

Andrew and Bernadette Goldstein are not your typical farmers. As owners of Wildflower Organics, a small farm located in the foothills of north Georgia, they are determined to work with the land, rather than work the land, and to "co-create with nature."

Their aim is to "create a balanced environment where plants can receive everything they need to be healthy and vibrant, so that they can give us food that is beautiful, nutritious, and delicious."

Andrew grew up in Atlanta and became a vegetarian at the age of nineteen. After creating and running a successful sprouts and greens business in Colorado, he had the opportunity to sell it and move back South. Bernadette was finishing her Master's Degree in psychology at West Georgia College, so a move to a Georgia farm seemed timely.

They started Wildflower Organics, joined the Georgia Organic Growers Co-op, and have established themselves as a source of information and inspiration for other organic gardeners in the state of Georgia.

I interviewed them on the deck of their small house, surrounded by the green of the foothills, the yellow of budding sunflowers, and the peace that seems to be an inherent part of a home and business so dedicated to preserving the glory of the natural world.

LCM: What does it mean to be an organic farmer?

ANDREW: Organic farming involves many aspects. For me, one of the most important components is that we take care of the land so that the land can take care of us.

BERNADETTE: We are working toward a harmony with nature, and it's a real pioneering effort to have a successful commercial farm this way. People have written many books about organic farming, but to bring oneself into balance with the land goes beyond that.

❧

Studies are showing that the more fertile the soil, when all the little microorganisms are working, the less insect infestations you'll have, and we see that ourselves.

❧

The approach we take is this: if we have an infestation of insects on a plant, instead of killing the insect, we try to look on it as a messenger that something is wrong in the garden, be it the soil, the plant, or the gardeners. We try to look beneath the surface to determine the root of the problem.

ANDREW: We are a commercial production farm, so sometimes we pick the bugs off by hand, but our idea is to not create a battlefield in the garden.

LCM: So, rather than try to find a substitute for chemical sprays and fertilizers, your idea is to find the root of the problem and try to recreate the balance of the land?

BERNADETTE: Yes. And the real situation is usually an imbalance of the soil.

Studies are now showing that the more fertile the soil, when all the little microorganisms in the soil are working, the less insect infestations you'll have, and we see that ourselves.

In weaker soils, the plants seem to be bothered more with insects.

LCM: How do you create a fertile soil?

BERNADETTE: We add natural amendments standard in organic practice, such as rock phosphate, greensand, green manures, composted manures, seaweed, organic cottonseed meal, and alfalfa meal. We don't use chicken litter because of the tremendous amounts of antibiotics that go into those chickens. We feel that the poisons they feed them will be in the litter. So, we've gone as far as importing bat guano and sea bird guano from California and Mexico, although we're getting away from that as well because we feel that the amount of energy that goes into getting it here is not beneficial for the planet.

We're looking to keep everything "in house" and cover cropping is one of the ways we are hoping to improve the soil. We plant nitrogen-fixing plants such as peas and vetches, which will give us both the nitrogen in the soil and organic matter. With a good cover cropping routine, that's all that one might have to do.

ANDREW: We're at the northern edge of the Cotton Belt, and cotton was grown on this land, so we're working with depleted soils.

LCM: You obviously work hard to improve your soils with organic products. What else is involved with gardening organically?

ANDREW: The term "organic" too often means different things to different people, but essentially, it means that first, no synthetic fertilizers, fungicides, pesticides, or herbicides have been used in the past three years on the land where an item was grown; and second, there is a systematic approach to building up the soil, thereby reducing or eliminating soil erosion and nutrient depletion, particularly the micronutrients.

Soon the term "organic" will be part of a national law where legally, you can not label something organic unless it is certified organic. There is a lot of controversy around the certification process. "Certified organic" entails a process whereby a certifying agency, typically the state agricultural department, inspects the farm and issues a certificate. Right now Georgia has an independent certifying agency.

Our farm has to be inspected every year. This entails a full twenty-page report on the farm and documentation of everything we sell. Every item of food that we sell has to be labeled as to what part of the farm it came from so it can be traced in case pesticides are found. We have to spend several hundred dollars for soil and water tests, and for the inspection itself. It's a full process used to guarantee people as much as possible that they are getting what they think they're getting.

BERNADETTE: Obviously, certain things are allowed and others are not. Some organic pesticides are permitted, although you can only use them in crisis situations. You have to use nontreated seed, and the seed starts have to be organic. But, it's more what you do than what you don't do. You have to be involved in a soil-building, sustainable practice.

ANDREW: You can't be an organic farmer just from neglect.

LCM: So, it's not just an absence of poisons, it's a matter of building?

ANDREW: Yes. You have to put in a long range farm plan each year describing what you're doing to build your soils, what are you doing to work with certain imbalances. For example, if you have a field with low potassium, what are you doing? Are you just adding potassium, or are you rotating crops so that you grow something there that uses less potassium?

❦

We are working for a harmony with nature and it's a real pioneering effort . . . to bring oneself into balance with the land. If we have an infestation of insects on a plant, instead of killing the insect, we try to look on it as a messenger that something is wrong in the garden, be it the soil, the plant, or the gardener.

❦

It's a thinking kind of thing. When you're in a situation like ours, where we're growing sixty different crops, it gets very intense.

LCM: Do you feel that the certification process is good, or do you think it's overdone?

ANDREW: I would like to see that the petro-chemical growers have to be certified and the organic growers are the norm.

LCM: I don't quite understand why there is so much red tape involved. Is it because the term organic has been abused?

ANDREW: That's part of it. There has been fraud, and some people have claimed that their product is something it is not, but it's also because of the higher prices organic growers command.

BERNADETTE: I think certification is a good thing. For people who don't like poisons in their food, it's well within their right to know that what they're buying does not contain poisons. It's a life and death issue. The fact that the organic issue is coming up in the farm bill indicates that it is getting bigger.

ANDREW: Pricing is the toughest issue we deal with. I'd rather deal with the bugs, as tough as they are, than deal with prices. We sell produce at the Organic Farmer's Market in Morningside, in Atlanta, and our prices are below those of the natural food stores in the area. However, for the most part, produce is cheap in this country, so organic food will seem expensive until the marketplace fully recognizes the environmental and health costs of chemically grown food.

LCM: You grow a lot of heirloom vegetables. Do you find that you have an educated market? Do people know that they're buying something special?

ANDREW: Some do, and some don't. For example, we grew Brandywine tomatoes this year, which are an heirloom and not highly productive, but are considered the best tasting. We sold every Brandywine we took in.

LCM: Here, toward the end of September, what will you take in?

BERNADETTE: Pumpkins and winter squashes, mustard greens, first fall lettuce, okra, peppers—we have great Italian heirloom peppers this year—basil, and a lot of flowers, which we sell to florists. We mix wildflowers, such as goldenrods and ironweed, with garden flowers such as zinnias and celosias.

ANDREW: We're big sunflower growers. Some weeks we do hundreds of stems. Typically, we'll do a mixture of snapdragon, zinnias, amaranth, dahlias, celosias, and sunflowers.

LCM: How do you encourage people to garden organically and to keep things in balance?

BERNADETTE: Soil, soil, soil. Work to get good soil. It is one of the most important ingredients.

ANDREW: Compost is the best thing you can do for the soil, and everyone can make compost. Or grow a cover crop. In late fall, we put in a winter crop such as annual rye, vetch, or Austrian winter peas. The Peaceful Valley catalog out of California is an excellent resource because they have a whole section on cover crops that explains what different crops will do what for the soil. So, if a gardener knew what nutrients were missing in his soil, he could then plant a particular cover crop to supply the nutrients.

For example, if you need nitrogen, you'd use one crop; if you need phosphorous, you would use something else. It's a whole science.

It's hard to give general advice because a garden is so site specific, and there are so many factors to consider.

BERNADETTE: Something else that people can do is to grow plants that are naturalized to the area, appropriate to the region, and easy to grow. For example, blueberries are easy here because they're native, and they do well.

We tried for years to have the first crop of snow peas, or the last crop of thus and so. One can do things like that, but it takes more energy. We're constantly trying to determine which crops take a lot of energy and which ones don't, and going with what's easier.

RESOURCES FOR ORGANIC GARDENING

BOOKS

Chaplan, Basil. *The Complete Manual of Organic Gardening.* London: Headline, 1992.

Coleman, Eliot. *The New Organic Grower: A Master's Manual of Tools and Techniques for the Home and Market Gardener.* Post Mills, Vermont: Chelsea Green Publishers, 1989.

Rodale's Successful Organic Gardening: Vegetables. Emmaus, Pennsylvania: Rodale Press, 1993.

Rodale's Successful Organic Gardening: Herbs. Emmaus, Pennsylvania: Rodale Press, 1993.

Wright, Machaelle Small. *Perelandra Garden Workbook: A Complete Guide to Gardening with Nature Intelligences.* Warrenton, Virginia: Perelandra Ltd., 1993.

MAGAZINES

Organic Gardening
Rodale Press
33 E. Minor Street
Emmaus, PA 18098

ORGANIZATIONS

Georgia Organic Growers Association
P.O. Box 567661
Atlanta, GA 31156
404-621-GOGA
Membership includes bimonthly newsletter.

Southern Sustainable Agriculture
  Working Group
P.O. Box 324
Elkins, AR
501-292-3714

SOURCES OF UNTREATED SEEDS

Abundant Life Seed Foundation
P.O. Box 772
Port Townsend, WA 98368
206-385-5660

Erth Food
1-800-849-ERTH
Chemical free fertilizer and soil conditioner.

Fertrell
Country Gardens
1415 Euharlee Road SW
Kingston, GA 30145
All natural and organic plant food and soil conditioner.

Healing Heart Herbs
2683 Hartwell Highway
Elberton, GA 30635
706-213-0455
Organic plant starts, perennials, herbs.

Mr. Natural
404-535-1511 (Atlanta)
800-287-2493 (north Georgia)
Organic landscaping products.

Necessary Trading Company
One Nature's Way
New Castle, VA 24127-0305
703-864-5103
Supplies, amendments, tools.

Peaceful Valley Farm Supply
P.O. Box 2209
Grass Valley, CA 95945
916-272-4769
Seeds, supplies, tools.

Seeds of Change
P.O. Box 15700
Santa Fe, NM
87506-5700
505-438-8080

DISPLAY GARDEN

Georgia Organic Growers Association, annual garden tour, 404-621-GOGA

CLASSES AND SEMINARS

Southern Sustainable Agriculture, annual conference in January, 501-292-3714

14

FRUITS AND VEGETABLES

VIRGIL ADAMS, JEFFERSON

Talk to Virgil Adams about gardening and you will learn as much about people as you will about plants. Virgil confesses that he can't remember a time when he didn't garden, and the lessons learned throughout a lifetime of digging in the dirt and nurturing plants has made him not only a great gardener, but a philosopher as well.

He attended Murray State College in Kentucky, and although he says he didn't even know how to spell journalism at the time, he knew he wanted to write and majored in English.

In 1952, he and his wife, Mary, moved to Jefferson, Georgia, to raise children and vegetables. At this time, Virgil served as news editor with the Cooperative Extension Service and wrote a weekly gardening column for the *Atlanta Journal/Constitution*'s home and garden section. In 1982 he retired to "garden a little, write a little, fish a little, and camp a little." He now says he needs to go back to work so he can get a little rest.

When I asked Virgil why he gardened, he had a quick and easy reply. "It's fun!"

I interviewed Virgil early in October, when his black-soiled vegetable beds held tiny green shoots of lettuce and dark green broccoli leaves. Walking up and down the paths between the beds, this man of the garden exuded love of the Earth and all things which grow in it.

LCM: For many years you wrote a very successful column for the *Atlanta Journal/Constitution*. Bill Broadway, your former editor, said that you were a great writer because you never turned in anything until the last word was just right.

Looking at your vegetable garden here, it seems as if you're just as careful in the garden. Do you think you'll always garden and always write?

VIRGIL: I have a good friend who is an art teacher at Jefferson High School and he's a pretty good artist. He told me one day, "I cannot *not* paint." I'm really trying to quit writing, but I cannot *not* write like I cannot *not* fish, or garden. I've been writing about forty years and I've been gardening all my life. My father and grandfather both gardened.

LCM: Gardened or farmed?

VIRGIL: Both. They farmed all day, then gardened when they got in from the fields. After we saw to the mules, then we would work the vegetable garden. This was in McLemoresville, Tennessee (population 311, if you counted dogs, cats, and chickens), during the Depression when if you didn't garden, you didn't eat. So, I learned to garden following the footsteps of my grandaddy and my daddy.

LCM: And do you garden as they did?

❧

Any fool knows that you can plant more seeds in a crooked row than you can in a straight row.

❧

VIRGIL: I'm getting back to gardening that way.

LCM: Which is how?

VIRGIL: We didn't have a lot of fertilizer when I was gardening with Papa and Daddy. What little we had was called guana. It was not bat manure, that's just what the old-timers called fertilizer in the late Thirties. We didn't have a lot of that because we couldn't afford it. So most of our fertilizer came out of the hog pen and the cow lot. We didn't have many insecticides either. Mostly we picked bugs off by hand.

Then I became educated and started gardening scientifically, which is altogether different from the way I had gardened with Papa and Daddy and the way I garden now. I garden now like I did sixty-five years ago as a kid.

LCM: What does that mean? You pick the bugs off by hand and use natural manures?

VIRGIL: I don't really even pick the bugs off anymore. I got back to that, but I'm a step beyond that now. I don't pick them off, I just leave them be.

LCM: And if you leave them be, there's enough for everyone?

VIRGIL: Yes. Are you into divas and those kind of things?

LCM: What do you mean?

VIRGIL: Like spirits?

LCM: Sure, I'm into spirits.

VIRGIL: Okay. If I had heard someone say twenty-five to thirty years ago what I'm fixing to say to you now, I would have said they were crazy as heck. But I have discovered that those bugs and birds and bees, and everything that's out there in my garden, they understand that I'm not trying to hurt them. When I tried to hurt them, with Sevin and Malathion, I had so damn many bug problems it was terrible.

Whether I have psyched myself up to believe I don't have any damage or whether I don't have any now, doesn't make any difference. It's sort of like happiness. A happy person is not a person in a certain set of circumstances, but a person with a certain set of attitudes.

It's like that chickweed. That stuff used to take over back there, and I'd fight it and lie awake nights worrying about what I was going to do about it. Then one day I realized that I wasn't going to lick it, so I changed my attitude and said, "Look, you're not my enemy, you're my friend," and I think that chickweed has made my soil what it is today, better than it's ever been. And I love chickweed. I even eat the stuff. So, it's really how you look at things.

LCM: What do you think brought you to this point, believing in divas and spirits?

VIRGIL: Um, I don't know. I was talking to a lady the other day who was complaining about her twenty-year-old son. She said she wished he would straighten up, get a job, get out of the house, and get his life together. I told her I wish I could encourage her, but I'm pushing seventy-three and I have no idea what I'm doing. And that's sort of where I am now.

You know, we're always in process. But I have jotted down on a piece of paper my philosophy as of today. It will change. It always changes, but right now it goes like this:

One thing I know and one thing I believe. I know the only years of my life are out ahead. I believe the best years of my life are out ahead. A small difference between knowing and believing.

I have decided to be done with the two useless emotions. One is guilt. It's always in the past. It's something you have done and you can't change. The other is worry. It's in the future, it hasn't happened yet, so be done with that.

No line is ever as long as it looks. That's straight out of the garden. One year I had a raised bed one hundred feet long, three feet wide in which I had planted winter rye. I usually turned it under in late February or early March. But that year it started raining, and that stuff started growing, and it grew and grew until it was three to four feet tall. And I said, "My gosh, my tiller won't handle that and it'll take me two days to do it with a sling blade." Well, I got the sling blade and flailed that stuff, and in thirty minutes it was done. So, no line is ever as long as it looks. It applies to every line you ever get in. The grocery line, or trials and tribulations, or the garden.

The best way to get a job done is to get it started.

I am not a victim. I cannot—I will not—blame God or anything or anybody for the troubles I've seen.

Everything I have is a gift from God—and I don't care who your god is. It can be a little "g" or a big "G." Doesn't make any difference to me. Everything I have is a gift.

My God takes pretty good care of what I have. Therefore, I must share it with others, else it is stolen property.

LCM: So, how did you get so philosophical?

VIRGIL: Everybody's so philosophical.

LCM: Why are you conscious of your philosophy, and why are you able to articulate it? Do you think gardening has influenced that?

VIRGIL: I don't think you can live and not be philosophical. But I guess there are some people who are alive and not aware that they are alive. You reckon?

LCM: Oh, yes.

VIRGIL: I think that I've learned to enjoy whatever I'm doing at the moment. I'm enjoying this interview, for some odd reason. There's nothing I'd rather be doing right now. When I get out in the garden, that's what I'm enjoying. My Daddy taught me to garden and to fish at about the same time. He was "sick" every Sunday of his life. He'd wake up every Sunday morning coughing and hacking and say, "I think I'm taking a cold." What he wasn't going to do was to go to Sunday school and church in McLemoresville, Tennessee. And he didn't.

☙

Gardening is spiritual and is done on faith. Gardening is nothing without worship, without awe, without mystery. Without a little philosophy. A little musing.

A little bull manure.

☙

But I can't remember when my mother didn't take me to Sunday school and church. The spiritual side of my life came from her, and the love of nature came from my Daddy.

You can't really put your finger on when I did this or that, or why I am the way I am. It's a journey we're on.

At one time I was after a certain amount of perfection in the garden. I realize now that I discouraged my own kids from helping because when they got out

there, the row they dug was never straight enough and the seeds were never spaced exactly right, and I was sort of a perfectionist when I was a scientific gardener. They got the feeling that in the garden, they never did anything right.

I'm doing a little better job with the grandkids. If they step on a row it's okay. We have four granddaughters and one grandson and all of them at one time have had their row out there. They put their name on it, and I leave them be.

LCM: And are there crooked rows and misplaced seeds?

VIRGIL: Yes. And any fool knows that you can plant more seeds in a crooked row than you can in a straight row. Think about that for a while.

LCM: How's the actual production of what you get out of your garden now compared to when you were gardening, as you put it, scientifically?

VIRGIL: It's more and better.

LCM: That's not just attitude? That's actuality?

VIRGIL: Well, I say it's actuality, but I guess it's partly attitude. And I don't really care which it is any more. I know that a scientist says that a plant doesn't know whether I grow it organically or inorganically, whether I used pure, unadulterated Kricket Krap™—actual cricket manure, analysis 4-3-2, totally organic—or whether I used chemical fertilizer 10-10-10. The scientist would say the plant would not know the difference and a taste test could not really determine which plants were grown organically, and that's all right. It doesn't bother me. The important thing is that I know.

It is important what the gardener does for the plant, but more important is what the plant does for the gardener. In other words, as you go through this journey, the important thing is the *gardener* growing. You can have a garden that may increase in production one hundred percent one year to the next because of management or irrigation or whatever, but if during the process the gardener goes backward or doesn't grow, then where's the success?

I stopped writing a column for the *Atlanta Journal/Constitution* several years ago. In my last column (which was never published), I had this advice for people:

> Listen up, please. Most gardeners aren't looking for some professional with all the answers, just a fellow human being to share stories with.

> I can't tell anyone how to garden. Nor do I want to. The idea is to find something that works, something you are comfortable with, and go with it. If you pick up a few new ideas and/or tips along the way, that's fine. But don't become addicted to them. A steady diet of tips is as unpalatable as zucchini three times a day.

> Loosen up. You don't make appointments with the garden. You don't punch a time clock at the garden gate. There is no deadline out there. There is a margin of convenience. Doing the work a little early or a little late makes only a little difference.

> The garden is one place down here where everything does not have to be all right. You don't have to bat a thousand—or even try. If you mess up, fine. You're still Number One. After all, it is your own back yard.

I guess all of us would like to turn gardening up a notch or two. We'd all like to bring increased awareness and sensitivity to the little spot of ground where we live, work, and play. We would like to experience growth on a higher level. Touch more deeply the source of our being.

Gardening is spiritual and is done on faith. Gardening is nothing without worship, without awe, without mystery. Without a little philosophy. A little musing. A little bull manure.

DAVID CHAMBERS, PINE MOUNTAIN: CALLAWAY GARDENS

Mr. Cason's vegetable garden at Callaway Gardens is as much a home for David Chambers as any place on earth. He literally grew up here among the vegetables and herbs, for he began working for Callaway Gardens while still a teenager.

It was an exciting school for a boy who loved to dig in the earth and watch things grow.

David's grandparents had a vegetable garden and, as David puts it, "they didn't grow much, but what they did grow, they grew well." David attributes to them his early love of gardening.

BEST TOMATO VARIETIES

'Rutgers'
'Celebrity'
'Better Boy'
'Supersonic'

I spoke with David in early September, harvest time for many of the vegetables.

"I assume this is your favorite time in the garden," I said, looking at the beautiful fruits and vegetables being pulled from the vine.

David pushed the cap back on his head and shook his head. "No, can't say that it is. Spring's my favorite. I'd rather see them young and growing."

And so it is with David Chambers. He is a man for whom growth is better than harvest, for whom the journey is preferable to the destination—and who is always ready for a new beginning.

LCM: When beginner gardeners ask you about starting a vegetable garden, what advice do you give them?

DAVID: Start small. I suggest that they do raised beds, or something that is framed in so they can easily improve the soil.

LCM: What is an ideal size vegetable bed for the beginning home gardener?

DAVID: If you're using a tiller, the beds should measure at least twenty feet by thirty feet; anything less than that you should dig by hand. In a small bed, if you use a tiller, you'll compact the soil more than you will help it.

Choose a size you're comfortable with, and then make sure that it's situated in a good site. For vegetables, you need a minimum of six hours of direct sunlight; any less than that and you won't have much luck. Some vegetables, such as lettuces and radishes, can get by with less light in spring, but most of the summer vegetables need full sun.

Stick with the easy. The first year, people look at catalogs and want to try whatever they see in those big, showy pictures, but those are not always the easiest things to grow.

I recommend the varieties marked All American. They have been tested throughout the United States to make sure that the seeds will germinate and the plants grow well. These are the varieties that work best for us, too.

If you don't have a greenhouse, buy the plants at a local nursery. It's really better to let someone else grow plants from seed, rather than try to do it yourself if you're not set up to do it right. Most people can get the seeds to germinate, but you need the correct light and moisture conditions for growing them so they won't bolt or get leggy. This is particularly true of plants that need to grow indoors for several weeks before they go into the garden.

LCM: What should you look for when you're purchasing plants from a nursery?

DAVID: Watch out for anything that shows a change in color in the leaf. Yellow or red in the leaves may be a sign that plants are getting old. Look for light green in leaves, which indicates new growth. You can tell if the plants have been watered daily by looking at the base. If you see yellow leaves at the bottom, the plants have probably been allowed to wilt between waterings.

LCM: So, sale plants aren't worth the money you save?

DAVID: I wouldn't think so. Good quality plants are going to cost more, but they're well worth it. Look for good, uniform size. Also, hybrids are probably going to cost more, but they are worth it because they will be faster growing and more resistant to insect and disease damage.

LCM: Can you give me an example of a hybrid vegetable which has worked well for you?

DAVID: Beets. You get a nice uniform size, they are ready for harvest in fifty days, rather than seventy to seventy-five. Also carrots. Several hybrid varieties have been developed for our climate. They germinate faster, come through the ground easier, resist cracking, and grow better in the heat.

There are advantages and disadvantages to using tomato hybrids. The hybrids usually ripen more uniformly and may look better, but they may not taste as good.

LCM: What are some of the more tasty hybrid tomatoes?

DAVID: 'Rutgers' is good, and 'Celebrity' is a disease-resistant hybrid that only produces in July, but it has a good taste. 'Better Boy' is always good, or 'Supersonic', which keeps growing and producing even in the heat of late July and August.

There's no easy way to get the perfect tomato to grow all summer long. You either have to spray with chemicals, or plant tomato varieties which have finished producing in late July when insects and diseases are at their worst. We always try both methods. We usually

plant a few tomatoes after the first of July, and some years we get a good late summer crop.

LCM: What other advice do you have for growing good tomatoes?

DAVID: Tomatoes are heavy feeders, so in addition to applying fertilizer about six inches away from the plant, we use calcium nitrate, which is slow release and lasts sixty to ninety days. It gives us more blossom set, and helps the fruit hold better. It will not burn the plants and is readily available to home gardeners. Put this on a month after planting, when the blooms start to form.

Calcium nitrate can also be used on squash and cucumbers, pansies, and other bedding plants. Just side dress it as you would with any other kind of granular fertilizer, or use it as a spray.

ADVICE FOR BEGINNERS

✧ Start small.

✧ Plant easy-to-grow vegetables.

✧ Use All America Selections.

✧ Buy good, healthy plants at a nursery.

✧ Don't plant too early in spring.

A substitute for this is Osmacote™, which offers the same benefits. You put it on one time, and it gradually releases the nutrients. Other fertilizers are gone within three to four weeks, especially if we have a heavy rain.

LCM: When do you start planting summer vegetables?

DAVID: People are always eager to get started and don't want to wait, but it doesn't do any good to plant too early. Even if the air temperature is warm, soil temperatures are more important because they effect germination. This year the soil stayed wet a long time and seeds would sprout, then wither and die. Anything you can do to warm the beds will help. For the most part, here at Callaway Gardens, we put out seeds in mid-April for summer crops.

If you plant early, a few things will help. Seeds of hybrid plants generally withstand cool weather better, and those painted with fungicide usually perform better.

LCM: What are planting dates for cool season crops?

DAVID: February 1 for spring crops, and the end of August or first of September for fall crops.

LCM: What are some of the cool season crops home gardeners can grow in spring and/or fall?

❧

We are using fewer and fewer chemicals. Instead, we are looking for quick growth and a fast harvest. Then we take the plant out before insects have a chance to bother it.

❧

DAVID: Many different kinds of lettuces, though we are limited to leaf lettuces or butterheads because of our climate. Don't try iceberg types. 'Buttercrunch' is probably the easiest and fastest growing. It almost forms a head and grows quickly without bolting. The red varieties can withstand more cold than the green varieties. Try 'Red Sails' or 'Red Fire'. The curly ones like 'Salad

Bowl' and 'Oak Leaf' both seem to have good taste and are easy to grow. The older varieties like 'Summer Bibb' and 'Bibb' are harder to grow.

Some cool season crops are more trouble than they're worth. Cauliflower takes up a lot of space and takes a long time to grow. And, unless you do a good job of growing it, it will look yellowish or brown, not anything like the bright white that commercial growers get.

Broccoli, on the other hand, grows faster and withstands heat even if you get it in late.

We can grow brussels sprouts in Georgia, but the flavor is often bitter.

Spinach seeds are slow to germinate, but once it comes up, it grows well. Transplants are readily available and make growing spinach easier. New varieties have leaves that are flatter, easier to clean, and have a milder flavor.

LCM: What do you do about pests and diseases?

DAVID: We are using fewer and fewer chemicals. Instead, we are looking for quick growth and a fast harvest, which allows us to remove the plant before insects have a chance to attack it.

Pests, such as cutworms, are found on the surface of the soil and eat the tender green outer layer of new plants in early spring. Putting a paper cup collar around the new plants might help, and if you can hang on until night temperatures are in the upper fifties, they will go away.

Squash borers are tough because they attack established plants, and the plant will be dead the next day. New varieties are supposed to be more resistant, but these are still being tested. Planting at just the right time lessens the chance of squash borer problems. If you plant too

❧

early, the plants will be weak as they begin to grow, creating perfect conditions for the borer. Of course, if the plants are stressed by too much heat in mid- to late summer, that also presents good conditions for the borer. So, you have a small window of time. Plant around the first of May and try to harvest by the end of June.

I do a little companion planting. For example, I plant bush beans as a trap crop to keep bean beetles off the more expensive pole beans. We also plant soybeans as a trap crop to keep insects off more valuable crops. We also use some of the older, smellier marigold varieties, which are useful for repelling nematodes.

LCM: What else do you recommend doing to improve the health of the plants?

DAVID: It's important to rotate crops and not grow the same crop in the same bed year after year. It's not as important to rotate fast growing crops, but those which take sixty to ninety days to grow and harvest should be rotated every year.

LCM: How do you group different vegetables in the garden?

DAVID: I try to plant crops together that have the same growth habits and cultural needs, or that somehow help one another. I plant radishes and carrots in the same row because the radishes actually loosen the soil for the weaker carrots. I plant spinach, lettuce, and beets in the same row because they have similar fertilizing and watering needs.

I'm careful not to use small plants next to larger ones which might give off too much shade.

LCM: Can you grow asparagus in Georgia?

DAVID: Yes. We had it here for fifteen to twenty years. After about ten years it began to loose vigor and weeds began to give us a lot of problems. It is a very heavy feeder. You need to add two inches of compost to it every winter to keep it actively growing.

LCM: How about corn for the home garden?

DAVID: Corn should really be grown in a block so it will pollinate correctly. A single row will not work. You may get some pollination, but not enough for a nice crop. A minimum sized bed would be four by eight. This, planted solid with corn, gives you enough for pollination. The ears will not be big, and you will have only one ear per stalk when you plant it close together, but this is a better method than planting in a single long row.

BEST LETTUCE VARIETIES

'Buttercrunch'
'Red Sails'
'Red Fire'
'Salad Bowl'
'Oak Leaf'

Squash, also, does better in circles and blocks rather than in rows, again for pollination purposes. Everything seems to like company.

LCM: What are some of the basic mistakes that gardeners make?

DAVID: People tend to spend more money than they have to. They buy an expensive fertilizer, for example, for a problem that composted leaves could fix.

Also, people will work to get the ground well tilled and light, then tramp back and forth on it and pack it back down. Even tractors do little compaction compared to foot traffic.

Some folks put in a plant and forget about it, then wonder why it didn't grow. People don't realize that planting a plant is just the beginning.

MICKEY HARP, FAYETTEVILLE: HARP'S FARMER'S MARKET AND NURSERY

Mickey Harp grew up in the rolling hills of Fayette County, just south of Atlanta. Born in a family of growers, Mickey has always been close to the soil. When he was nineteen years old, he planted 1,000 Christmas trees to earn a little extra cash while he worked for the airlines.

When the airlines asked him to transfer to a different state, Mickey was faced with a tough decision. He could either make a career with the airlines, or he could stay in Fayette County and farm the land he grew up on.

Fortunately for all who find Harp's Farmer's Market and Nursery a wonderful

resource for plants and "pick your own fruits," Mickey decided to stay.

Although Mickey originally grew only fruits and vegetables, the lure of flowering plants proved to be too strong to resist. A few years ago, he and his wife, Tammie, began selling an outstanding collection of daylilies, perennials, and native plants at their Farmer's Market. The Market—upscale country—provides both produce, plants, and gardening paraphernalia.

I interviewed Mickey in early summer in his office, which was full of flowering plants, children, and kittens. Outside, peaches were just beginning to turn a reddish gold, and blueberries hung like dewdrops on the vine.

LCM: Your "pick your own" crops look beautiful and must be wonderfully productive. Can you recommend some good vine and shrub fruits to grow in Georgia?

MICKEY: Blackberries, blueberries, muscadines, and strawberries are all easy for the home gardener to grow.

LCM: Let's start with the muscadines, because there seem to be many home gardeners who want to grow them. What are some good varieties to grow and what is the difference between a muscadine and a scuppernong?

MICKEY: A lot of people think that the scuppernong is white and the muscadine is black, but muscadines are either red, white, or black. The scuppernong is actually a kind of muscadine that only grows naturally in the southeastern United States.

LCM: Can you grow muscadines in all parts of Georgia?

MICKEY: Pretty much so, although they don't like temperatures below zero degrees.

The vines have to have good soil drainage and good air circulation, but they're not too picky about the kind of soil they grow in as long as it is not too alkaline. This is a plant that likes our acidic soils. The best pH is between 6.0 and 6.5.

You need to prepare the soil just as you would for planting corn or tomatoes. Get rid of as many weeds as possible before you plant.

If space allows it, plant the vines in long, straight rows. If you're planting on a slope, you might have to contour the plantings and curve them on the hillside. The vines ought to get full sun. They can take a little shade, but production will not be as good.

Set the plants out after the really cold weather is over, probably after the first of March in the Atlanta area. If you plant any earlier, put about six to eight inches of soil around the trunk to protect it from the cold. After April first, remove this extra dirt.

After you plant, be sure to keep water on the roots so they won't dry out.

Muscadines have to have support to grow. You can make a trellis out of anything, but treated wood posts and single wires are used most often.

When you choose your plants, remember that if you don't have a self-fertile variety, you will have to plant a pollinator within at least fifty feet from a female vine. The ratio is generally four female plants to every male plant.

Prune the vines during winter months, preferably before February. Have the main stem running down the wire; [two vines,] ten foot on each end; and prune everything else back to three to four inches long.

You will get fruit in two years after you plant, but count on at least three years before you get much production from the vines.

LCM: What are the best blackberry varieties to grow?

MICKEY: There are several different types of blackberries—thornless, thorny, upright, and trailing. The best thorny type is 'Shawnee'; the best thornless is 'Navajo', which has big, flavorful berries. The only drawback is that the canes do not come back as well, and after a few years you will have skips in your rows. After seven or eight years, you will have to start a new planting of blackberries.

LCM: When do you plant black-berries?

MICKEY: Anytime before April 1. Put them in a sunny spot and make sure there are no wild blackberry vines around. Once a new cane comes up and grows to about waist high, pinch out the tops so they will branch out. Then, about twice during the year, trim back those limbs that have branched out because they will be very vigorous. During winter months, prune out all the dead canes.

LCM: Do you interplant new plants to keep continuous production in the black-berries?

MICKEY: No, because you don't want to spread disease. I would start new plantings at a different location after about three years.

LCM: How about raspberries?

MICKEY: They are a little trickier to grow than the other brambles, but you can grow them anywhere in the state. 'Dorma Red' has large red berries and can be grown as far south as northern Florida. The flavor is okay, and the berries can be used for pies, jams, and jellies.

LCM: What kind of conditions do blueberries need?

MICKEY: Blueberries are actually one of the easiest fruits to grow. They have

BEST VINE AND SHRUB FRUITS

Blackberry 'Shawnee' (thorns), 'Navajo' (thornless)

Blueberry 'Climax' (early season), 'Brightwell' (mid-season), 'Tiftblue' (late season)

Muscadines 'Supreme', 'Darlene'

Strawberries 'Everbearing Ozark', 'Tennessee Beauty'

Figs 'Celeste' (cold hardy), 'Brown Turkey'

Raspberry 'Dorma Red'

fewer problems with disease and insects, and are less work.

They should be planted in full sun in well-drained, slightly acidic soils. Blueberries live a long, long time—up to about forty years—so be sure to choose a site that you like. Blueberries like acidic soils; they do not like sandy soils because sand cannot hold water or nutrients long enough.

Prune to a uniform height and cut back any stray branches that shoot up above the shrub. After about five to seven years, start taking out some of the old canes.

Most of the blueberries grown commercially are either 'Climax', which ripens early, or 'Tiftblue', which ripens late, but the one rated for the best flavor is 'Brightwell', which ripens midseason.

Blueberries need to cross-pollinate, so it's important to plant at least two different kinds.

LCM: For a home gardener with limited space, which fruits do you recommend?

MICKEY: Strawberries are one of the best fruits for the home garden because you can plant them on a tiered platform made of railroad ties or landscape timbers, and they don't take up much space. You have to protect them from frost, and sometimes if we have a lot of rain, you'll have problems with diseases, but other than that, it's a good crop to grow. Some of the best varieties are the 'Everbearing Ozark' and 'Tennessee Beauty'.

LCM: Are figs easy to grow?

MICKEY: Figs are pretty easy to care for; nothing much bothers them. You can buy fig plants in containers, but usually people just put them in bare root in March. You don't need to prune figs unless they get too tall and you want to keep the height down. It takes about two to three years before you have enough figs for canning purposes.

'Brown Turkey' is the best all-round variety to grow in the state. It's a good eating fig, or good to dry or use for preserves. 'Celeste' is another good one. It's a little more cold hardy, but the fruit is smaller in size.

LCM: What other fruits do you recommend for the home gardener?

MICKEY: Kiwi. You can grow it as far north as Atlanta. If you take good care of it the first couple of years, then even if it gets cold, the vines will come back. It produces a good fruit and a lot of it.

LCM: What about peaches?

MICKEY: There are hundreds of varieties of peaches to choose from. What you grow depends on where you live. Some of the varieties they grow in south Georgia won't do well even as far north as Atlanta.

One of the best peaches we grow here in Fayette County is 'Jefferson'. It's flavorful and cling-free, meaning it will break away from the seed. From Atlanta north, 'Crest Haven' is a good variety because it blooms later and there will be less trouble with frost.

You need at least two peach trees for pollination purposes. If you plant about seven different varieties, you can have peaches in this area from the first of June through mid-September.

'Derby' is a good early variety, followed by 'Windblow', 'Crest Haven', 'Jefferson', 'Georgia Bell' (a white peach with a great flavor), then 'Old Henry', and 'Lorraine'.

LCM: How about some of the melons?

MICKEY: They take a lot of space, full sun, and the right amount of water. If you have too much water, the flavor won't be as good.

'Hales Jumbo Best' is a good cantaloupe with a great flavor. 'Crimson Sweet' is a good watermelon. The seedless varieties are good but not any better than this one. I've been growing watermelon since I was a kid, and 'Crimson Sweet' is just hard to beat.

LCM: How much room do you need?

MICKEY: For watermelons, you need an area about nine feet by ten feet. Put in two to three hills, plant five seeds, then thin the seedlings out to two plants. For the homeowner, the hills can be three feet apart.

Cantaloupes can go in a slightly smaller area, say five foot by six foot.

We don't pick off blooms, but if you are interested in getting really good sized melons, you could do that. Melons need really warm weather so we don't plant watermelon or cantaloupe here until after April 15.

LCM: Can you grow any of these fruits in the shade?

MICKEY: You know, there are just times that you have to have sunshine, and growing fruits is one of those times. It could be that there are some varieties that will grow okay with some shade, but no one has done any research on it as far as I know. Probably your best bet would be with the muscadines and blueberries.

LCM: What do you suggest people do about pests in small garden areas?

MICKEY: Netting is a lot of trouble, but it seems to work if you tie the net down to the ground with stakes or even rocks or boards. Some people have luck with the blow-up owls or snakes, but they only last a short period of time.

LCM: What about diseases?

MICKEY: The only real problem I have is with blackspot on the muscadines, and I suggest that people use products recommended by the local nursery. Just be sure to be careful and follow the label directions as to when to spray.

LCM: Do you have any general recommendations for growing small fruits?

MICKEY: Work with the soil, add soil conditioner or ground pine bark, get all the weeds out, and till it well. Know that it will take time to grow some of the fruits, but stick with it. You can do it.

WALTER REEVES, ATLANTA: COOPERATIVE EXTENSION SERVICE

Radio personality, newspaper writer, county extension agent, and enthusiastic plantsman, Walter Reeves has shared his knowledge and humor with Georgians for many years. When asked if he had a degree in horticulture, Walter grins and shakes his head.

❦

I try to do things so that I don't have to spray. This involves building the soil and digging stuff into the earth so my plants are healthy enough to win their own fights.

❦

"No, my horticulture background was helping my mother and father with a large vegetable garden, and my flower background came from my grandmother, who had a huge flower garden. And I learned things from the ground up.

"My mother was convinced that if you ate vegetables grown on land that contained the correct amounts of trace minerals, you would be better off and healthier. So now I spend my time teaching people what my mother was so interested in, which is, what to add to the garden to get healthy soil. Karma just goes around."

After leaving south Fayette County, Walter went to the University of Georgia and earned a B.S. degree in chemistry. His real love was in biology and botany, though, and when he realized that chemists had little interaction with people (a basic necessity for someone with Walter Reeves' personality), he approached the Cooperative Extension Service and asked if they would be interested in hiring him

as a county agent to work with 4-H clubs. He was hired promptly; eventually his job encompassed horticulture and Walter found his true love.

I interviewed Walter in his garden northeast of Atlanta in early fall.

LCM: You write and speak knowledgeably about so many different aspects of horticulture. Do you have a particular area of interest or expertise?

WALTER: My greatest interest is in growing plants, and how you can do it with the least amount of work. For example, I'm not a big pesticide person because frankly, just preparing the pesticide and getting out to spray is troublesome. I try to do things so that I don't have to spray. That involves building the soil and digging organic matter into the earth so my plants are healthy enough to win their own fights.

It's like the bean beetles. They ate the heck out of the leaves on my beans this year, but I had plenty of beans, so we just kind of coexist. I don't have any problem using chemical sprays as long as I know exactly what I'm spraying for, and I use the right precautions. I do spray things such as poison ivy.

LCM: How does a gardener begin to learn how to use chemical sprays if they have little information or experience?

WALTER: In general, knowledge is always the key. If you can at least identify the bug, you can find out whether or not you need to treat it, and how.

LCM: Are there books available for identifying different pests?

WALTER: Yes. The extension service has several good pamphlets, although they are not in color. Rodale has an excellent book, *Rodale's Color Handbook of Garden Insects*, by Anna Carr.

❦

Knowledge is the key. For example, if you have a leaf-cutter bee that's cutting holes in the edges of your redbud leaves, anyone with any knowledge will know that leaf-cutter bees are not a major problem. In fact, the effect on the leaves is darn pretty. They leave perfectly scalloped edges and create beautiful patterns, especially on the young leaves.

And there's no use getting all worked up about tent caterpillars, because they won't bother you. Or orange-striped oak worms, because they won't cause permanent damage.

But cabbage loopers eat the stew out of cabbage leaves, so you should probably do something about them.

LCM: Are there organic pesticides available?

WALTER: There are more now than there used to be. Neem is one of the newer ones, you can get it under the trade name Bioneem™ or Neemesis™. Neem is supposedly [a deterrent to feeding] and a good insecticide as well. I use it on plants because it is organic. The neem tree has been used as a pesticidal tree in India for a thousand years. Even today kids there take a branch and brush their teeth with it because it has fungicidal properties. Oil from the nuts and extracts from the leaves are thought to have insecticidal properties.

People are also using more organic horticultural oils. If you spray these insecticidal oils on the leaves of fruit trees, it suffocates the insects without hurting the plant. Up until recently, though, you couldn't use the oils during the summer because they would scorch the leaves. The refining process is better now, so an ultrafine oil like Sunspray™ can be used in Georgia in 90-degree temperatures and it does a good job.

LCM: Do you recommend buying seeds for plants that have been bred to be disease resistant?

WALTER: I would recommend it, but they are sometimes difficult to find. The vegetables that are bred to be resistant to various pests and diseases don't produce the biggest tomatoes or longest beans, and frankly, gardeners generally want quantity as well as quality. So, until the consumer demands it, finding seeds for disease resistant vegetables might be difficult.

LCM: What do you recommend doing about furry creatures like squirrels?

DEER RESISTANT FLOWERS

(Although deer have been known to eat just about anything, the following seem to be their least favorites. This list was extracted from one composed by the California extension service. For the complete list, contact your local extension service.)

Hollyhock *Althaea rosea*

Columbine *Aquilegia* sp.

Pot marigold *Calendula officinalis*

Cornflower *Centaurea cyanus*

Chrysanthemums *Chrysanthemum* sp.

Clematis *Clematis* sp.

Larkspur *Delphinium ajacis*

Bleeding heart *Dicentra spectablisis*

Foxglove *Digitalis* sp.

Lenten rose *Helleborus* sp.

Iris *Iris* sp.

Lantana *Lantana* sp.

Narcissus *Narcissus* sp.

Spiderwort *Tradescantia virginiana*

Tulip *Tulipa* sp.

THE WELL-STOCKED GARDEN TOOL CHEST

- ✧ Shovels: round-pointed, narrow-bladed, and flat
- ✧ Medium weight hoe
- ✧ Spading fork
- ✧ Trowel
- ✧ Spade
- ✧ Bulb planter
- ✧ Hand pruners
- ✧ Hedge trimmer
- ✧ Rakes: steel, leaf

WALTER: We have planted corn three years running and have never eaten an ear of corn out of our garden because the squirrels or chipmunks or something climbs up and eats them. I never see them, but the husks are pulled down and everything is eaten up. I can only guess it's squirrels.

Actually, in most cases, you just learn to coexist. If you get really obsessive, you can fence and put out human hair and other natural repellents, but we try to take the attitude, "If they get some, they get some."

As far as berries and the birds, some years they eat them up, other years they don't seem to mess with them. But overall, I think netting is more trouble than it's worth.

LCM: How about deer?

WALTER: It's not as big a problem here in suburban Atlanta as it is in other areas. Deer will eat anything in the garden, though the extension service has put out a list of plants that are considered deer repellent.

LCM: Is there anything you can do about voles?

WALTER: We try to keep the area around plants free of mulch. Voles are very secretive and they like to get underneath the mulch and burrow. Hosta people take big plastic drums, cut them into sections, and then plunge the ring around the hosta plant, leaving two inches above ground, and about three to four inches below.

The below-ground part keeps the voles from burrowing, the above ground part gives the gardener an area to keep clean and covered with sand. Voles don't like to be out in the open, exposed to predators. So it's a reasonable control, even under pine trees. See? Even something as beneficial as mulch, you have to know when to use it and when not to.

LCM: What are your basic recommendation for building the soil?

WALTER: If you're smart, you start with a soil test and follow the recommendations given. Gardeners can do a great deal to improve their soil. A lot of people don't realize the importance of lime and how much emphasis should be placed on the pH of the soil.

The most dramatic evidence I have seen are pictures showing the same plants grown in soils with a .5 change in pH. The plant tops all look healthy enough, but the root systems change dramatically with more appropriate pH. The roots may actually triple in size, and with a bigger root mass, the plants will be more resistant to disease, insects, drought, and so on. So, lime is very, very important.

But you have to get lime down to the root level. Lime moves so slowly in the soil, the roots may stay at the same pH level for fifty years unless people really dig in the lime.

LCM: What do you do about adding lime for established plants?

WALTER: Just dig it in the best you can. It's hard to do with established beds. I just use cheap lime; pelletized doesn't release any faster, although it is easier to spread. It takes both the pelletized and the powdered lime about six months to do any good.

LCM: When should you add lime?

WALTER: It may move a little faster when the weather's warm but you can lime any time of year. Just remember to add lime whenever you plant.

LCM: In addition to lime, what else do you recommend adding to the soils in the Georgia Piedmont area?

WALTER: Phosphorus, because it's very important for photosynthesis and helps plant energy formation. You can add it either directly with superphosphate, 0-46-0, or indirectly with organic matter. Straight compost and manure are high in phosphorus. But, like the lime, the phosphorous is slow to move. Unless you dig it in, it stays around on the top six inches of soil.

Adding regular fertilizer that contains nitrogen, phosphorus and potassium is also good. If you need phosphorous in the soil, be sure to choose a fertilizer with the middle number up above five, indicating that it is high in phosphorous.

LCM: Is there any danger of overdosing, adding too many nutrients to the soil?

WALTER: Not really. Even if you use straight superphosphate, you'd have to add tons before the plant would show toxicity. When your soil test comes back with certain elements showing high, some people think that they need to take stuff out of the soil, but these high levels only indicate that these are elements that do not need to be added to the soil.

If the soil test comes back showing that your soil is low in something, then seventy percent of the time, the plants will benefit from your adding these missing elements to the soil.

LCM: How about adding a substance such as granite dust?

WALTER: I have used granite dust to improve the texture of the soil and drainage, but I'm convinced that in clay soils, organic matter is the easiest thing to find, use, dig in, and work with, so I don't use much granite dust any more. It's hard to find and heavy as heck to get into the garden; frankly, compost is much easier. I am using organic matter more. But I have to keep adding it to the soil because it disappears over time.

LCM: Are there things you should not put into a compost pile?

WALTER: Plants that have nematodes on them, or diseased plants.

LCM: Grass clippings, kudzu vines— can you compost things like that?

WALTER: Yes. From experience, I learned that you don't put a big bunch of grass clippings in one big pile because it will stink up the entire neighborhood. I still use grass clippings, but I do it in moderation. I stockpile pine needles in the fall. If they're fresh, I use them for mulch. If they're rotted, I use them for compost.

LCM: Do you layer it with soil?

WALTER: I'm a lazy person. When I compost, Mother Nature is my big partner. I just dump stuff in a pile and let it go.

LCM: If you were just starting out gardening, what are some of the basic tools you would need?

WALTER: You really ought to have several shovels, a regular round-pointed one, and also a narrow-bladed shovel about four to five inches wide and fourteen to sixteen inches long. Because it's so narrow it is helpful for trenching around things. It's great if I'm trying to cut that last root underneath a shrub. Also, a flat shovel is good for scraping out the bottom of my trailer, and a child's shovel is good for transplanting small plants.

I like a medium- to heavyweight hoe. If it's too light, you spend the day trying to chop weeds out of the garden. I don't weed until the plants are over my head, so I need a big hoe.

You need a spading fork for digging in heavy, clay soils where a shovel might not go in as easily. And you need pruning saws, loppers, and a heavy-duty trowel. A $3 trowel just doesn't last as long as a $9 trowel. I use my bulb planter a lot for doing transplants. You could probably use two to three hand pruners and a hedge shear.

LCM: Are there times of the year when you should not prune?

WALTER: That's pretty much an old wive's tale. It's rare that you could markedly hurt a plant by pruning at the "wrong" time. There are times that are less good than others, and there are times that you achieve effects that you don't like, but you're not going to hurt a plant by pruning.

There are a few special cases. If you prune an overgrown boxwood, you'll likely kill it. If you prune azaleas in fall, you'll knock off all the new blooms. And you need to prune hydrangeas right after they bloom to allow the blooms for next year to form on new growth.

LCM: Any last bit of philosophy or encouragement?

WALTER: Just really work with the soil. Folks don't understand how organic matter disappears in the soil. Digging it in increases the productivity of the soil, but also speeds up the rate at which the

organic matter disappears. If you think of organic matter as burning very slowly in the soil, what you have after a couple of years is a little bit of ash. Adding oxygen to the soil makes organic matter disappear faster. Sometimes the chunkier you get stuff, the longer it will last. If I had new ground that I was working, I wouldn't put fine, well-aged compost into it. I would look for chunky things with chips a half-inch wide. It will last longer, and in time it will break down and eventually the soil will become blacker and browner. It takes time to build the soil, but that's the best investment you can ever make in a successful garden.

STEPHEN MYERS, ATHENS: COOPERATIVE EXTENSION SERVICE

Because he grew up in a family whose primary objective was scientific exploration, it is no surprise that Stephen Myers and all his brothers are now involved in careers that still involve scientific pursuits.

"We never knew an attitude of indifference," Steve said. "We were encouraged to be curious, and we always had some pretty unusual pets like snakes, skunks, goats, and flying squirrels.

"My father, originally a chemist, was a dentist and loved science. Once he showed us how to make hydrogen gas from hydrochloric acid, and we sent up balloons that were found two states away.

"I loved working in the garden with my grandfather. My parents had a wonderfully landscaped yard and garden. For rural South Carolina, we had some pretty unusual plants—a zoysia lawn, dawn redwood trees, and crabapples."

While he was growing up, Stephen and his brother David had a plant collection in the woods. Today both enjoy grown-up versions of their boyhood hobby in their horticulture-related work. David works in plant geography, and Stephen is a professor in the Horticulture Department at the University of Georgia.

"I like teaching because the students keep you sharp, and the research is fun because of the excitement of exploration and the idealistic goal of trying to improve things."

I interviewed Steve in late spring at the University of Georgia. He spoke of the joys and challenges of growing fruit in the state of Georgia.

LCM: Georgia is known as the Peach State. Can you grow peaches in all parts of the state?

STEPHEN: We have a great diversity of growing conditions in the state, and if you're careful to plant the right cultivars, you can grow peaches throughout Georgia. Matching the number of chill

hours required by a specific cultivar with the different regions is important. Without a sufficient number of chill hours—the time below 45 degrees needed for the trees to break dormancy—the tree will not flower or grow normally in the spring.

The extension service has divided the state into five different regions, and there are peach varieties which are suitable for each of these. South Georgia is most suited for low-chill peaches such as 'June Gold', 'Gold Prince', and 'Springcrest'. The best zone 4, middle Georgia, cultivars include 'Scarlet Pearl', 'Harvester', 'Swanee', 'Redskin', and 'Flame Prince'.

Zone 3, from Macon to Augusta, has the most varieties to choose from both because of the climate, and because this is the zone in which most of the research has been done. Here you can grow 'Redhaven', 'Windblown', 'Cresthaven', 'Jefferson', and 'Encore'. These varieties are also good for zones 1 and 2, which includes all of north Georgia.

LCM: What do you need to consider when buying trees?

STEPHEN: Be sure you get good plants from a reputable nursery. We have several excellent nurseries in the state. Lawson's in Ball Ground specializes in antique apple varieties; Johnson's in Ellijay is good for peaches, apples, and pears.

Commercial growers typically purchase and plant bare-root trees.

LCM: Can you buy container-grown plants as well?

STEPHEN: Yes. Again, just make sure you know what you're buying. Many plant sources don't name the rootstock on which the trees are grafted, but this is very important, for this determines [whether or not] the tree is dwarf, early bearing, its mature size, its susceptibility to disease, and so on. The rootstock should be accurately marked on any plant you buy.

For south Georgia, purchase peach trees on 'Nemagard' rootstock. In more northern areas of the state, you should purchase trees on 'Lovell' rootstock.

LCM: How do you recommend planting fruit trees?

STEPHEN: The first thing you need to do is take a soil test. Get the soil from at least six to eight inches deep to accurately test the root zone.

Most of our soils are low in phosphorous and are acidic. Fruit trees do best in neutral soils of pH between 6.0 and 7.0. However, if you put lime and phosphorous on top of the soil, in twenty years it will have only moved an inch or two. Anytime you prepare soil for a perennial planting, you need to incorporate these amendments into the soil throughout the root zone before planting. Otherwise, it's not possible to get the material to the root zone without harming the plant.

STEPS FOR·PLANTING FRUIT TREES

1. Take a soil test.
2. When soil is dry, dig lime, phosphorous, and other nutrients into root zone.
3. Select cultivars adapted to your area.
4. Purchase quality trees that are true to name.
5. Plant trees the same depth as they were grown in the nursery. Do not plant too deeply.
6. Water thoroughly and mulch.
7. Protect trees from stress of drought, weed competition, and pests.

Something else that people do incorrectly is to work the soil when it's too wet. If you dig a hole in clay soil, which many of our soils are, it will push the particles of clay together, resulting in compaction and poor drainage. That's why clay makes good pots—because the particles of soil can be compacted and become watertight. We don't have freezing and thawing like they do in the north, which helps move the earth. If you ball up a hand full of soil and drop it and it shatters, it's okay to dig and plant. If it stays in a ball, it's too wet to work.

Another rule of thumb is not to plant too deep. Plant the tree the same depth that it was grown in the nursery, with the upper roots near the surface of the soil. Even on bare-root trees, you should be able to see where the soil line was in the nursery. If you must, err on the side of being too high rather than too deep. If you plant fruit trees too deep, particularly in our heavy soils, the roots may die of oxygen deprivation.

Plant trees in the least stressful time of the year, which for Georgia is in the fall. Late winter to early spring is the second choice. Avoid planting in the summer when high temperatures can increase transplant shock. An old peach growers' saying is that trees should be in the ground by Christmas.

LCM: Do you recommend adding organic matter?

STEPHEN: Not generally, because the plants have to adapt to the native soils. You would have to amend the entire root zone, and this is rarely practical. Most fruit trees will do okay as long as the nutritional levels are correct, so don't amend for soil texture, but for soil fertility.

LCM: How about fertilizing the trees?

STEPHEN: The rate depends on the age of the plant. Generally, you should not fertilize until the ground around a newly planted tree has settled after a good rain. Even then, it's important to keep the fertilizer away from the trunk, because the fertilizer can mix with the rain, run down the trunks, and kill the plant with an overdose.

I often use a starter solution of 20-20-20. A little dose of that in spring will stimulate root activity.

If you mulch heavily, you might end up with a nitrogen deficiency. If you use a lot of organic matter, you might have to compensate with extra nitrogen. I don't think there is much difference in nitrogen sources as long as the pH is maintained near 6.5. Calcium nitrate, however, is a favorite fertilizer. It is neutral and won't change the pH, but it is expensive and hard to find.

LCM: Is it necessary to spray fruit trees on a regular schedule?

STEPHEN: Actually, no. Just like commercial growers, gardeners should spray on an as-needed basis. There are times when you need to be particularly watchful. Brown rot is a big problem on mature fruit, and generally if you don't spray for that, the losses will be terrible.

Most growers today are progressive and show leadership in regards to integrated pest management [IPM]. For example, they have learned to protect good insects by spraying only under certain conditions, and allowing these insect predators to do their jobs.

Controlling pests is very difficult because there are specific sprays for specific pests. The first step is identifying the pest. The next thing you need to do is determine all the options for control. In integrated pest management, a wide range of control methods may be at your disposal, from hand picking to using soaps and dormant oils.

LCM: Can you grow peaches organically?

STEPHEN: It is very difficult to do with peaches because the climate here is hot and humid and the growing season is long, creating good conditions for problems with insects and disease.

DON HASTINGS, JR., ROSWELL

Seedsmen, plantsmen, and horticultural wizards, the Hastings could easily be considered the first family of Georgia gardening. Don Hastings, Jr., following in the footsteps of his grandfather, H.G. and his father, Donald, is the third generation to carry on the tradition of horticultural excellence in this state.

But Don has not limited his influence to the state of Georgia. In 1976, after selling the Hastings Company to outside interests, he began developing major export-oriented fruit and vegetable farms in tropical and sub-tropical countries. This enterprise led him all over the world, to Egypt and the Philippines, to Malaysia,

Jamaica, Antigua and Morocco, and has resulted in a world-wide reputation in fruit and vegetable production.

❦

I think that the gardeners of

the 1930s were the best because

they didn't have the quick fix.

In those days, cottonseed meal,

cow manure, bone meal, and

blood meal were the way

you grew things.

❦

Don is the author of a three-volume series of books, *Gardening in the South*, and was a long-time radio gardening host. With Kathy Henderson, he starred in a syndicated TV series, also known as *Gardening in the South*.

I interviewed Don in early fall, and listened as he spoke of the traditions of gardening, and of the joys of passing on this tradition from one generation to another.

LCM: You and your family have been well-known in the gardening community of this state for a long time. Do you think that people today are as interested in gardening as they used to be?

DON: Gardening is a phenomenon that goes up and down. In the 1930s there were a lot of gardeners, but after World War II, it faded away, and people became more active in other things. But I think it's back. People get a lot of pleasure out of gardening. It may be more important to people now than it ever has been before. I've known many doctors

and airline pilots who tell me that gardening is their release from stress.

LCM: Can you tell me what it was like growing up as a part of the Hastings family?

DON: It was tough [laughing]. My great-grandfather was a newspaper man from Ohio. He became ill and his doctors said he should move to a different climate, so he moved his family to Interlochen, Florida, and started a newspaper there. My grandfather, Harry G. Hastings, worked for him selling subscriptions to the paper. When he was age eighteen or nineteen, he had an idea—sort of like my own sons—of how to do things better. He devised a promotion plan for selling newspapers and gave a little package of seeds away with every subscription that was bought.

He soon found out that people were buying the subscription for the seeds more than for the newspaper. Well, H.G. was a very thinking person, and he decided to look into the seed business.

LCM: Were there other seed companies at this time?

DON: There weren't many of them. Rueters in New Orleans, and T.W. Wood in Richmond were both doing basically the same thing. In 1889, H.G. started the business and published a catalog listing the seeds he had, and the whole thing just prospered. But he had trouble getting mail out of Interlochen, Florida, quickly, so he moved to Atlanta and set up shop on Mitchell Street. All through the early 1900s he worked to develop a widespread seed business. H.G. was a character and a very strong man; he had a lot of influence on Southern farmers. His goal was to get the farmer away from planting a single crop, like cotton, which was wearing out the land.

His three boys—my father and his two brothers, Stanley and Ray—all went into the business. Stanley eventually left the business, and Ray, who was an innovative person, started the All America Seed Selection. My father stayed and married my mother, who was a biology major at Agnes Scott and a fabulous gardener. She was probably the best gardener of the whole crowd.

LCM: And a great flower arranger and garden club lady, yes?

DON: Yes, that's what she was known for. But as far as gardening was concerned, she had a veritable green thumb. All the field workers would laugh and say Mrs. Hastings was the only one who knew how to grow azaleas. She was a very strong person and she knew what she wanted. The gardens at Lovejoy [the family farm] were really spectacular. We always had formal gardens there, and they were beautiful.

LCM: Have you always loved gardening?

DON: When I was a little boy, I hated gardening. I went to the fields to work when I was twelve or thirteen—mostly to get away from having to garden. Mother was very exacting. I budded roses and hoed things and cut weeds and became a nurseryman and worked until I went to college.

LCM: And where was that?

DON: Cornell. I have a degree in ornamental horticulture. I graduated in 1950 and came back and went into the business with my father.

LCM: Having been in the gardening business all your life, do you see certain trends that people repeat over and over?

DON: The nursery trade goes through phases like anything else. I think that the gardener of the 1930s was the best gar-

dener, because he didn't have the quick fix. In those days, cottonseed meal, cow manure, bone meal, and blood meal were the way you grew things. But Southern soils are unique, especially in the Piedmont. They are heavy and they need organic matter. On a scale of one to ten, if the 1930s gardener was up around level ten, and the late 1940s and '50s gardeners were down to about two, I'd say today's gardener is back up to about a six or seven.

What I find really exciting in Georgia is that the commercial people have accepted flowers and plants. Post Properties is the real reason it started, because they built a reputation on flowers and good landscaping. I think there's a great deal of hope in gardening that it will continue to improve.

DON HASTINGS' EASY SUMMER VEGETABLES

(*From seed unless indicated*)
Tomatoes (Start from plants)
Peppers (Start from plants)
Eggplant (Start from plants)
Cucumbers
Yellow crookneck squash
Zucchini squash
Pole beans
Okra
Sweet corn
Bush snap beans
Bush lima beans
Cow peas, like blackeyes

As long as human beings live, there will be people who will want things beautiful. I'm really happy to see the trend away from the quick cure, spraying with liquid fertilizer. Gardening is an experience; it's not something you buy and sell, more now than ever.

LCM: What specific gardening mistakes do you see people make?

DON: The biggest mistake is poor soil preparation. My father always said, "Plant a one-dollar plant in a ten-dollar hole." Starting plants correctly by preparing the soil well is the main key to success.

LCM: How do you prepare vegetables beds for spring planting?

DON: A vegetable garden is similar to a sunny annual bed; it should have rich, well-drained soil and at least six hours of sunlight daily. The area must be tilled deeply and amendments added if the soil is poor. Take a soil test to determine exactly what needs to be added, but generally, the area will need to be limed. I apply fertilizer at planting time, and continue applications every six weeks during the season.

DON HASTINGS' EASY SPRING VEGETABLES

(*Should be started from transplants*)
Green onions
Onions
Broccoli
Beets
Turnips
Greens

I create my vegetable beds by removing soil from a central channel and making wide ridges to plant in. This is essential for root crops, but is also beneficial for other crops because it encourages better root growth and higher production. I also run my rows in a north-south direction so that the sun falls evenly on the plants.

LCM: What are some easy spring vegetables to grow?

DON: Onion sets for spring [green] onions, onion plants for large bulbs, broccoli [from transplants], beets, turnips, and various greens.

LCM: How about some easy summer vegetables?

DON: I would try tomato, pepper, eggplant, cucumber, yellow crookneck squash, zucchini squash, pole beans, okra, sweet corn, bush snap beans, bush lima beans, and a cow pea, like blackeyes.

LCM: How do you put the beds down for winter?

DON: After frost, all vegetables and annual flowers should be removed from their beds. I prefer to grow crimson clover or Austrian winter peas in bare areas, especially in the vegetable garden. When root diseases have been a problem in any area, I like to plant [annual] ryegrass for the winter. Grasses seem to have the ability to reduce root disease infections.

LCM: Any last bit of gardening advice or philosophy?

DON: I think that gardening as a family, if it's done right, can be a very enriching experience and can help bind a family together. It keeps the kids away from the television and computer games. But you can't make little slaves out of your children. You can't expect them to till the garden when you want to sit around and drink lemonade.

Betsy and I were not particularly smart parents, but we were lucky parents. I loved to garden when the boys were little, and they were always out there with me. They did whatever they wanted to do in the garden. As a result, we all love the garden and each of us has a specialty.

It's good if you can help them develop so that they believe that the garden is as much theirs as yours, as much the family's as it is any one person's. I think the next generation—your children's children—are going to need it. People need beautiful things. People need plants.

RESOURCES FOR FRUITS AND VEGETABLES

BOOKS

Adams, William D., and Thomas R. Leroy. *Growing Fruits and Nuts in the South.* Dallas: Taylor Publishing Company, 1992.

Chambers, David, and Lucinda Mays. *Vegetable Gardening.* New York: Knopf Publishing/Pantheon Books, 1996.

Hastings, Don. *Gardening in the South with Don Hastings.* Dallas: Taylor Publishing Company, 1988.

Ison, William G. *All About Muscadines, Blueberries, Blackberries for the Growers of These Fine Berries.* Brooks, Georgia: Self-published, 1988.

McEachern, George Ray. *Growing Fruits, Berries, and Nuts in the South.* Houston: Gulf Coast Publishing Co., 1978.

PAMPHLETS

University of Georgia Cooperative Extension Service puts out many pamphlets on growing individual fruits, including peaches and nectarines, pears, figs, blueberries, raspberries and blackberries, bunch grapes, apples, and muscadines.

Other useful pamphlets include: *Minor Fruits and Nuts in Georgia* and *Disease and Insect Control in Home Orchards.*

Information sheets on growing individual vegetables are also available at Callaway Gardens, as well as at select garden centers.

SOURCES OF PLANTS

Harp's Farmer's Market and Nursery
1692 Highway 92 South
Fayetteville, GA
770-719-9588

Ison's Nursery
Brooks, GA
770-599-6970
Muscadine grapes, fruits, and berries.

Johnson's Nursery
Rt. 5, Box 29 J
Ellijay, GA 30540
706-276-3187
Fruit trees, ornamental trees, deciduous shrubs.

Lawson's Nursery
Rt. 1, Box 472
Yellow Creek Road
Ball Ground, GA 30102
770-893-2141

DISPLAY GARDENS

Atlanta Botanical Garden summer vegetable garden, Atlanta

Georgia Station Research and Education Garden, Griffin

Harp's Farmer's Market and Nursery, Fayetteville

Mr. Cason's Vegetable Garden, Callaway Gardens, Pine Mountain

PLANT CATALOG

Acer rubrum (Maple)
Large tree with colorful fall foliage.
Grows 40–50 feet.
Needs full sun.
Other species: *A. floridanum*, Florida maple,
A. leucoderme, Chalkbark maple, *A. palmatum*.

Achillea × 'Coronation Gold' (Achillea)
Perennial with finely cut foliage and golden-
yellow flower heads.
Grows 2–3 feet.
Needs full sun.

Achillea millefolium 'Oertel's Rose' (Yarrow)
Perennial with deep green fernlike foliage, pink
flowers which fade to white.
Grows 12–18 inches.
Will grow in full sun or part shade.
Thought to be same species as *A. millefolium*
'1869'.

Aconitum uncinatum (Monkshood)
Native perennial with several hooded, violet-
blue flowers in late summer, early fall.
Grows 2–4 feet.
Needs shade or part shade and moist, well-
drained soil.

Acorus gramineus variegatus (Sweet flag)
Dwarf form of groundcover with evergreen,
striped grass-like leaves.
Grows 3–5 inches.
Prefers partial shade.

Actinidia deliciosa (Kiwi vine)
Fruit-bearing perennial vine.
Grows up to 25 feet long.
Needs full sun to partial shade.

Adiantum capillus-veneris (Southern maiden-
hair fern)
Low growing fern.
Prefers shade and rich, moist soil.

Adlumia fungosa (Allegheny vine)
Perennial vine. Pearly pink flowers in summer;
large, attractive foliage.
Needs full sun or partial shade.

Aesculus parviflora (Bottlebrush buckeye)
Deciduous shrub. Large white blooms in
summer.
Grows 8–10 feet tall, 10–15 feet across.
Needs full sun or part shade, in moist, acidic
soil.
Other species: *A. pavia*, red buckeye.

Agarista populifolia (Florida leucothoe)
Evergreen shrub, glossy-green foliage and fra-
grant creamy white flowers in early summer.
Grows 12 feet tall.
Prefers full to partial shade; moist, acidic soils.

Ajuga reptans (Ajuga)
Perennial groundcover.
Height varies from 4–12 inches.
Best in partial shade, needs good air circulation
and well-drained soil.
Cultivars: 'Catlin's Giant'—works best in sun,
'Bronze Beauty'—metallic bronze foliage,
'Burgundy Glow'—foliage shades of pink, rose
and green.

Alcea rosea (Hollyhock)
Old-fashioned annual in every color except
blue.
Grows 4–6 feet.
Needs full sun.

Allegheny Vine (see *Adlumia*)

Allium schoenoprasum (Chives)
Perennial herb grown from a small bulb, pro-
duces pungent, grass-like foliage. Rose-lavender
flowers.
Grows to 12–18 inches.
Needs full sun.

Amsonia tabernaemontana var. *montana*
(Bluestar)
Perennial: narrow leaves, rich, blue flowers.
Grows 24–30 inches tall.
Full sun or partial shade.

Anacharis (see *Elodea canadensis*)

Andropogon virginicus (Broomsedge)
Perennial native grass. Golden brown in fall.
Grows 2–4 feet.
Needs full sun.

Anemone × *hybrida* 'Honorine Jobert'
(Japanese anemone)
Perennial with white blossoms in early fall.
Grows 12–18 inches.
Needs part shade, rich soils.

Anemone vitifolia 'Robustissima' (Fall
anemone)
Perennial; mauve pink flowers. Blooms in fall.
Grows 18–36 inches.
Needs part shade, rich soils.

Anethum graveolens (Dill)
Self-seeding annual herb. Feathery, blue-green
foliage.
Grows 36 inches.
Needs full sun.

Anise tree, Florida (see *Illicium floridanum*)

Anthriscus cerefolium (Chervil)
Hardy annual herbs, grown for foliage which
produces subtle taste.
Grows 24 inches.
Needs partial shade, moist humus.

Antirrhinum majus (Snapdragon)
Cool weather annual; plant with pansies and
Johnny-jump-ups.
Grows 7–36 inches.
Prefers full sun.

Apple (see *Malus*)

Aquilegia canadensis (Columbine)
Native woodland perennial, readily self-sows.
Attractive blue-green foliage, yellow and red
spurred flowers.
Grows 12–18 inches.
Needs partial shade.

Arachnoides simplicia 'Variegata' (East Indian
holly fern)
Triangular leaves, 2 feet long.
Needs shade, moist, rich soil.

Arisaema triphyllum (Jack-in-the-Pulpit)
Woodland perennial. Green and brown attrac-
tive spathe, arched over spadix.
Grows 1–3 feet tall.
Needs full to partial shade.
Other species—*A. ringens, A. cochiana,
A. tuberosa.*

Artemisia abrotanum (Southernwood)
Perennial herb with gray-green aromatic
foliage.
Full sun, moderately rich soils.

Artemisia absinthium (Wormwood)
Spreading perennial with gray-green leaves,
covered with hairs.
Grows 24–30 inches.
Needs full sun, part shade, will grow in heavy
soils.

Artemisia dracunculus sativa (French
tarragon)
Perennial herb. Difficult to grow in Georgia
except in northern areas.
Grows to 24 inches.
Full sun, well-drained soil.

Artemisia × 'Powis Castle' (Artemisia)
Perennial grown for attractive grey-green
foliage.
Grows 12–18 inches.
Full sun.

Asarum canadense (Wild ginger)
Perennial groundcover, large glossy leaves up
to 7 inches across.
Grows 6–8 inches tall.
Prefers partial to full shade.
Other species: *A. shuttleworthii* 'Callaway' has
mottled evergreen leaves.

Asclepias incarnata (Swamp milkweed)
Perennial with clusters of deep pink flowers in
summer.
Grows 1–4 feet.
Needs full sun and moist soils.

Asclepias tuberosa (Butterfly weed)
Native perennial with clusters of beautiful
orange flowers.
Grows 24–30 inches.
Needs full sun and dry conditions.

Asimina triloba (Pawpaw)
Native deciduous tree, edible greenish-yellow
berries.
Grows 20 feet tall.
Prefers moist, rich, acidic soils, full sun.

Asparagus officinalis (Asparagus)
Cool season biennial vegetable.
Grows 36 inches.
Full sun.

Asperula odorata (Sweet woodruff)
Native perennial with small white flowers in
late spring.
Partial shade, rich soils.

Aster sp. (Aster)
Perennials, generally fall blooming, with small
daisy-like blossoms.
Aster carolinianus—climbing, with small
mauve flowers.
A. tataricus—grows 6 feet tall, blue flowers in
late fall.
A. lateriflorus—white or purplish flowers.
A. oblongifolius—blue or purplish flowers.
A. divaricatus—clusters of white flowers, 1–2
feet tall.
A. laevis—purple foliage, blue flowers, yellow
centers.
A. × 'Hella Lacy'—purple flowers, 3–4 feet
tall.
Most species need full sun or partial shade.

Astilbe chinensis pumila (Astilbe)
Attractive perennial with spires of flowers in
white, peach, pink, or red in late spring.
Grows 24–36 inches tall.
Needs part shade and moist, rich soil.

Atamasco lily (see *Zephyranthes atamasco*)

Athyrium nipponicum 'Pictum' (Japanese
painted fern)
Deciduous perennial fern, attractive foliage.
Grows 12–18 inches tall.
Grows in full to part shade, but foliage colors
will be best with a little sunlight.

Autumn fern (see *Dryopteris ludoviciana*)

Azalea (see *Rhododendron* sp.)

Bachelor's buttons (see *Centaurea cyanus*)

Banana shrub (see *Michelia figo*)

Baptisia australis (Baptisia)
Perennial with blue flowers in early summer.
Grows 3–4 feet tall.
Needs full sun or part shade.
Other species: *Baptisia minor*, similar but
smaller leaves; *B. alba*, white flowers; *B.
sphaerocarpa*, yellow flowers.

Barbara's button (see *Marshallia obovata*)

Barberry, Japanese (see *Berberis thunbergii*)

Basil (see *Ocimum basilicum*)

Bay (see *Laurus nobilis*)

Beautyberry, American (see *Callicarpa
americana*)

Beebalm (see *Monarda didyma*)

Begonia, angel wing (see *Begonia
semperflorens*)

Begonia semperflorens (Angel wing begonia)
Annual bedding plant with white, pink, red
flowers, green or bronze foliage.
Grows 12 inches.
Part sun to shade.

Berberis thunbergii (Japanese barberry)
Small, deciduous shrubs, generally deep red
foliage, with small thorns.
Needs full sun, considered tough and adaptable.
Recommended varieties: 'Aurea'—chartreuse
foliage.
'Red Bird'—deep red foliage, only grows to 5
feet.
'Royal Cloak'—deep purple-red leaves and
arching branches.

Betula nigra (River birch)
Medium- to fast-growing deciduous tree.
Alternate, simple, pointed leaves.
Grows 40–70 feet, with equal spread.
Prefers moist soils, found naturally along
stream banks and in flood zones.

Birch, river (see *Betula nigra*)

Black mondo grass (see *Ophiopogon
planiscapus*)

Black-eyed Susan (see *Rudbeckia* sp.)

Blackberry (see *Rubus* sp.)

Blazing star (see *Liatris aspera*)

Bleeding heart (see *Dicentra spectabilis*)

Blue fan flower (see *Scabiosa caucasica*)

Blue star (see *Amsonia tabernaemontana*)

Blue-eyed grass (see *Sisyrinchium
angustifolium*)

Blueberry (see *Vaccinium* sp.)

Brachycome iberidifolia (Swan River daisy)
Annual with masses of blue or violet flowers,
somewhat short lived.
Grows 12–18 inches.
Needs full sun, warm temperatures.

Brassica oleracea (Ornamental cabbage)
Annual grows for its large, attractive leaves
tinged with pink, cream, or purple.
Grows 10–12 inches high, 12–15 inches
across.
Plant in fall for cool season color, needs full
sun, rich soils.

Brassica oleracea var. *botrytis* (Broccoli)
Annual cool season vegetable.
Production in spring or fall.
Needs full sun.

Brassica oleracea var. *captitata* (Cabbage)
Annual cool season crop.
Needs full sun.

Brassica oleracea var. *gemmifera* (Brussels
sprouts)
Long growing season makes this a difficult crop
to grow in Georgia.

Broccoli (see *Brassica oleracea* var. *botrytis*)

Broomsedge (see *Andropogon virginicus*)

Brussels sprouts (see *Brassica oleracea* var. *gemmifera*)

Buckeye, bottlebrush (see *Aesculus parviflora*)

Buddleia davidii (Butterfly bush)
Perennial shrub with beautiful lavender, pink or white spires of flowers in summer.
Must have full sun, prefers moist, rich soils.
Cut back to the ground in late winter.

Butterfly bush (see *Buddleia*)

Cabbage (see *Brassica oleracea* var. *capitata*)

Calendula officinalis (Pot marigold)
A cool season annual, bright orange or yellow flowers.
Grows 10–12 inches.
Needs full sun or light shade, will not tolerate high temperatures and humidity.

Callicarpa americana (American Beautyberry)
Deciduous shrub; violet to magenta fruits in fall (white form also available).
Grows 4–6 feet.
Full sun to part shade.

Camellia japonica (Camellia)
Evergreen broadleafed shrub. Attractive winter blooms (November–March).
Grows to be a small tree 10–15 feet.
Grows best in partial shade.
Other species: *Camellia sinensis*.

Camellia sasanqua (Camellia)
Broad-leafed evergreen shrub. Blooms September through December.
Grows 6–10 feet.
Grows in full sun or filtered shade.

Campion, rose (see *Lychnis coronaria*)

Camptosorus rhizophyllus (Walking fern)
Long, tapering fronds, not dissected as many other ferns.
Grows 4–18 inches.
Prefers moist, rich soils and shade.

Canna hybrids
Tender perennial with broad, tropical looking foliage. Large flowers in summer.
Grows 6–8 feet.
Needs full sun, ample moisture.

Cantaloupe (see *Cucumis melo*)

Cardinal flower (see *Lobelia cardinalis*)

Carex glauca (Blue sedge)
Perennial ornamental grass with blue-gray foliage.
Grows 6 inches.
Needs full sun to part shade.

Carrot (see *Daucus carota sativus*)

Cassia corymbosa (Cassia)
Shrub with yellow flowers in summer.
Grows 10 feet.
Needs full sun, well-drained soils.
Other cultivars: *C. corymbosa*, blooms in fall; *C. bicapsularis*, somewhat tender.

Catnip (see *Nepeta cataria*)

Cattail (see *Typha* sp.)

Celandine poppy (see *Chelidonium majus*)

Celosia spicata (Celosia)
Shrubby summer annual, produces terminal spikes of flowers.
Grows $3^{1}/_{2}$–4 feet.
Needs full sun or partial shade, blooms May to frost.
Recommended cultivars: 'Purple Flamingo Feather'—reddish-purple flowers.
'Pink Candle'—pink flowers.

Centaurea cyanus (Bachelor's buttons)
Annual. Bright blue flowers in late spring.
Grows 12–36 inches.
Needs full sun.

Cercis canadensis (Redbud)
Deciduous tree.
Grows 20–40 feet.
Needs full sun.
Cultivar 'Forest Pansy'—attractive dark red
foliage.

Chasmanthium latifolium (River oats grass)
Luxuriant grass-like growth.
Shade tolerant.

Cheiranthus cheiri (Wallflower)
Perennial, treated as a cool season annual with
yellow, orange, or mahogany flowers.
Grows 12–30 inches.
Will grow in full sun or partial shade, does not
like hot weather.

Chelidonium majus (Celandine poppy)
Perennial with deep yellow flowers in summer.
Grows 12–24 inches.
Needs shade to part shade, moist, rich soil.

Chervil (see *Anthriscus cerefolium*)

Chimonanthus praecox (Wintersweet)
Attractive deciduous shrub, fragrant yellow to
purple flowers in winter.
Grows 10–15 feet.
Needs full sun, partial shade, well-drained
soils.

Chinese foxglove (see *Rehmannia elata*)

Chionanthus virginicus (Grancy gray-beard or
fringetree)
Attractive native tree, produces fragrant white
blossoms in May.
Mature height 12–20 feet.
Performs best in full sun, but will also do well
with partial shade.

Chives (see *Allium schoenoprasum*)

Christmas fern (see *Polystichum acrosticoides*)

Chrysanthemum leucanthemum (Ox-eye
daisy)
Perennial, naturalized throughout. White blossoms in spring, early summer; readily reseeds.
Grows 12–16 inches.
Needs full sun, partial shade, will tolerate moderately well-drained soils.

Chrysanthemum maximum (Daisy)
Perennial, showy white flowers in summer.
Grows 12–24 inches.
Full sun.

Chrysanthemum × *maximum* (Daisy)
Perennial with large white daisies in summer,
strong stems.
Grows 3–3$^1/2$ feet.
Needs full sun, well-drained soil.
Recommended varieties 'Ryan' and 'Becky'.

Chrysanthemum nipponicum (Nippon daisy)
Fall blooming daisy.
Grows 24–30 inches.
Needs full sun or light shade, will tolerate poor
soils.

Chrysanthemum parthenium (Feverfew)
Annual herb with a mass of small white daisy-
like blossoms. Reseeds prolifically.
Grows 24–36 inches.
Needs full sun.

Chrysogonum virginianum (Green-and-gold)
Woodland perennial groundcover. Produces
bright yellow flowers in spring, then blooms off
and on in May and June.
Grows 10–12 inches tall.
Recommended cultivar: 'Eco Laquered Spider'.

Cimicifuga racemosa (Cohosh, snakeroot)
Perennial; tall, white spires in late summer.
Grows 6–8 feet.
Needs moist, rich, acidic soils in shade.

Citrullus vulgaris (Watermelon)
Summer fruit-bearing vine.
Needs full sun.
Recommended: 'Crimson Sweet'.

Clematis × *hybrida*
Popular perennial vines with flowers in pink,
red, white, blue, and purple in summer and
early fall.
Needs full sun or part shade; rich, well-drained
soils and ample moisture.
Other species: *Clematis maximowicziana*,
sweet autumn clematis, is a vine which produces an abundance of creamy white blossoms
in late summer.

Clethra alnifolia (Clethra)
Deciduous shrubs with spires of fragrant white
blossoms in summer, attractive fall foliage.
Grows to 8 feet.
Needs full sun to partial shade.
Pink-flowered cultivars: 'Pink Spires', 'Ruby
Spice', and 'Fern Valley Pink'.
Dwarf-form: 'Hummingbird', grows 3–4 feet
tall.

Clover leaf fern (see *Marsilea uncinata*)

Cohosh (see *Cimicifuga racemosa*)

Coleus × *hybridus*
Summer annual grown for beautifully marked,
colored foliage.
Grows 6–18 inches.
Traditionally a shade plant, new cultivars ('Sun
Lover' series) will grow in full sun.
New varieties introduced include ruffled
leaves, 'Red Ruffles', and miniature leaves,
'Thumbelina'.

Colocasia esculenta (Green-stemmed taro)
Tender perennial water plant grown for huge,
arrow-shaped, dark green foliage.
Grows 3–5 feet.
Will grow in wet soils, or in water up to 12
inches deep.

Columbine (see *Aquilegia canadensis*)

Comfrey (see *Symphytum officinale*)

Confederate rose (see *Hibiscus mutabilis*)

Consolida orientalis (Larkspur)
Annual with spikes of white, blue, purple, or
pink.
Grows 2 feet or more.
Needs full sun or partial shade.

Coreopsis lanceolata (Coreopsis)
Native perennial with bright yellow daisy-like
flowers in summer.
Grows 18–24 inches.
Needs full sun; drought tolerant.

Coreopsis verticillata 'Zagreb'
Perennial with small, bright yellow flowers and
dense, thread-like foliage.
Grows 12–18 inches.
Needs full sun.

Coriander (see *Coriandrum sativum*)

Coriandrum sativum (Coriander)
Annual herb with bright green leaves, finely
grooved stem.
Grows 2–3 feet.
Grows in full sun, part shade; moderately rich
soils.

Cornus florida (Flowering dogwood)
Beautiful small tree with showy white bracts in
spring.
Generally grows about 20 feet tall, may be
taller in some areas.
Acidic, well-drained soils and partial shade,
though will tolerate full sun with sufficient
moisture.

Corylopsis glabrescens (Winterhazel)
Deciduous shrub, pale yellow flowers in April,
good for shrub border.
Grows 8–15 feet.
Needs full sun or part shade.

Cosmos bipinnatus (Cosmos)
Pink or white daisy-like flowers borne in
summer.
Grows 18–36 inches.
Needs full sun; moderately rich, well-drained
soils.

Cosmos sulphureus (Cosmos)
Bright yellow or orange blossoms.
Grows only to 2 feet.
Needs full sun.

Cotinus coggygria (Smoketree)
Deciduous tree with beautiful red-purple
foliage, flowers create a smoke effect in summer.
Grows 10–15 feet.
Performs best in full sun.

Crabapple, southern (see *Malus angustifolia*)

Cranberry (see *Vaccinium macrocarpon*)

Crataegus aestivalis (Mayhaw)
Native hawthorn; fruit makes excellent jams
and jellies.
Grows to 30 feet.
Needs full sun or part shade.

Crape myrtle (see *Lagerstroemia indica*)

Crinum sp. (Crinum lily)
Bulbs producing tropical looking, lily-like flow-
ers in spring and summer.
Produces clumps of leaves that are 3–4 feet
long, and 3–4 inches wide.
Needs rich, moist soils and full sun.
Other species: *C. bulbispermum* and *C. moor-
ei* are hardy to zone 8.

Cryptomeria japonica (Japanese cedar)
Attractive, graceful evergreen tree. Beautiful
reddish-brown bark.
Grows 50–60 feet tall, 20–30 feet wide.
Prefers rich, well-drained soil, full sun, should
be protected from high winds.

Cucumis melo (Cantaloupe)
Annual vine producing melons.
Needs full sun.
'Hales Jumbo Best'—recommended variety.

Cyrtomium falcatum (Holly fern)
Evergreen fern.
Grows 18–24 inches.
Needs full to part shade and moist, rich soil.

Daisy, shasta (see *Chrysanthemum maximum*)

Daphne odora (Daphne)
Small evergreen shrub with extremely fragrant
rosy flowers in February.
Grows to 3 feet.
Needs full sun or partial shade.

Daucus carota sativus (Carrot)
Biennial vegetable, grown as annual.
Needs full sun and very fine, well-worked soil.

Daylily (see *Hemerocallis* sp.)

Dianthus barbatus (Sweet William)
Short-lived perennial. Clusters of white, pink
or red fragrant flowers in summer.
Grows 10–18 inches.
Needs full sun or partial shade, neutral pH
soils.

Dianthus gratianopolitanus 'Bath's Pink'
(Dianthus)
Evergreen perennial groundcover, with single
pink flowers on 6–8 inch stems in spring.
Foliage only grows to $1/2$ inch tall.
Needs full sun.

Dicentra spectabilis (Bleeding heart)
Woodland perennial. Beautiful pink and white
flowers on arching stem in spring.
Grows 18–24 inches tall.
Likes moist, rich soil in partial shade.
Other species: *Dicentra eximia,* native perennial with several deep pink, drooping heart-
shaped flowers in spring, grows 10–18 inches
tall, needs shade and rich soils.

Digitalis purpurea (Foxglove)
Biennial, purple and white blooms in spring,
self-sows.
Grows 4–5 feet tall.
Needs semi-shade, moist soils.
Recommended varieties: 'Foxy' and *Digitalis* ×
'Emerson'.

Dill (see *Anethum graveolens*)

Diospyros virginiana (Persimmon)
Fruit-bearing tree.
Grows 40–50 feet tall.
Needs full sun.

Dogwood, flowering (see *Cornus florida*)

Dryopteris erythrosora (Autumn fern)
Evergreen fern.
Grows 18–30 inches tall.
Needs full to part shade and moist, rich soil.
Other species: *Dryopteris celsa* (log fern),
D. marginalis (marginal wood fern).

Dryopteris ludoviciana (Florida wood fern)
Deciduous fern.
Grows 48 inches tall.
Needs full to part shade.

Dutch lavender (see *Lavandula*)

East India holly fern (see *Arachnoides simplicia* ' Variegata')

Echinacea purpurea (Purple coneflower)
Hardy perennial with light pinkish-purple
daisy-like blossoms in summer (white variety
available).
Grows 30–36 inches tall.
Needs full sun or part shade.

Elm, winged (see *Ulmus alata*)

Elodea canadensis (*Anacharis*)
Small aquatic plant.
Produces white flowers.

Erigeron pulchellus (Fleabane)
Moderately showy perennial wildflower.
Lavender flowers, one inch across, blooms
early summer.
Grows 18–24 inches tall.
Will not perform in too rich soils, needs full
sun, partial shade.

Eucalyptus gunnii (Eucalyptus)
Tender perennial—must be taken indoors dur-
ing cold months.
Needs full sun.

Eupatorium maculatum (Joe-pye weed)
Very tall perennial with umbels of mauve
flowers in fall.
Grows to 6 feet or more.
Prefers full sun, moist soils but will adapt to
drier soils.

False Solomon's Seal (see *Smilacina racemosa*)

Fennel, bronze (see *Foeniculum vulgare*
'Purpureum')

Feverfew (see *Chrysanthemum parthenium*)

Ficus carica (Fig)
Fruit-bearing shrub.
Grows 8–12 feet tall.
Needs full sun.
Recommended varieties: 'Celeste' and 'Brown
Turkey'.

Fig (see *Ficus carica*)

Filipendula rubra (Queen-of-the-Prairie)
Native perennial with clusters of feathery pink
flowers in summer.
Grows 3–6 feet tall.
Needs full sun.

Fleabane (see *Erigeron pulchellus*)

Florida leucothoe (see *Agarista populifolia*)

Florida wood fern (see *Dryopteris ludoviciana*)

Foam flower (see *Tiarella cordifolia*)

Foeniculum vulgare 'Purpureum' (Bronze fennel)
Tender perennial herb, grown as an annual in Georgia. Feathery, bronze foliage.
Grows 48 inches.
Needs full sun and well-drained soil—does not do well in clay soils.

Forsythia × intermedia (Forsythia)
Deciduous shrub; early spring yellow flowers.
Grows 6–10 feet tall.
Needs full sun to part shade.

Fothergilla gardenii (Fothergilla)
Deciduous early blooming shrub, leathery summer foliage.
Grows 3–5 feet tall.
Best flowers and fall foliage from plants grown in sun, but can be grown in partial shade.
Recommended varieties: 'Mt. Airy', 'Blue Mist'.

Four o'clocks (see *Mirabilis jalapa*)

Foxglove (see *Digitalis purpurea*)

Fringetree (see *Chionanthus virginicus*)

Gaura lindheimeri (Gaura)
Perennial summer bloomer. Small white flowers are found on a long narrow stalk above foliage.
Grows 3–4 feet.
Needs full sun or part shade.

Gentian (see *Gentiana saponaria*)

Gentiana saponaria (Gentian)
Native perennial with light blue, slightly opened flowers in late summer.
Grows 12–24 inches.
Needs shade or part shade and moist soils rich in organic matter.
Other species: *Gentian villosa*.

Geranium (see *Pelargonium × hortorum*)

Ginger, wild (see *Hexastylis speciosa*)

Globe amaranth (see *Gomphrena globosa*)

Golden club (see *Orontium aquaticum*)

Goldenrod (see *Solidago* sp.)

Gomphrena globosa (Globe amaranth)
Summer annual, also used as dried flower.
Flowers are white, pink, or red.
Grows 9–12 inches.
Needs full sun.
Good plant for coastal gardens. Will withstand temperatures to 0° F.

Grancy Gray-beard (see *Chionanthus virginicus*)

Green-and-gold (see *Chrysogonum virginianum*)

Gum, black (see *Nyssa sylvatica*)

Hamamelis × intermedia (Witchhazel)
Deciduous small tree with yellow, fringe-like blossoms in winter.
Grows 15–20 feet.
Needs full sun or shade.

Heavenly bamboo (see *Nandina domestica*)

Helianthus angustifolius (Narrow-leaf sunflower)
Very large perennial sunflower, with small yellow petals and purple centers.
Grows to be 6 feet tall.
Needs full sun and prefers moist soils.
Other species: *Helianthus giganteus*, 10 feet, prefers moist soils; *Helianthus salicifolius*, 3–6 feet, likes dry areas.

Helleborus orientalis (Lenten rose)
Perennial, grown for dark green leathery foliage and pink to white nodding flowers which appear in December or January.
Grows 12–18 inches.
Needs rich, moist soils, does not like to be moved.

Hemerocallis sp. (Daylily)
Diverse group of perennials with long, narrow leaves and lily-like flowers in a wide range of colors. Blooms in summer.
Grows 18–30 inches tall.
Needs full sun or part shade.

Hepatica americana (Hepatica)
Woodland perennial wildflower.
Small, liver-shaped leaves and bluish-white blossoms in spring.
Grows 6–9 inches.
Needs full or partial shade.

Hepticodum minocodum (Seven son flower)
Rare shrub from China, white flowers in fall, yellowish fall foliage, exfoliating bark.
Grows 10–15 feet, maybe taller.
Best in partial shade in Georgia.

Heuchera micrantha (Alumroot)
Perennial, grown for attractive mottled foliage.
Grows 12–24 inches.
'Palace Purple' has deep purple ivy-shaped foliage.

Hexastylis speciosa (Harper's wild ginger)
Native evergreen perennial, produces glossy heart-shaped leaves and large flower.
Grows 6 inches.
Needs shade and moist soils.
Other species: *H. shuttleworthii,* more variegated leaf.

Hibiscus coccineus (Swamp hibiscus)
6-inch, dark red flowers produced on tall, shrub-like plant, mid-summer to fall.
Grows 6–7 feet.
Prefers moist soils and full sun or light shade.

Hibiscus mutabilis (Confederate rose)
Large tree-like shrub, produces white flowers that turn to pink.
Grows 8–10 feet.
Prefers full sun or partial shade.

Holly fern (see *Cyrtomium falcatum*)

Hollyhock (see *Alcea rosea*)

Hosta sp. (Hosta)
Shade-loving perennials, grown primarily for foliage, which varies from dark green to light green to gold or striped or edged.
Needs shade and well-drained, rich soils.

Hydrangea macrophylla (Hydrangea)
Deciduous shrubs. White, pink, or blue flower.
3–7 feet in height.
Needs full sun or partial shade.

Hydrangea quercifolia (Oak-leaf hydrangea)
Southern native. White flowers turn pink, then brown as they mature.
Grows 6–8 feet tall.
Grows best in part shade.

Hypericum olympicum (St. John's-wort)
Perennial with 2-inch-wide yellow flowers in late spring.
Grows 9–12 inches.
Needs full sun to bloom well.
Other species: *Hypericum densiflorum* (dense St. John's-wort), perennial with narrow leaves; and *H. frondosum.*

Ilex verticillata (Winterberry)
Deciduous holly with an abundance of red berries. One male cultivar is recommended for every five female plants to assure good berry production.
Ranges in size from 3 to 12 feet tall.
Prefers full sun to part shade, but some varieties should be given protection from hot afternoon sun.

Illicium floridanum (Florida anise tree)
Broadleaf evergreen shrub. Foliage smells like anise; dark red flowers bloom in late spring.
Grows 6–10 feet tall.
Prefers partial to full shade.

Impatiens wallerana (Impatiens)
Summer annual in shades of pink, red, white, and lavender.
Grows 12–24 inches tall.
Needs ample moisture and partial shade. Will not bloom well in full shade.

Indian hawthorn (see *Raphiolepis indica*)

Interrupted fern (see *Osmunda claytoniana*)

Iris sp.
Excellent genus of plants, species can be chosen to provide bloom in Georgia from late November through June.
Species range in size from the dwarf, less than 15 inches, to the tall bearded iris, which grows 28 inches or more.
Generally, iris prefer moist conditions and full sun to partial shade.
Recommended native varieties: *Iris versicolor*, *I. fulva*, *I. virginica*, *I. prismatica*, *I. verna*.

Iris cristata (Dwarf crested iris)
Woodland perennial. Small, with purplish-blue flowers marked with yellow.
Grows only 8–12 inches tall.
Needs partial shade and very well-drained soils.

Jack-in-the-Pulpit (see *Arisaema triphyllum*)

Jacob's ladder (see *Polemonium reptans*)

Japanese anemone (see *Anemone × hybrida*)

Japanese apricot (see *Prunus mume*)

Japanese cedar (see *Cryptomeria japonica*)

Japanese painted fern (see *Athyrium nipponicum* 'Pictum')

Joe-pye weed (see *Eupatorium maculatum*)

Johnny-jump-up (see *Viola tricolor*)

Kalmia latifolia (Mountain laurel)
Attractive broad leaf evergreen shrub. Whorls of alternate, simple leaves. Outstanding flowers vary in color from white to deep pink, appear in clusters in late spring. Many cultivars available.
Grows 7–9 feet.
Needs acidic, cool, well-drained soils. Will tolerate sun or shade but flowers better in sun.

Kerria japonica (Kerria rose)
Deciduous, spreading shrub with single or double yellow flowers in spring.
Arching stems stay green during winter.
Grows 24–36 inches.
Needs full sun to partial shade.
Cultivar: 'Picta'—leaves edged in white, single yellow flower.

Kiwi vine (see *Actinidia deliciosa*)

Kosteletzkya virginica (Seashore mallow)
Perennial with large $1^1/_2$–$2^1/_2$ inch pink flowers in summer.
Grows 1–3 feet tall.
Prefers brackish or wet soils, but adaptable to drier conditions.

Lactuca sativa (Lettuce)
Cool season vegetable.
Recommended butterhead varieties: 'Buttercrunch', 'Red Sails', 'Red Fire', 'Oak Leaf'.
Recommended older varieties: 'Summer Bibb' and 'Bibb'.
Heading types not recommended for Georgia.

Lagerstroemia indica (Crape myrtle)
Small deciduous tree with interesting bark and multiple stems.
Foliage only found on upper half.
Grows 15–25 feet.
Prefers hot, sunny areas.

Lamb's ears (see *Stachys byzantina*)

Lamium maculatum (Lamium)
Perennial groundcover. Green leaves with white markings.
Needs partial shade and well-drained soil.
Performs best where nights stay cool and evenly moist.

Lantana camara (Lantana)
Tender perennial with dark green foliage and showy clusters of flowers in summer.
Varieties: 'New Gold'—prolific bloomer.
'Miss Huff'—perennial, with yellow blossoms turning orange, then pink, should withstand Georgia winters as far north as Canton. Blooms May to frost.
Do not remove old wood until after last spring frost.

Larkspur (see *Consolida orientalis*)

Lathyrus odoratus (Sweet pea)
Annual vine; fragrant blossoms in purple, rose, red, white, pink or blue in summer.
Needs full sun, rich soil and plenty of water.
If growing from seed, soak overnight.

Laurus nobilis (Bay)
Medium sized tree, shiny dark green leaves.
Grows 10 feet.
Full sun, part shade, hardy to Piedmont area.

Lavandula angustifolia (Lavender)
Perennial herb.
Grows to 36 inches.
Needs full sun, well-drained soil.
Other species: *Lavandula × intermedia* 'Dutch' (Dutch lavender), *Lavandula stoechas* (Spanish lavender).

Lavender (see *Lavandula angustifolia*)

Lemon verbena (see *Lippia citriodora*)

Lettuce (see *Lactuca sativa*)

Lemon balm (see *Melissa officinalis*)

Leucojum vernum (Snowdrop)
Bulb with small white blossoms in early spring.
Grows 6–12 inches.
Needs full sun or part shade.

Liatris scariosa (Gayfeather)
Tall perennial with purple spike-like blooms.
Cultivars with purple or white flowers.
Grows 3 feet.
Needs full sun, well-drained soils.
Other species: *L. aspera*, Blazing star, spike of rounded lavender flowers.

Ligularia stenocephala (Ligularia)
Large perennial with yellow flower spikes.
Very difficult to grow in Georgia because of the heat.

Lippia citriodora (Lemon verbena)
Tender perennial shrub (hardy to zones 9–10).
Container grown in cooler regions.
Grows 5 feet tall.
Needs full sun.

Liriodendron tulipifera (Tulip poplar)
Deciduous tree with large lobed leaves and attractive greenish-yellow flowers.
Grows to 90 feet.
Prefers deep, moist, well-drained soils.

Lizard's tail (see *Saururus cernuus*)

Lobelia cardinalis (Cardinal flower)
Perennial native plant, bright red spikes of flowers in summer.
Grows 2–6 feet.
Needs full to partial shade, prefers moist conditions.
Other species: *L. siphilitica*.

Lonicera fragrantissima (Winter honeysuckle)
Deciduous shrub with loose, arching branches and very fragrant flowers in late January and February.
Grows 6–10 feet.
Full sun, partial shade, very well-drained soil.

Loropetalum chinense (Loropetalum)
Shrubs with year-round, deep red-purple foliage. Pink or white blossoms in spring.
Grows in deep shade to full sun.
Recommended varieties: 'Burgundy', 'Rubrum', 'Plum Delight', 'Zuchoi fuschia'.

Lotus (see *Nelumbo lutea*)

Lungwort (see *Pulmonaria longifolia*)

Lychnis coronaria (Rose campion)
Perennial with small gray-green wooly leaves,
rosy red flowers throughout summer.
Grows 24–36 inches.
Needs full sun and well-drained soil.

Lycopersicon pimpinellifolium (Tomato)
Summer vegetable.
Grows up to 10 feet tall, will need staking or
support.
Needs full sun.
Recommended varieties: 'Rutgers', 'Celebrity',
'Better Boy', 'Supersonic'.
Will bear best before the heat of midsummer.

Macleaya cordata (Plume poppy)
Perennial with large, lobed leaves and plumes
of feathery pinkish flowers in summer.
Grows 7–8 feet tall, considered a vigorous
grower.
Needs full sun or partial shade.

Magnolia grandiflora (Southern magnolia)
Beautiful broad leafed evergreen tree. Leaves
glossy dark green above, light green or brown
below.
Grows 60–80 feet with 30–50 foot spread.
Prefers rich, porous, acidic, well-drained soils,
full sun or partial shade.
Other species: *Magnolia ashei, M. virginiana*
(silver bay).
Plant in late winter, early spring.

Mahonia bealei (Mahonia)
Attractive evergreen shrub with long, sharp-
spined leaves and late-winter yellow flowers
and dark blue berries.
Grows 3–6 feet.
Needs full to partial shade.

Maidenhair fern, southern (see *Adiantum
capillus-veneris*)

Malus sp. (Apple)
Fruit tree.
Grows 25–40 feet.
Needs full sun.

Malus angustifolia (Southern crabapple)
Pink buds open to fragrant white blossoms.
Blooms early (late winter) in south Georgia.
Rounded, small tree to 20 feet.

Maple, red (see *Acer rubrum*)

Marigold, pot (see *Calendula officinalis*)

Marjoram (see *Origanum majorana*)

Marsh pink (see *Sabatia bartrami*)

Marshallia obovata (Barbara's button)
Perennial with pink or purple flowers in late
spring.
Grows 4–6 inches.
Needs full sun, grows naturally in heavy clay
soils in the South.
Other garden-worthy species: *M. trinervia* and
M. morhii.

Marsilea uncinata (Clover leaf fern)
An unusual perennial fern with clover like
leaves.
Grows 6–12 inches.
Needs full or part shade.

May haw (see *Crataegus aestivalis*)

Melampodium paludosum (Melampodium)
Annual with mass of yellow daisy-like flowers
from early summer to frost. Heat tolerant.
Grows 12–16 inches.
Needs full sun.

Melissa officinalis (Lemon balm)
Fragrant, lemon-scented herb. Grown for
green, crinkly foliage.
Grows 24 inches.
Needs full sun to partial shade.

Mentha sp. (Mint)
Square stems, opposite fragrant leaves. Much variation.
Grows in full sun, part shade, rich soil.
Also: *M.* × *Piperita*—peppermint;
M. Spicata—spearmint.

Mertensia virginica (Virginia bluebells)
Perennial with wonderful blue flowers in late spring, leaves disappear by midsummer.
Grows 12–24 inches.
Needs moist, shady areas.

Michelia figo (Banana shrub)
Attractive evergreen shrub with spring flowers which smell like bananas.
Grows 6–8 feet.
Full sun to part shade.

Milkweed, swamp (see *Asclepias incarnata*)

Mint (see *Mentha* sp.)

Mirabilis jalapa (Four o'clocks)
Old-fashioned summer annual, trumpet-shaped flowers in white, red, yellow, pink or violet.
Grows 15–36 inches.
Needs full sun to part shade.

Miscanthus sinensis (Zebra grass)
Green and yellow striped ornamental grass, perennial.
Grows 5–6 feet tall.
Needs full sun or partial shade.

Monarda didyma (Beebalm)
Perennial; bright red spidery flowers on top of stems in June and July.
Grows 2–3 feet.
Full sun or part shade.
Recommended variety: 'Jacob Cline'.

Monkey flower (see *Torenia fournieri*)

Monkshood (see *Aconitum uncinatum*)

Mountain laurel (see *Kalmia latifolia*)

Muscadine (see *Vitis rotundifolia*)

Myosotis scorpioides (Forget-me-not)
Low growing perennial with masses of blue flowers, yellow centers in spring.
Grows 8–12 inches.
Needs partial shade, rich, moist soils.

Myrica cerifera (Southern wax myrtle)
Broadleaf evergreen large shrub.
Grows 10–15 feet tall with similar width.
Full sun to part shade.

Nandina domestica (Heavenly bamboo)
Small shrub with delicate foliage and bright red berries in fall.
Grows 4–6 feet.
Will grow in full sun to full shade.

Narcissus sp. (Narcissus)
Spring blooming bulbs.
Grow 6–14 inches.
Full sun to part shade.

Nasturtium (see *Tropaeolum majus*)

Nelumbo lutea (American lotus)
Native to North America, light yellow blossoms. Circular leaves, 1–2 feet across.
Grows 3–5 feet.
Grows in water, needs full sun.

Nepeta cataria (Catnip)
Perennial fragrant herb, flowers white with purple-pink spots, or in some cultivars, blue.
Grows 9–12 inches.
Performs best in poor, well-drained soils, full sun or partial shade.

Nicotiana alata (Flowering tobacco)
Summer annual with pink, yellow, purple, red, green, or white blossoms.
Grows 10–18 inches.
Needs full sun and well-drained soils.

Nymphaea sp. (Water lilies)
Attractive water plants with large, flat leaves
and attractive single or double flowers in
white, pink, red and yellow.
Hardy water lilies are less showy than tropical
ones, but can be left in the water throughout
the year.

Nyssa sylvatica (Black gum)
Attractive native tree, pyrimidal shape when
young.
Grows 30–50 feet tall, 20–30 feet wide.
Prefers moist, acidic, well-drained soils.

Oak, black (see *Quercus velutina*)

Oak, southern red (see *Quercus falcata*)

Oak, white (see *Quercus alba*)

Oak, willow (see *Quercus phellos*)

Ocimum basilicum (Basil)
Annual herb with fragrant leaves often used in
cooking.
Needs full sun, well-drained soils, will not
tolerate cold temperatures.
'Dark Opal' has dark purple leaves.
O. basilicum minimum has tiny, very flavorful
leaves.

Oenothera perennis (Sundrops)
Perennial with attractive yellow blossoms on
tall flowering stalk.
Grows 12–24 inches.
Prefers full sun, dry soils.

Ophiopogon planiscapus (Black mondo grass)
Groundcover with narrow dark purple leaves
and metallic blue fruit.
Grows about 6 inches.
Tolerates full sun, prefers partial shade and
moist conditions.

Oregano (see *Origanum vulgare*)

Origanum majorana (Marjoram)
Fuzzy leaves, bushy tender perennial.
Grows 1 foot.
Full sun; light, well-drained soil.

Origanum vulgare (Oregano)
Fragrant perennial herb, valued for leaves.
Grows 1–2 feet tall.
Needs full sun.

Orontium aquaticum (Golden-club)
Perennial bog plant, grows well at edge of pool
or stream, but will grow in water up to 6 inches deep. Produces golden tipped white spikes
above blue-green leaves.
Needs partial shade, wet soils.

Osmanthus fragrans (Tea olive)
Large shrub or small tree grown for fragrant
fall flowers.
Grows 20–30 feet tall.
Performs best in sun but will adapt to partial
shade.

Osmunda claytoniana (Interrupted fern)
Deciduous fern which turns golden yellow in
fall.
Grows 24–48 inches tall.
Needs shade to part shade, moist conditions.
Other species: *Osmunda regalis* (royal fern).

Pansy (see *Viola* × *wittrockiana*)

Papaver nudicaule (Iceland poppy)
Annual, multi-colored plants, seeds sown in fall
produce good spring display.
Grows 12–18 inches.
Needs full sun.

Papaver somniferum (Opium poppy)
Short lived perennial which reseeds readily.
Grows 2–3 feet.
Needs full sun.

Parsley (see *Petroselinum crispum*)

Pawpaw (see *Asimina triloba*)

Peach (see *Prunus persica*)

Pelargonium × *hortorum* (Geranium)
Popular summer bedding annual. Single or double flowers in white, red, or pink. Heart-shaped leaves.
Grows 24 inches tall.
Scented geraniums (*Pelargonium* sp.) Often used in potpourri.

Pentas sp. (Penta)
Annual with bright pink or red flowers in summer.
Grows 18–22 inches.
Needs well-drained soil and full sun.

Perovskia atriplicifolia (Russian sage)
Deciduous, semi-woody subshrub with attractive gray-green foliage and pinkish purple flowers in late summer, should be used in mass plantings, good for winter interest.
Grows 3–5 feet.
Needs full sun, very well-drained soils.

Persian shield (see *Strobilanthes dyeranus*)

Persimmon (see *Diospyros virginiana*)

Petroselinum crispum (Parsley)
Biennial, grown for its pungent foliage. Both flat (Italian) and curly leaf grow well in Georgia.
Grows to 18 inches.

Petunia × *hybrida* (Petunia)
Old-fashioned annual with many new cultivars, blooms in every color, come in two classes: multiflora with smaller numerous blossoms, grandiflora with larger, fewer blossoms.
Needs sun and well-drained soil.
Recommended variety: 'Purple Wave', multiflora covered with bright purple blossoms.

Philadelphus coronarius (Sweet mock orange)
Somewhat leggy shrub with beautifully scented white flowers in May and early June.
Grows 10–12 feet.
Needs full sun or light shade.

Phlox stolonifera (Phlox)
Evergreen perennial groundcover 'Bruce's White' has pure white fragrant flowers in spring.
Grows 6–18 inches tall.
Needs partial shade.
Other species: *Phlox maculata* (wild Sweet William), *P. divaricata* (wild blue phlox), *P. amoena* (hairy phlox).

Pieris japonica (Pieris)
Slow growing large shrub with spreading habit. Attractive glossy green foliage, white flowers in spring.
Eventually reaches height of 9–12 feet.
Needs full to part shade, well-drained soil.

Pineapple sage (see *Salvia rutilans*)

Pinus virginiana (Spruce pine)
Evergreen tree.
Grows to 40 feet.
Adaptable and will grow on poor, clay soils.
Needs full sun.

Plectranthus argentatus (Plectranthus)
Annual with thick yellowish-green leaves.
Grows 9–12 inches tall.
Will grow in sun or shade.

Plum (see *Prunus angustifolia*)

Plume poppy (see *Macleaya cordata*)

Polemonium reptans (Jacob's ladder)
Woodland perennial with clusters of blue-bell-shaped flowers in spring.
Grows 12–18 inches.
Needs shade to part shade and rich, moist soils.

Polygonatum commutatum (Great Solomon's-seal)
Perennial with clusters of small, greenish white flowers beneath arching stems.
Grows 3–6 feet.
Prefers moist soils and shade.

Polystichum acrostichoides (Christmas fern)
Evergreen native fern.
Grows 12–18 inches.
Needs full to part shade and moist, rich soil.

Polystichum polyblepharum (Tassel fern)
Evergreen fern.
Grows 18–24 inches.
Needs full to part shade, and moist, rich soil.

Poppy, Iceland (see *Papaver nudicaule*)

Poppy, opium (see *Papaver somniferum*)

Portulaca oleracea (Purslane)
Sprawling plant with reddish stems, yellow
flowers in summer.
Groundcover, stems 12 inches long.
Needs full sun and hot, dry conditions.

Poterium sanguisorba (Salad burnet)
Bushy perennial.
Grows 3 feet.
Needs full sun or partial shade.

Prunus angustifolia (Plum)
Fruit-bearing tree.
Needs full sun.
Recommended varieties: 'Santa Roses'—good
green plum, 'Morris'—good ripe.

Prunus mume (Japanese apricot)
Ornamental tree, very early bloomer, produces
fragrant pale rose flowers in late winter.
Grows to 30 feet.
Full sun or part shade.
Recommended variety: 'Peggy Clarke'.

Prunus persica (Peach)
Fruit-bearing tree.
Grow 10–15 feet.
Needs full sun.
Varieties: 'June Gold', 'Gold Prince', 'Spring
Crest', 'Florida King', 'Harvester', 'Swanee',
'Red Skin', 'Flame Prince', 'Crest Haven',
'Windblown'.

Pulmonaria longifolia (Lungwort)
Perennial with attractive spotted or mottled
leaves and blue flowers in spring.
Grows 9–18 inches.
Prefers partial shade.
Recommended varieties: 'Bertram Anderson',
'Sissinghurst White'.

Purple coneflower (see *Echinacea purpurea*)

Purple sage (see *Salvia officinalis*)

Purslane (see *Portulaca oleracea*)

Queen-of-the-Prairie (see *Filipendula rubra*)

Quercus alba (White oak)
Shade tree.
Grows 60–100 feet.
Grows in full sun to part shade.
Other species: *Quercus velutina* (black oak),
Q. phellos, (willow oak), *Q. falcata* (southern
red oak).

Raphiolepis indica (Indian hawthorn)
Evergreen shrub, attractive dark green leaves,
produces white or pinkish flowers in mid-
spring.
Grows 3–4 feet.
Needs full sun or part shade.

Raspberry (see *Rubus idaeus*)

Redbud, eastern (see *Cercis canadensis*)

Rehmannia elata (Chinese foxglove)
Perennial with yellow and purple blossoms.
Grows 4–5 feet.
Needs partial shade, light, rich soil and ample
moisture.

Rhododendron sp.
Evergreen shrubs, over 900 species worldwide
and many, many cultivars. Produces white, red
or yellow blossoms, primarily in spring and
early summer. All azaleas are in the rhododendron genus.

River oats grass (see *Chasmanthium latifolium*)

Rosa sp. (Rose)
Probably the most popular flower grown today, roses show great variation in form, size and color. There are bush and climbing roses, those grown for a single spectacular bloom, and those grown for an abundance of smaller blossoms.
Needs full sun; rich, well-drained soil; and careful attention to prevent pests and disease.

Rosemary (see *Rosmarinus officinalis*)

Rosmarinus officinalis (Rosemary)
Pungent evergreen herb, valued for leaves.
Grows 2–4 feet tall.
Needs full sun or partial shade.

Rubus sp. (Blackberry)
Fruit-bearing bramble.
Full sun.
Cultivars: 'Shawnee' (with thorns), 'Navajo' (thornless).

Rubus idaeus (Raspberry)
Perennial fruit-bearing vines.
Grows 3–5 feet.
Needs full sun.
'Dorma Red'—recommended.

Rudbeckia laciniata (Cutleaf coneflower)
Lemon yellow flowers with green cones.
Grows 5–6 feet tall.
Needs full sun or part shade.
Other species and varieties: *R. Graminifolia,* a red-flowered black-eyed Susan; *R. fulgida* 'Goldsturm', long-lived native perennial with yellow flowers in July and August; *R. hirta,* a black-eyed Susan, short-lived native perennial with bright, orangish-yellow flowers in July and August, needs full sun.

Rumex acetosa (French sorrel)
Perennial herb with wide, crinkly leaves.
Grows 24 inches.
Needs full sun.

Russian sage (see *Perovskia atriplicifolia*)

Sabatia bartrami (Marsh pink)
Native perennial with pink flowers in summer.
Needs full sun.

Sage (see *Salvia officinalis*)

Saint John's-wort (see *Hypericum olympicum*)

Salad burnet (see *Poterium sanguisorba*)

Salvia azurea (Salvia)
Attractive garden perennial. Produces spikes of blue flowers in fall. Usually hardy throughout Georgia.
Grows 3–4 feet tall.
Needs well-drained soils and full sun.

Salvia blepharophylla (Salvia)
Produces scarlet blooms in summer.
Grows 30 inches.
Needs full sun.

Salvia buchannii (Salvia)
Produces fuchsia blooms in summer, early fall.
Grows 18–24 inches.
Needs full sun.

Salvia clevelandii (Salvia)
Produces blue blooms in summer.
Grows 4^1/$_2$ feet.
Needs full sun.

Salvia farinacea (Mealy cup sage)
Perennial with either white or blue spikes in summer.
Grows 1–2 feet tall.
Needs full sun and well-drained soil.

Salvia Greggii (Salvia)
Produces red, white, rose, peach, pink blooms in summer.
Grows 30 inches.
Needs full sun.

Salvia × 'Indigo Spires'
Deep blue flower spires.
Grows 3–4 feet.
Needs full sun.

Salvia karwenskii (Salvia)
Produces bright red, winter blooms.
Grows 6 feet tall, 6 feet wide.
Needs full sun.

Salvia koyamae (Japanese yellow sage)
Produces yellow blossoms in fall.
Grows 5 feet.
Prefers partial shade.

Salvia leucantha (Mexican sage)
Produces violet-purple flowers with white
corollas in fall.
Can grow very large, up to 4–5 feet tall, 3–4
feet across.
Needs full sun.
Susceptible to the cold, but withstands heat
and drought well. Treated as an annual in
north Georgia.

Salvia madrensis (Salvia)
Produces yellow blooms in fall.
Grows 8 feet tall, 8 feet wide.
Needs full sun.

Salvia officinalis 'Purpurascens' (Purple sage)
Hardy perennial, drought resistant. Wooly
leaves are gray-green edged with dark purple.
Needs full sun.

Salvia rutilans (often seen as *S. elegans*)
(Pineapple sage)
Fall blooming tender perennial. Produces red
tubular flowers at end of strong stems.
Foliage smells like pineapple, hardy but winter
mulch recommended.
Full sun or partial shade.

Salvia uliginosa (Bog sage)
Produces sky blue flowers in summer.
Grows 4 feet.
Prefers wet soils, full sun to partial shade.

Salvia vanhoutti (Salvia)
Produces deep red flowers in late summer.
Grows 4 feet.
Needs full sun.

Santolina chamaecyparissus (Santolina)
Aromatic leaves, yellow blooms.
Grows 24 inches.
Needs full sun, well-drained soil.

Saponaria ocymoides (Soapwort)
Perennial with pale pink flowers in spring.
Grows 6–9 inches tall.
Difficult to grow in hot summers, or poorly
drained soils.
Needs full sun.

Sarcococca confusa (Sweetbox)
Small evergreen shrub with fragrant winter
blossoms. Attractive glossy green foliage.
Grows 3 feet.
Shade, needs moist, rich soils.

Saururus cernuus (Lizard's tail)
Aquatic perennial with small, fragrant white
flowers on long, curved spike in summer.
Grow in full sun or partial shade in wet soil or
water up to 6 inches deep.

Scabiosa caucasica (Blue fan flower)
Perennial with blue flowers in late summer.
Grows 18–24 inches.
Needs partial shade.

Scilla siberica (Scilla)
Bulb with blue flowers in spring.
Grows 3–6 inches tall, spreads easily.
Will grow in full sun or partial shade.

Scuppernong (see *Vitis rotundifolia*)

Scutellaria incana (Skullcap)
Native perennial, produces blue flowers in
summer.
Grows 18–24 inches.
Needs full sun.

Seashore mallow (see *Kosteletzkya virginica*)

Sedum spectabile 'Autumn Joy' (Sedum)
Perennial with late summer or autumn flowers
pink turning rusty red with age.
Grows 2–2$^{1}/_{2}$ feet tall.
Needs full sun or partial shade.

Sellaginalla uncinata (Spikemoss)
Perennial groundcover with blue-green foliage.
Grows 2–3 inches.
Prefers shade and moist conditions.

Serissa foetida (Yellow rim)
Evergreen shrub with dark green leaves, small
white flowers in late spring.
Grows 3–4 feet.
Needs sun and well-drained soils.

Seven son flower (see *Hepticodum
minocodum*)

Sisyrinchium angustifolium (Blue-eyed grass)
Native wildflower. Narrow, grass-like leaves
and blue, star-shaped flowers in May and June.
Grows 4–20 inches.
Needs full sun or partial shade.

Skullcap (see *Scutellaria incana*)

Smilacina racemosa (False Solomon's seal)
Perennial woodland wildflower. Large, oval
leaves on gracefully arched stem, small white
flowers underneath.
Grows 2–3 feet.
Needs shade, moist soils.

Smoketree (see *Cotinus coggygria*)

Snapdragon (see *Antirrhinum majus*)

Snowdrops (see *Leucojum vernum*)

Soapwort (see *Saponaria ocymoides*)

Solidago rugosa (Rough-stemmed goldenrod)
Small, slightly arching stems bear light yellow
blossoms in late summer and fall.
Grows 1–6 feet.
Needs full sun or partial shade.
Other species: *S. caesia* (wreath goldenrod),
grows 3 feet tall; *S. rugosa* 'Fireworks',
produces golden yellow flowers in spring.

Solomon's seal, false (see *Smilacina racemosa*)

Solomon's seal, great (see *Polygonatum
commutatum*)

Sorrel, French (see *Rumex acetosa*)

Southern shield fern (*Thelypteris normalis
kuentii*)

Southernwood (see *Artemisia abrotanum*)

Spanish lavender (see *Lavandula stoechas*)

Spikemoss (see *Sellaginalla uncinata*)

Spinacia oleracea (Spinach)
Cool season vegetable.
Grows 2 feet.
Needs full sun.

Spinach (see *Spinacia oleracea*)

Spiraea × *bumalda* 'Limemound'
Deciduous shrub, spring foliage is yellow
flushed with red, turning chartreuse when
mature.
Grows 2–3 feet.
Needs full sun.
Other species: *S.* × *vanhouttei*, vase shaped
growth, 8–10 feet tall, white flowers.

Spruce pine (see *Pinus virginiana*)

St. John's wort (see *Hypericum olympicum*)

Stachys byzantina (Lamb's ear)
Perennial with light green wooly leaves.
'Primrose Heron' has primrose-yellow foliage
in spring, fades to green in summer.
Grows 12–15 inches.
Needs full sun, good air circulation, and well-
drained soils.

Stewartia monadelpha (Stewartia)
Tree with summer flowers, attractive autumn
color and interesting exfoliating bark.
Grows 40–60 feet.
Heat-tolerant species. Needs partial shade.

Stokesia laevis (Stoke's aster)
Perennial with blue or white flowers in summer, many cultivars.
Grows 12–24 inches.
Prefers filtered sunlight and well-drained soil.

Stoke's aster (see *Stokesia laevis*)

Strobilanthes dyeranus (Persian shield)
Metallic purple foliage, annual.
Needs full sun.

Sundrops (see *Oenothera perennis*)

Sunflower, narrow-leaf (see *Helianthus angustifolius*)

Swamp milkweed (see *Asclepias incarnata*)

Swan River daisy (see *Brachycome iberidifolia*)

Sweet mock orange (see *Philadelphus coronarius*)

Sweet pea (see *Lathyrus odoratus*)

Sweet woodruff (see *Asperula odorata*)

Sweetbox (see *Sarcococca confusa*)

Symphytum officinale (Comfrey)
Perennial herb, dies back in winter. Large, coarse plant; small blue flowers in summer.
Grows 3–5 feet.
Needs partial shade or full sun.

Tagetes lucida (Texas tarragon)
Perennial herb, often grown instead of French tarragon.
Grows 24 inches.
Full sun.

Tanacetum vulgare (Tansy)
Dark green fern-like leaves with yellow flower heads.
Grows 3–4 feet.
Needs average soil, sun to part shade.

Tansy (see *Tanacetum vulgare*)

Taro, green-stemmed (see *Colocasia esculenta*)

Tarragon, Texas (see *Tagetes lucida*)

Tarragon, French (see *Artemisia dracunculus sativa*)

Tassel fern (see *Polystichum polybelpharum*)

Tea olive (see *Osmanthus fragrans*)

Thalia dealbata (Thalia)
Aquatic perennial with long oval leaves.
Grows 3–4 feet tall in container.
Needs to grow in moist soils, or in water up to 12 inches deep. Will grow in sun or part shade.

Thelypteris normalis kuentii (Southern shield fern)
Deciduous fern.
Grows 24–36 inches.
Will grow in sun or shade, prefers moist, rich soils.

Thelypteris noveboracensis (New York fern)
Large plume like fronds.
Grows 24–30 inches.
Needs shade or part shade.
Other species: *T. kunthii* (southern wood fern).

Thyme (see *Thymus vulgaris*)

Thymus vulgaris (Thyme)
Perennial herb, grown for foliage.
Grows 3–15 inches.
Needs full sun or partial shade.
Other species: *T. Glabrescens* (long leaf grey thyme), vigorous grower.

Tiarella cordifolia (Foam flower)
Woodland perennial. Heart shaped mottled leaves, small racemes of pinkish-white flowers in spring.
Needs full to partial shade, moist, rich organic soils.

Tithonia rotundifolia (Mexican sunflower)
Very large annual with bright orange daisy-like
flowers in summer.
Grows 3–6 feet.
Needs full sun; drought and heat resistant.

Toad lily (see *Tricyrtis formosana*)

Tomato (see *Lycopersicum pimpinellifolium*)

Torenia fournieri (Monkey flower, wishbone
flower)
Summer annual. Purple, violet or blue flowers,
lime green seed pods.
Bushy, low growing plants, 8–12 inches.
Needs full to partial shade, rich well-drained
soils.

Tricyrtis formosana (Toad lily)
Perennial woodland plant, produces funnel-
shaped lilac flowers in fall.
Grows 12–24 inches.
Prefers moist soils and shade.

Trillium vaseyi (Vasey's trillium)
Native woodland perennial with reddish-
brown, pleasant smelling flowers in spring.
Grows 10–18 inches.
Needs shade and rich, moist soil.

Tropaeolum majus (Nasturtium)
Summer annual. Red, yellow, orange, mixed
blooms.
Grows 6–12 inches.
Needs full sun and well-drained soil.

Tulip poplar (see *Liriodendron tulipifera*)

Typha sp. (Cattail)
Aquatic plants grown for strong, vertical foliage
and elongated brown catkins.
Needs full sun to partial shade.
Will become invasive if not grown in a con-
tainer.
Other species: *T. angustifolia* (narrow-leaved
cattail), graceful, slender leaves.

Ulmus alata (Winged elm)
Medium-sized tree. Dark green, leathery
leaves.
Grows to 40 feet tall.
Prefers well-drained soil, partial shade.
Susceptible to mildew.

Vaccinium macrocarpon (Cranberry)
Perennial trailing shrub, pinkish white flowers
in summer. Natural habitat is open bogs,
swamps and lake shores, but has proven to be
very adaptable to drier conditions.
Prefers full sun.

Vaccinium sp. (Blueberry)
Perennial fruit-bearing shrub.
Needs full sun to part shade.
Cultivars: 'Climax'—upright with spreading
stems, medium sized berries.
'Brightwell'—similar to 'Climax' but ripen
later.
'Tiftblue'—good productivity, flavorful berries.

Verbena × *Hybrida*
Perennials with attractive clusters of flowers in
summer.
Grow 6–12 inches.
Need full sun.
'Abbeville'—lavender and white; 'Evelyn
Scott'—red; 'Homestead Purple'—bright pur-
ple, quite vigorous cultivar; 'Sara Groves'—
pink.

Veronica × 'Goodness Grows'
Perennial with blue flowers in spring, long
flowering.
Grows 10–12 inches tall.
Needs full sun.

Veronica longifolia 'Icicle'
White flowers in summer.
Grows 24–30 inches.
Full sun to part shade.

Viburnum dilatatum (Viburnum)
Deciduous shrub. Produces red berries in fall,
white flowers in early summer.
Grows 6 feet tall, spread 10 feet.
Needs full sun or part shade, moist acidic soils.

Vinca rosea (Vinca)
Summer annual with pink, red or white blossoms.
Grow 6–10 inches.
Needs full sun.
'Pretty' series recommended.

Viola cornuta (Viola)
Cool season annual with purple, yellow, cream-colored blossoms from early spring until summer.
Grows 4–6 inches.
Will grow in full sun to part shade.
'Sorbet' series recommended.

Viola tricolor (Johnny-jump-up)
Cool season annual, producing small yellow-and-purple blossoms from fall to spring.
Grows 6–18 inches.
Prefers rich, moist soils and full sun to part shade.

Viola × *wittrockiana* (Pansy)
Very popular cool season annual in many colors. Plant in fall for color through spring, will tend to get leggy when weather turns warm in early summer.
Grows 3–6 inches.
Will grow in full sun or part shade.

Virginia bluebells (see *Mertensia virginica*)

Virginia chain fern (see *Woodwardia virginica*)

Vitis rotundifolia (Scuppernong)
Grape-producing vine.
Full sun.

Vitis rotundifolia (Muscadine)
Perennial grape-producing vine, sometimes 50 feet long.
Needs full sun.

Walking fern (see *Camptosorous rhizophyllus*)

Wallflower (see *Cheiranthus cheiri*)

Water lilies (see *Nymphaea*)

Watermelon (see *Citrullus vulgaris*)

Wax myrtle, southern (see *Myrica cerifera*)

Winter honeysuckle (see *Lonicera fragrantissima*)

Winterberry (see *Ilex verticillata*)

Winterhazel (see *Corylopsis glabrescens*)

Wintersweet (see *Chimonanthus praecox*)

Witchhazel (see *Hamamelis* × *intermedia*)

Woodsia obtusa (Blunt-nosed woodsia)
Perennial fern, sterile fronds remain green throughout winter.
Grows 8–20 inches.
Needs full to part shade, rich, moist soils.

Woodwardia virginica (Virginia chain fern)
Perennial fern, often found in swampy places in the South.
Grows 2–3 feet.
Needs shade and very moist soils.
Other species: *Woodwardia areolata* (netted chain fern).

Wormwood (see *Artemisia absinthium*)

Yarrow (see *Achillea millefolium*)

Yellow rim (see *Serissa foetida*)

Zebra grass (see *Miscanthus sinensis*)

Zephyranthes atamasco (Atamasco lily)
Beautiful lily, white flowers early spring.
Grows 12 inches.
Full sun to part shade, likes moist conditions.

Zinnia linearis (Narrowleaf zinnia)
Summer annual with orange or white blossoms on weak, sprawling stems.
Grows 6–18 inches.
Will grow in full sun or part shade.

GEORGIA GARDENERS'
RESOURCE GUIDE

PUBLIC GARDENS IN GEORGIA

Appalachian Arboretum
University of Georgia Mountain Branch
Experiment Station
Blairsville, GA 30512
706-745-2655
Hours: Daylight to dusk
Fee: None
Display of native plant communities.

Atlanta Botanical Garden
Piedmont Park at The Prado
Atlanta, GA 30357
404-876-5858
Hours: Tuesday through Sunday 9:00 A.M. to
7:00 P.M. (April through September), 9:00 A.M.
to 6:00 P.M. (rest of the year).
Fee: Adults $6; Seniors $5; Students (with ID)
and children 6–12 $3; children under 5 and
Garden members free.
*Thirty acres of gardens and woodland near
Piedmont Park in downtown Atlanta. Includes
rose garden; Japanese garden; rock, herb, and
vegetable gardens; and a conservatory.*

Atlanta Decorator's Showhouse Garden
Annual spring event (location changes every
year)
*Several gardens usually landscaped by local
designer; gardens included with showhouse
ticket.*

Atlanta History Center
130 West Paces Ferry Road
Atlanta, GA 30305
Hours: Open seven days a week, 10:00 A.M. to
5:30 P.M. Monday through Saturday; noon to
5:30 P.M. Sunday. Closed on some holidays.
Fee: Adults, $9; Seniors over 65 and students
with ID $7; youth 6–17, $6; children under 5
free. Admission ticket includes all exhibits,
house tours, gardens, and museum. Tickets are
$2 less if you opt not to tour the houses.
*Series of gardens including Asian-American
garden, Tullie Smith garden, Swan Woods
Trail, and Gardens for Peace.*

Barnsley Gardens
597 Barnsley Gardens Road
Adairsville, GA 30103
770-773-7480
Directions: One hour north of Atlanta. I-75
north, exit 128. Follow signs.
Hours: Open February through mid-December;
Tuesday through Saturday, 10:00 to dark;
Sunday noon to dark.
Fee: Adults, $6.50; Seniors (62 over) $5.50;
students $4; children 12 and under, free.
*Thirty acres of gardens first planted in 1840.
Water and bog gardens, fernery, woodland
gardens, rockeries, and small boxwood
parterre.*

Berry College Horticulture Garden
Berry College Campus
Mt. Berry
706-236-1737
Hours: Daylight.
Fee: None.
Three-acre experimental and display beds.

Birdsong Nature Center
Route 3, Box 1077
Thomasville, GA 31792
912-377-4408
Hours: Wednesday and Friday mornings 9:00
to 12:00; Saturdays, 9:00 to 2:00; Sundays,
1:00 to 5:00.
Fee: Adults, $5; children ages 4–12, $2.50.
*565-acre tract of land located halfway
between Tallahassee, Florida, and
Thomasville, Georgia; the educational branch
of Tall Timbers Research Station, specializing
in ecology and natural history.*

Callaway Gardens
Highway 27, P.O. Box 2000
Pine Mountain, GA 31822
800-282-8181 or 706-663-5060
Hours: 7:00 A.M. to 7:00 P.M. daily.
Fee: Prices vary from season to season and for
special events. Call for prices before going to
the gardens.
*1,500 acres of azaleas, hollies, rhododen-
drons, dogwoods, butterfly house and garden,
conservatory, huge annual and perennial beds.*

Catalpa Plantation
Goodwyn-Bailey-Smith House
2295 Old Poplar Road
Newnan, GA 30263
404-253-3806
Hours: Tours are given by appointment.
Fee: Donations are accepted.
Directions: Take Exit 10 off I-85, turn left onto
Route 154, go two miles and take a right onto
Lower Fayetteville Road; take first left onto
Parks road. Catalpa Gardens at the end of this
road.
*Small gardens adjacent to mid-nineteenth-
century plantation house.*

Chatham County Garden Center and
   Botanical Garden
1388 Eisenhower Drive
Savannah, GA 31406
912-355-3883
Hours: Daylight.
Fee: None.
*1840's farmhouse, 11 1/4 acres including
roses, vegetables, perennials, herbs.*

Coastal Gardens, Historic Bamboo and
   Horticultural Collections
Canebrake Road, near Savannah
Hours: Daylight to dusk.
Fee: None.
912-921-5461
Located between Highway 17 and I-95. Take
exit 16 off I-95 and go east. Turn right at the
first light on Southgate Boulevard. Turn left on
Cranebrake Road and go approximately half a
mile to gate.
*Display and experimental beds, strong educa-
tional program.*

Cobb County Backachers Garden
County Farm Road
Marietta, GA
770-528-4070
Hours: Open to groups only, call for appointment.
*Demonstration gardens built and maintained
by Cobb Master Gardener program; features
theme gardens and printed information about
plantings in each garden area.*

Columbus Museum
Olmsted Gardens
1251 Wynnton Road
Columbus, GA 31906
706-649-0713
Hours: Tuesday through Saturday 10:00 A.M.
to 5:00 P.M., and Sunday 1:00 P.M. to 5:00 P.M.
Fee: None to garden or museum.
*Three-acre garden with woody and herba-
ceous plant material.*

Crescent
904 North Patterson Street
Valdosta, GA 31603
912-244-6747
Hours: Monday through Friday, 2:00 P.M. to
5:00 P.M. by appointment only. Closed weekends.
Fee: $2 donation per person requested.
Owned and operated by the Valdosta Garden
Clubs, the garden is made up of individual
plots maintained by different clubs.
Perennials, annuals, woody shrubs, display
garden for the American Hemerocallis Society.

Dekalb College Botanical Garden
3251 Panthersville Road
Atlanta, GA 30034-3897
404-244-5077
Hours: 10:00 A.M. to 3:00 P.M., 7 days per
week.
Fee: None.
Display gardens showing extension collection
of native plants for both shade and sun.

Eddie Bowens Garden at Seabrook Village
660 Trade Hill Road
Midway, GA 31320
912-884-7008
Hours: Daylight hours.
Fee: None.
Directions: (30 miles south of Savannah) Take
Exit 13 off I-95, go east for about 5 miles.
Historical country garden with unusual old-
fashioned plant material, including scarlet wis-
teria (Sesbania punicea) and strawberry tree
(Cudrania tricuspidata).

Fernbank Science Center and Museum of
    Natural History
156 Heaton Park Drive
Atlanta, GA 30307
404-378-0127
Hours: Forest is open Sunday through Friday
from 2:00 P.M. to 5:00 P.M. and Saturday 10:00
A.M. to 5:00 P.M.
Fee: None to Fernbank Forest, Garden,
Briarcliff Greenhouse.
Staton Rose Garden is open during daylight
hours from Monday through Friday. All facili-
ties are closed for the Labor Day weekend.

Founders Memorial Garden
325 A. Lumpkin Street
Athens, GA 30602
706-542-3631
Hours: Daylight.
Fee: None.
Small enclosed garden at site of original
Garden Club of Georgia headquarters.

Gardens for Peace, Atlanta locations
Atlanta History Center, Swan Woods Trail
Agnes Scott College Campus (behind Anna
Young Alumnae House)
141 E. College Avenue
Decatur, GA 30030
404-355-2197
Fee: None.
Hours: Daylight.
Gardens for Peace is a non-profit organization
created to promote international gardens as
symbols of peace and places of meditation.

Georgia Southern Botanical Garden,
    Magnolia Gardens
Georgia Southern University
Statesboro, GA 30460
912-871-1777
Hours: Daylight.
Fee: None.
Directions: Entrance is off Fair Road, Highway 67.
Ten-acre farm/garden with camellia collec-
tion, woodland display. Emphasis is on pro-
moting plants native to Georgia coastal plain.

Georgia Station Research & Education Garden
The University of Georgia
Georgia Experiment Station
1109 Experiment Street
Griffin, GA 30223-1797
770-228-7243
Hours: Monday through Friday from 8:00 A.M.
to 5:00 P.M. by guided tour only. Call for
appointment.
Fee: Tax-deductible donations requested.
New garden, opened in 1995, includes both
experimental and display beds.

Guido Gardens
600 North Lewis Street (Rt. 121 N)
Metter, GA 30439
912-685-2222
Hours: Daylight.
Fee: None.
Three-acre garden with waterfall, gazebo, sea-sonal flowers.

Hamilton Rhododendron Garden
Highway 76, P.O. Box 290
Hiawassee, GA 303546
706-896-4191
Hours: Daylight.
Fee: None.
Best bloom in late April, early May. Located at Georgia Mountain Fair site, Hiawassee.

Indian Springs Hotel Garden
Butts County Historical Society
P.O. Box 215
Jackson, GA 30233
770-775-2493
Hours: Daylight. March through November.
Fee: None.
Directions: Georgia Hight 42, five miles south of Jackson, 45 miles south of Atlanta.
Dedicated to Mrs. Elizabeth Harris, 1990, 110 by 30 foot garden, contains herbs, annuals, perennials, roses.

John Cranshaw's One Horse Farm and Garden
186 Sandefur Road
Kathleen, GA 31047
912-987-3268 (Early morning, around noon, or after 8:00 P.M.)
Hours: Open summers only, 10:00 A.M. to 6:00 P.M.
Fee: None.

Lockerly Arboretum and Botanical Gardens
1534 Irwinton Road
Milledgeville, GA 31061
912-452-2112
Hours: Weekdays, 8:30 A.M. to 4:30 P.M., Saturday, 1:00 P.M. to 5:00 P.M.
Fee: None.
Forty-seven acres of woodlands, pond, trails.

Massee Lane Gardens
American Camellia Society Headquarters
One Massee Lane
Fort Valley, GA 31030
912-967-2358
Hours: Open from 9:00 A.M. to 5:00 P.M. Monday through Saturday; 1:00 P.M. to 5:00 P.M. on Sunday.
Fee: Ages 12 and older, $2. Children under 12, free.
Beautiful collection of camellias and companion plants.

Middle Georgia Trial Gardens
Wesleyan College Campus
Macon, GA 31297
912-751-6338
Planted spring, 1996. Trial beds for annuals, perennials, vegetables, herbs. Built and maintained by Master Gardener Program.

North Georgia Tech Interpretive Gardens
5198 Ross Road
Acworth 30102
770-975-4077
Exits 120 and 121.
Hours: Daylight.
Fee: None.
Directions: Located on east side of I-75 between Exits 120 and 121.
One-acre fenced garden, small arboretum, trial beds for educational purposes.

Oak Hill
189 Mount Berry Station
Rome, GA 30149
706-291-1883
Hours: Tuesdays through Saturdays, 10:00 to 5:00 P.M.; Sunday 1:00 to 5:00 P.M. Buildings are closed on Mondays, but gardens are open.
Fee: Adults $3, children 6 to 12 years, $1.50.
Directions: North of Rome on U.S. 27 across from Berry College Campus.
1847's plantation house and gardens.

Penny's Garden
Black's Creek Road
Mountain City, GA 30562
706-746-6918
Hours: Open April to mid-December 9:00 to
5:00 Monday through Saturday; closed January
through March.
Fee: None.
Directions: Three miles north of Clayton off
Highway 441 / 23.
Display herb garden and shop.

Piccadilly Farm
1971 Whippoorwill Road
Bishop, GA 30621
706-769-6516
Hours: 10:00 A.M. to 4:30 P.M., Thursday,
Friday, and Saturday, April through mid-June.
Fee: None.
Beautiful display gardens and nursery.

Promina Cobb Hospital
Horticulture Therapy garden
Austell, GA 30001
770-732-4000
Hours: Daylight.
Fee: None.
Directions: Corner of East-West Connector and
Austell Road.
One-acre handicap-accessible garden, three
theme gardens: butterfly, texture, fragrance.
Initial landscaping and installation by Post
Properties.

Rock City Gardens
1400 Patten Road
Lookout Mountain, GA 30750
706-820-2531
Hours: Open every day except Christmas; 8:00
A.M. to 8:00 P.M. Memorial Day through Labor
Day; 8:30 A.M. to 5:00 P.M. rest of year.
Fee: Adults $8.95; children 3–12 $4.95; 2 and
under free. Group rates are available with
advance reservations.
Directions: I75N to I24W to Exit 17, straight
ahead off exit to Broad Street, turn left, follow
signs.
Ten acres of rock formations, wildflowers,
native plants, and shrubs.

Sea Island Trial Beds
Behind the Cloister Hotel
Sea Island, GA 31561
912-638-3611
Hours: Daylight.
Fee: None.
Experimental beds displaying perennials,
annuals, and herbs.

Shepherd Center
Horticulture Therapy Garden
2020 Peachtree Road
Atlanta, GA 30309
404-350-7785

State Botanical Garden of Georgia at the
University of Georgia
2450 S. Milledge Avenue
Athens, GA 30605
706-542-1244
Hours: The Garden is open daily from 8:00
A.M. to sunset. The Visitor Center/Conservatory
is open Monday through Saturday from 9:00
A.M. to 4:30 P.M., and on Sundays from 11:30
A.M. to 4:30 P.M., except for certain holidays.
Fee: None.

Tim Bell Daylily Garden
1305 Griffin Road
Sycamore, GA 31790
912-567-4284
Call for appointment.

Transplant Nursery
Parkertown Road
Lavonia, GA 30553
706-356-8947
Hours: 8:00 A.M. to 5:00 P.M. Monday through
Friday. In fall and spring, gardens open Monday
through Saturday 9:00 A.M. to 5:00 P.M.; Sunday
2:00 P.M. to 5:00 P.M. Call for an appointment.
Fee: None.
Directions: I-85N to exit 59, turn right, go 1/4
mile to a 4-way stop, go straight 1/2 mile, the
second paved road is Parkertown Rd., turn
right, go 1.6 miles on left.
Wonderful display garden and nursery, show-
ing rhododendrons, azaleas, and native aza-
leas with companion planting.

University of Georgia Trial Gardens
Next to Pharmacy School, University of
 Georgia
Athens, GA 30602
Hours: Daylight hours.
Fee: None.
*Trial beds for the All America Selections, gaze-
bo, seasonal displays.*

Vines Botanical Garden
3500 Oak Grove Road
Loganville, GA 30249
770-466-7532
Hours: Hours vary according to season; the
garden is open special hours during peak
blooming seasons, call for details.
Fee: Adults $3; Seniors $2; children 5 to 12
$1; children under 5 free.
*Twenty-five acres of developed gardens,
including 3.5-acre lake.*

Wildwood Farms
5231 Seven Islands Road
Madison, GA 30650
706-342-4912
Hours: No real regular hours; schedule always
changes, call for schedule. Open a few weekends in Spring and Fall.
Fee: None.
*Good display beds, some planted according to
plant family. Pond, woodland area, nursery.*

Wilkerson Mill Gardens
9595 Wilkerson Mill Road
Palmetto, GA 30268
770-463-9717
Directions: Take I-85 South from Atlanta and
follow "Spur 14" to third stop light (Cascade
Palmetto Road). Turn left and go two (plus)
miles to Wilkerson Mill Road. Turn right.
Nursery is two miles on right.
*Wonderful ornamental and native shrub
"orchard", old mill, woodland, and trails.*

GARDEN LIBRARIES

Cherokee Garden Library
Atlanta History Center
130 West Paces Ferry Road
Atlanta, GA 30305
404-814-4046

Sheffield Garden Library
Atlanta Botanical Gardens
Piedmont Park at the Prado
Atlanta, GA 30357
404-876-5858

Vines Botanical Garden Library
3500 Oak Grove Road
Loganville, GA 30249
770-466-7532

Fernbank Science Center Library
156 Heaton Park Drive
Atlanta, GA 30307
404-378-0127

American Camellia Society Library
One Massee Lane
Ft. Valley, GA 31030
912-967-2358

Chatham County Garden Center Library
1388 Eisenhower Drive
Savannah, GA 31406
912-355-3883

PLANT SOCIETIES AND
ORGANIZATIONS

American Begonia Society, Atlanta Branch
Mr. Russell Richardson
1854 Chancery Lane
Chamblee, GA 30341
770-457-0371

American Camellia Society
One Massee Lane
Fort Valley, GA 31030
912-967-2722

American Daffodil Society
1686 Grey Fox Trail
Milford, OH 45150
513-248-9137

American Gourd Society
P.O. Box 274
Mt. Gilead, OH 43338-0274
419-946-3302

American Herb Association
P.O. Box 353
Rescue, CA 95672

American Horticultural Society
7931 East Boulevard Drive
Alexandria, VA 22308

American Horticulture Therapy Association
362 A. Christopher Avenue
Gaithersburg, MD 20879
For information on Georgia Horticulture
Therapy gardens call:
Ranita Keener
Augusta Regional Hospital
706-790-2799 or,
John Paul Breault
North Georgia Regional Hospital
706-295-6709 (ext. 6080)

American Hosta Society
5300 Whiting Avenue
Edina, MN 55435

American Hydrangea Society, Atlanta Chapter
Penny McHenry
2477 Fairknoll Drive
Atlanta, GA 30345
770-636-7886

American Iris Society
7414 East 60th Street
Tulsa, OK 74145

American Ivy Society, Atlanta Chapter
6515 Bridgewood Valley Road
Atlanta, GA 30328
404-255-9618

American Pomological Society
103 Tyson Building
University Park, PA 16802

American Rhododendron Society
Mrs. Barbara Hall
P.O. Box 1380
Gloucester, VA 23061
804-693-4433

American Rock Garden Society
15 Fairmead Road
Darien, CT 06820

American Rose Society
P.O. Box 30,000
Shreveport, LA 71130-0030
318-938-5402

Atlanta Bonsai Society
Tony Smith
1412 West Peachtree Street
Atlanta, GA 30309
404-872-2217

Azalea Society of America
Ralph T. Bullard, Jr.
6159 Ridge Way
Douglasville, GA 30135
770-949-0494

Chattahoochee Unit Herb Society
Chris Adams
P.O. Box 434
Lilburn, GA 30247
770-921-0358

Coastal Georgia Herb Society
Don Bass
912-354-7299

Dahlia Society of Georgia
Mr. Edward K. Mercer
2782 Redding Road
Atlanta, GA 30319
404-455-8422

Georgia Botanical Society
Mikell Jones
2490 F. Windsor Wood Lane
Norcross, GA 30071-2336
770-448-7613

Georgia Chrysanthemum Society
Hall C. Goode
1758 Brandon Hall Drive
Dunwoody, GA 30350
770-396-0911

Georgia Daffodil Society
Bonnie Campbell
590 Sandy Creek Road
Fayetteville, GA 30213
770-461-7066

Georgia Green Industry
P.O. Box 369
Epworth, GA 30541
706-492-4664

Georgia Horticulture Society
Joyce Latimer
Horticulture Department
Georgia Experiment Station
Griffin, GA 30223
770-228-7243

Georgia Hosta Society
110 Dawn Drive
Fayetteville, GA 30214
770-292-4609

Georgia Native Plant Society
1100 Edgewater Drive
Atlanta, GA 30328
For information, call Jim Harrington 770-667-9918

Georgia Organic Growers Association
Deborah Pelham
1185 Bend Creek Trail
Suwannee, GA 30174
770-476-0473

Georgia Organic Grower's Association Message
Center
P.O. Box 567661
Atlanta, GA 31156
770-621-4642

Georgia Perennial Plant Association
P.O. Box 13425
Atlanta, GA 30324
404-393-3451

Georgia Wildlife Federation
1930 Iris Drive
Conyers, GA 30207
770-929-3350

Greater Atlanta Hemerocallis Society
Ray B. Stephens
2446 Cofer Circle
Tucker, GA 30084
770-938-9633

Herb Society of America
9019 Kirtland Chardon Road
Kirtland, GA 44094
216-256-0514

Herb Society of America, Chattahoochee Unit
P.O. Box 53323
Atlanta, GA 30355
For information call Carol Strickling,
770-475-9876

Master Gardeners International Corp.
2904 Cameron Mills Road
Alexandria, VA 22302
703-683-6485

National Chrysanthemum Society
10107 Homer Pond Drive
Fairfax Station, VA 22039-1650

Seed Savers Exchange
Rural Route 3 Box 239
Decorah, IA 52101

Southern Garden History Society
Flora Ann Bynum
Old Salem Inc.

Drawer F Salem Station
Winston-Salem, NC 27108
919-724-3125

Southern Nurserymen's Association
1000 Johnson Ferry Road
Suite E - 130
Marietta, GA 30068
770-973-9026

Water Lily Society, Georgia Chapter
Shirley L. Covington
P.O. Box 242
Roswell, GA 30077
770-640-7900

INDEX

ORDER FORM

10% DISCOUNT on orders of $50 or more —
20% DISCOUNT on orders of $150 or more —
30% DISCOUNT on orders of $500 or more —
On cost of books for fully prepaid orders

NAME

ADDRESS

CITY/STATE   ZIP/POSTCODE

PHONE   COUNTRY (outside of U.S.)

TITLE	QTY	PRICE	TOTAL
Peace in Everyday Relationships (paperback)		@ $14.95	

Prices subject to change without notice

Please list other titles below:

		@ $	
		@ $	
		@ $	
		@ $	
		@ $	
		@ $	
		@ $	
		@ $	

Check here to receive our book catalog ☐ free

Shipping Costs

By Priority Mail: first book $4.50, each additional book $1.00
By UPS and to Canada: first book $5.50, each additional book $1.50
For rush orders and other countries call us at (510) 865-5282

TOTAL	
Less discount @ _____%	(_____)
TOTAL COST OF BOOKS	
Calif. residents add sales tax	
Shipping & handling	
TOTAL ENCLOSED	
Please pay in U.S. funds only	

☐ Check ☐ Money Order ☐ Visa ☐ MasterCard ☐ Discover

Card # _____

Exp. date _____

Signature _____

Complete and mail to:

Hunter House Inc., Publishers
PO Box 2914, Alameda CA 94501-0914
Website: www.hunterhouse.com
Orders: (800) 266-5592 or email: ordering@hunterhouse.com
Phone (510) 865-5282 Fax (510) 865-4295

Hunter House books on
Trauma and Recovery in Children
pg. 3

TRAUMA IN THE LIVES OF CHILDREN: Crisis and Stress
Management Techniques for Counselors, EMTs, and Other
Professionals *by Kendall Johnson, Ph.D. ... New 2nd Edition*

Written by one of the foremost trauma experts in the
country, this book explains how schools, therapists, and
families can and must work together to help children
traumatized by natural disasters, parental separation, violence, suicide, the death of a loved one, or any other
trauma a child may face.

352 pages ... Paperback $19.95

**GROW: Growth and Recovery Outreach Workbooks for
Children** *by Wendy Deaton, MFCC, and Ken Johnson, Ph.D.*

A creative, child-friendly program for children ages 6–12,
these popular workbooks are filled with original exercises to
foster healing, self-understanding, and optimal growth. They
are written by a winning author team for professionals to
use with children. The workbooks are designed for one-on-
one use between child and professional. Tasks are balanced
between writing and drawing, thinking and feeling, and are
keyed to the phases and goals of therapy: creating a therapeutic alliance, exploring delayed reactions, integrating, and
strength-building.

Each workbook is formatted to become the child's very
own, with plenty of space to write and draw, friendly line
drawings, and a place for the child's name right on the colorful cover. Each also comes with a "Therapist's Guide" that
includes helpful references to Dr. Johnson's book *Trauma in
the Lives of Children.*

Some of the titles in the series:

LIVING WITH MY FAMILY — helps children traumatized by
domestic violence and family quarrels to identify and
express their fears

NO MORE HURT — provides children who have been physically or sexually abused with a "safe place" to explore their
feelings and find their own resources

I AM A SURVIVOR — for children who have survived a natural disaster such as a flood, tornado, fire, hurricane, or earth-
quake and who need to deal with shock and loss

A SEPARATION IN MY FAMILY — for children whose parents
are separating or have already separated or divorced

Call for more details and a complete list of workbooks.
Workbooks $9.95 each ... Workbook Library (all 10 in the series) $75.00